ELT
Power-Ups

Just-in-Time Professional Learning
for Teachers of Multilingual
Learners of English

Janet Eichenberger Hiatt and Cindra Porter

tesol press

Companion Site

 This book has a companion website. Go to
www.tesol.org/ELT-power-ups for additional resources.

DEDICATION

To K–12 teachers of multilingual learners of English,
whose voices made this book possible.

bookstore.tesol.org

TESOL International Association
1925 Ballenger Avenue, Ste. 550
Alexandria, VA 22314 USA
www.tesol.org

Associate Director of Publications: Tomiko Breland
Copy Editor: Elizabeth Adler
Reviewers: Robyn Brinks Lockwood, Jessica Burchett, Khanh-Duc Kuttig
Cover and Interior Design: AM Graphic Design
Head of Education and Events: Sarah Sahr

Recommended citation:
Eichenberger Hiatt, J., & Porter, C. (2025). *ELT power-ups: Just-in-time professional learning for teachers of multilingual learners of English*. TESOL Press.

ISBN 978-1-953745-26-2
ISBN (ebook) 978-1-953745-27-9

Library of Congress Control Number 2024943233

Table of Contents

Acknowledgments

We would like to express our sincere gratitude to Tomiko Breland, TESOL International Association associate director of publications, and other TESOL Press staff for their invaluable assistance in revising and editing this book. Their keen attention to detail, insightful suggestions, and dedication greatly enhanced the quality of this work. We are truly thankful for their expertise and support throughout this process.

From Janet Eichenberger Hiatt

I would like to thank my colleague and friend, Cindra Porter, for the collaborative effort in cowriting this book. It has been a joy to write every iteration as your *book-writing partner*. I also thank my former colleague and mentor, Stephaney Jones-Vo, whose collaboration and encouragement played a pivotal role in fostering the belief that I could also be an author. Additionally, I am humbled by the opportunities I have had to collaborate with and learn from distinguished experts who support teachers of multilingual learners of English, including Shelley Fairbairn, Wendy Robinson, Diane Staehr Fenner, Sydney Snyder, Michelle Benegas, and Amy Stolpestad. Thank you for sharing your expertise. I also thank TESOL International Association for their professional guidance. *The 6 Principles for Exemplary Teaching of English Learners: K–12®* and *Standards for Initial TESOL Pre-K–12 Teacher Preparation Programs* provided a solid roadmap for this book's professional learning opportunities. In addition, sincere gratitude goes to K–12 teachers and leaders of multilingual learners of English who continually ask insightful questions and work diligently to ensure their students receive an equitable education. Your dedication is truly inspiring. Finally, I am forever grateful for my loving family, especially my husband, Mike Hiatt, who encouraged and uplifted me along the way. Thank you for supporting me on this journey.

From Cindra Porter

Many people have shaped my journey as an educator in the field of English language teaching and encouraged me to contribute to a book about teaching and learning. I sincerely thank Janet Eichenberger Hiatt, my colleague, writing partner, and friend, for inviting me to collaborate on this project. Working with you has been incredibly transformative, and I appreciate the chance to learn and grow together. I'd also like to express my gratitude to Shelley Fairbairn, Wendy Robinson, Kevin Schlomer, Celeste Rosas-Stirgus, and Macy Visser—colleagues in education whose thoughtful conversations have greatly contributed to my professional development. The shared observations, exchange of ideas, and collaborative spirit have been instrumental in shaping my perspective as an educator devoted to serving multilingual learners of English and their families. I want to thank my family, whose love and support remind me of the importance of ensuring every student and family feels valued and supported in our schools. The combined impact of this group of individuals, along with many other educators too numerous to name, is apparent in this book. I'm sincerely grateful for the opportunities to learn and grow together.

Introduction

About This Book

How This Book Came to Be

Teachers are our society's most tenacious, dedicated, and creative professionals. While teachers do not give up, and their determination is unwavering, they would benefit from a tangible and practical path to support their learning and efforts. To bolster learning, today's teachers need professional learning that is flexible, accessible, and feasible in small increments of time. That is where this book's concept of a professional learning guidebook for teachers of multilingual learners of English emerged.

Drawing upon over 50 years of collective experience as English language development (ELD) teachers, teacher leaders, professional learning providers, coaches, and consultants, we (the authors) have realized that today's teachers need a different approach to learning about multilingual learners of English in our schools. In the schools we serve, there is a noticeable increase in the enrollment of immigrant and refugee students; however, the teachers at these schools often need help accessing information or support to inform their instructional planning and teaching practices with multilingual students learning English.

This book came to be because we felt some areas of English language teaching (ELT) education were most relevant and necessary for teachers serving multilingual learners of English. By designing these crucial areas of information into smaller areas of learning, we launched this guidebook in the hope that teachers needing additional preparation could access the learning they deserve to feel more prepared to serve multilingual learners of English in their classrooms every day.

The Purpose of This Book

This book aims to provide K–12 teachers who feel they need additional preparation in serving multilingual learners of English with immediately accessible professional learning opportunities that best fit their work in supporting students in their classrooms. Guided by *The 6 Principles for Exemplary Teaching of English Learners: Grades K-12, Second Edition* (TESOL International Association, 2024b) and, when applicable, the *Standards for Initial TESOL Pre-K–12 Teacher Preparation Programs* (TESOL International Association, 2019), this book provides teachers of multilingual learners of English opportunities to build their knowledge in five crucial areas of ELT: (1) sociocultural considerations, (2) English language acquisition, (3) high-quality lesson design, (4) assessment and evaluation, and (5) professionalism and leadership.

This book is also an introduction for teachers responsible for supporting multilingual learners of English. We acknowledge several contexts within teaching and learning, and different audiences will approach this book with different purposes and levels of prior experience. Our approach to each section of the book is to share introductory considerations related to crucial areas of culture, language acquisition, lesson design, assessment, and leadership while welcoming adaptability to multiple teaching contexts.

Audience

This book has three primary audiences: professional learning providers, ELD teachers, and general education teachers. We define these three roles in this section of the book.

Professional learning providers (e.g., curriculum consultants, instructional coaches, and teacher leaders) are integral in planning and facilitating professional learning opportunities for their colleagues. Professional learning providers are often former teachers who have become teacher educators. In addition, ELD teachers are often responsible for facilitating professional learning content. The lessons and activities in this book provide content for brief professional learning sessions in small-and large-group contexts (e.g., at a faculty meeting, in a professional learning community, and in a grade- or content-level meeting).

The book is also for *ELD teachers* who specialize in English language development for multilingual learners of English. ELD teachers provide instruction that is specifically designed for multilingual learners of English to develop productive (speaking and writing) and receptive (listening and reading) skills in English. ELD teachers also collaborate with general education teachers to support the academic success of multilingual learners of English. The book helps refine the skills of ELD teachers and provides them with tools to support their general education colleagues.

A third audience for the book is *general education teachers* who are responsible for providing core content and academic language instruction in primary and secondary general education classrooms. The book's content is especially relevant for general education teachers who may have needed more preservice education pedagogy or in-service professional learning opportunities to support multilingual learners of English. Based on our experiences working in rural and urban K–12 schools, we have realized it is sometimes challenging for schools to deliver professional learning when there is limited time in their schedules. As a result, schools often sacrifice professional learning that addresses the needs of multilingual learners of English for more pressing topics, and general education teachers are often left on their own for professional learning that addresses teaching and learning for their language learners. When this gap exists in professional learning opportunities for general education teachers, we include them as an audience.

Our Title

This book stems from a great deal of love and respect for teachers who work with multilingual learners of English in their schools and classrooms daily. However, we know that many teachers without an ELD credential have yet to have the opportunity to gain a comprehensive understanding of language acquisition and how to design instruction for multilingual learners of English, be it during their preservice preparation or in their current in-service teaching positions. The title of this book, *ELT Power-Ups: Just-in-Time Professional Learning for Teachers of Multilingual Learners of English*, reflects its purpose of providing timely and guided professional learning opportunities for teachers serving multilingual learners of English. We hope that teachers will find this book to be a resource that feeds their most salient learning needs regarding support for multilingual learners of English at the precise moment when they need it.

Clarification of Terms

There are several terms to unpack in the title *ELT Power-Ups: Just-in-Time Professional Learning for Teachers of Multilingual Learners of English* and other additional terms integral to this book. The terms that guide the thinking for this book (in the order mentioned in the title) include the following:

- *ELT*: ELT stands for the field of *English language teaching* to multilingual learners of English. For this book, ELT could refer to language development that happens
  - in the ELD classroom with an ELD teacher;
  - in the general education classroom, when using a collaborative approach between general education and ELD teachers;
  - in the general education classroom, when the general educator identifies and instructs the academic language needed for multilingual learners of English to access content.
- *Power-ups*: For this book, power-ups refer to professional learning that helps increase the preparedness or readiness levels of teachers of multilingual learners of English. When teachers grow in their preparedness or readiness to serve multilingual learners of English, they power up or become more empowered to meet their students' linguistic, academic, and cultural needs. Throughout this book, teachers are invited to complete a variety of pre- and post-self-assessments to determine their current and changing perceived levels of preparedness to serve multilingual learners of English.
- *Just-in-time*: Teachers of multilingual learners of English have increasing demands for their time. Often, teachers request support at the point of need or when they are struggling with the best approaches to support the academic, cultural, and linguistic needs of their multilingual learners of English. This book provides professional learning opportunities for that point of need. In addition, professional learning opportunities are readily accessible within or outside the school boundaries and, at times, convenient to teachers. The topics also implement a flexible design based on each teacher's learning needs.
- *Professional learning*: As experts have noted (Baecher, 2021; Kamali, 2021), the term *professional development* is a preferred term over *training* because "training ends while professional development continues and is concerned with goals, learning, and the future" (Kamali, 2021). Similarly, professional learning connotes ongoing learning that does not stop after preservice coursework, allowing in-service teachers to continue to hone their teaching practice. In this book, professional development and professional learning are synonymous.
- *Teachers*: In this book, teachers include the following:
  - Professional learning providers who are teachers (or former teachers) responsible for facilitating professional learning opportunities for other teachers in the buildings they serve.
  - ELD teachers who have received an approved teaching license specialization or endorsement in English language development. ELD can refer to the teacher (ELD teacher) or subject (ELD classroom). ELD teachers are also referred to as English as an additional language (EAL) teachers, English as a second language (ESL) teachers, and English to speakers of other languages (ESOL) teachers. For more information about common acronyms in the English language teaching profession, see TESOL International Association's webpage "Common Acronyms in the English Language Teaching Field" (www.tesol.org/common-acronyms-in-ELT).

- General education teachers who have received an approved teaching license in an area other than English language development and are responsible for ensuring multilingual learners of English at the elementary and secondary levels are progressing in English language proficiency and meeting content standards. General education teachers are also known as content, in-service, or practicing teachers.

- *Multilingual learners of English*: Multilingual learners of English are K–12 students with a language other than English present in their home environment who have been identified by a language screener and are eligible for support in English language development until they reach full language proficiency as determined by an approved language assessment (Every Student Succeeds Act, 2015). Multilingual learners of English are also known as *English learners* (*ELs*) or *English language learners* (*ELLs*). TESOL International Association now prefers the more assets-based term *multilingual learners of English*.

Table *Defining Multilingual Learners of English for the Purposes of This Book*

Multilingual Learners

This book focuses on...	This book does not focus on...
Multilingual learners of English *who are eligible for English language development support from an ELD teacher based on an approved language screener:* • Gifted and talented multilingual learners of English • Students with limited or interrupted formal education • Multilingual learners of English with disabilities • Experienced multilinguals* (or students who have not reached English language proficiency within 5 years of initial identification) • Newcomer multilingual learners of English • Dual language learners from linguistically and culturally diverse backgrounds	***Other multilingual students*** *who are not eligible for English language development support from an ELD teacher:* • Heritage language learners • Exited language learners • Never multilingual learners of English (or never English learners) from linguistically and culturally diverse backgrounds • Dual language learners from English-speaking backgrounds

Note. ELD = English language development.

Based on Gottlieb (2021).

*Huynh and Skelton (2023) recommend the more assets-based term *experienced multilinguals* for students who were formerly known as long-term English learners. They refer to the Every Student Succeeds Act (2015) federal definition for long-term English learners based on a 5-year time period of not reaching English language proficiency or being classified as multilingual learners of English for 6 or more years.

- We avoid using acronyms for students (e.g., MLs for multilingual learners of English) as much as possible to help promote person-centered language. Person-centered language reminds us, first and foremost, that multilingual learners of English are general education students.
- Multilingual learners make up a very heterogeneous student population. The Table highlights the breadth of diversity among multilingual learners. The Table also emphasizes that this book focuses on multilingual learners of English who are eligible for English language development support from an ELD teacher (left column) versus other multilingual learners who are not eligible for ELD support from an ELD teacher (right column).

Additional Terms (in Alphabetical Order)

- *Administrators of multilingual learners of English*: K–12 principals and other leaders whose schools have enrolled students learning English. They are responsible for supporting multilingual learners of English and teachers in their buildings and are also integral in advocating for professional learning opportunities for their colleagues.
- *Guidebook*: We hope this book serves as a guidebook that provides tips and multiple pathways to navigate professional learning for teachers of multilingual learners of English. We offer various opportunities for you to choose your own pathways and destinations. Along the way, we also offer a variety of resources for teachers seeking additional knowledge.
- *Language acquisition*: For this book, language acquisition refers to the academic language development of multilingual learners of English in primary and secondary school contexts.
- *Limited English proficient:* This term will appear in the book only when it refers to federal legislation. In its revised acronyms webpage, TESOL International Association (2024; www.tesol.org/careers/career-tools/beginning-your-career/common-acronyms-in-the-english-language-teaching-profession) states "although this term is still used in some U.S. legislation, this term is deficit based (i.e., pointing out what is lacking instead of celebrating what is known) and should be avoided when talking about multilingual learners of English." Please note that TESOL does not use this term and strives to use only asset-based terminology.
- *TESOL*: TESOL usually refers to teaching English to speakers of other languages. For this book, TESOL refers to the organization TESOL International Association.

Companion Site

Throughout this book, many of the printed resources, including all activities and many of the tables and figures, are also available on the companion site (www.tesol.org/ELT-power-ups), and many of these are available as customizable templates.

Professional learning providers may choose to download activities, tables, and figures from the companion site for professional learning sessions with teachers. We also encourage other readers to use these online resources to enhance their learning.

Chapter Overview

Chapter 1: Professional Learning for Teachers of Multilingual Learners of English

In the first chapter, we justify the need for professional learning for teachers of multilingual learners of English. We then introduce five professional learning pathways for teachers and various professional learning opportunities that align with each pathway and share additional considerations for effective professional learning. Finally, we conclude the chapter by sharing the structure of each professional learning pathway, discussing some pre- and post-self-assessments, and providing recommendations for how to use this book to meet your professional learning needs specific to serving multilingual learners of English.

Chapter 2: Sociocultural Considerations

Chapter 2 provides multiple professional learning opportunities. You will have opportunities to identify dimensions of your identity and consider how culture impacts instruction for multilingual learners of English. In addition, you may choose to implement a method to collect and organize relevant background information for your multilingual learners of English to help inform instruction and assessment. There are also opportunities to explore the importance of relying on an assets-based perspective and how to leverage the assets multilingual learners of English bring to the classroom to enhance learning. Finally, you will consider how to promote a welcoming environment for your multilingual learners of English and families. Chapter 2 has five bite-sized professional learning opportunities:

- Know Your Own Identity
- Recognize How Culture Impacts Learning
- Know the Backgrounds of Your Multilingual Learners of English
- Embrace and Leverage Resources Multilingual Learners of English Bring to the Classroom
- Create Welcoming Classroom Environments

Chapter 3: English Language Acquisition

Chapter 3 introduces you to the process of language acquisition and, in particular, how schools have adopted English language assessments and standards for use with their multilingual learners of English. Our goal in this chapter is to reduce the apprehension of learning about language acquisition by introducing you to the basics and showing how this knowledge may inform your work with multilingual learners of English in your classroom. First, you will explore how students are selected to receive academic English support and how teachers can use the stages of language acquisition and information about student backgrounds to plan their initial work in planning language support for every student. Next, we define language standards and assessments to help teachers understand how English language proficiency is defined and measured. You will also learn to record and monitor language growth to guide instructional practices with multilingual learners of English. Finally, we identify and evaluate potential barriers to English language acquisition and consider which barriers may be most relevant for the students in our classrooms and schools. Chapter 3 has three professional learning opportunities:

- Academic Language Acquisition for Multilingual Learners of English
- Analyze Annual Academic English Language Growth
- Identify Barriers to Academic English Language Acquisition

Chapter 4: High-Quality Lesson Design

In Chapter 4, you explore various aspects of designing lessons for multilingual learners of English. The chapter begins with an overview of an equitable content lesson plan for multilingual learners of English. Next, we provide a professional learning opportunity for scaffolding appropriately for multilingual learners of English to enhance receptive and productive language while providing access to core content. Finally, we offer a framework for putting it all together when planning instruction for multilingual learners of English. Chapter 4 has three bite-sized learning opportunities:

- The Equitable Content Lesson Plan for Multilingual Learners of English
- Scaffold to Make Core Content Accessible
- Putting It All Together

Chapter 5: Assessment and Evaluation

Chapter 5 examines the impact of bias on assessing multilingual learners of English, the accessibility of assessments in schools, and strategies to enhance formative assessment for these students in general education classrooms. It addresses barriers to accurately assessing the knowledge and skills of multilingual learners of English aligned with content standards guiding classroom instruction. The chapter also offers ideas to increase accurate measures of learning and ways to design assessments that will allow multilingual learners of English to use their current levels of English language proficiency to demonstrate content area knowledge and skills. As you read through these topics, we invite you to reflect on your current assessment practices and identify topics you may wish to delve deeper into as you engage in the chapter's three bite-sized professional learning opportunities:

- Assessment Bias
- Making Assessments Accessible
- Formative Classroom Assessments

Chapter 6: Professionalism and Leadership

In Chapter 6, you will learn about the role of professionalism and leadership as a teacher of multilingual learners of English. This chapter provides opportunities to build background on the rights and policies that impact instruction and daily interaction with multilingual learners of English and families. In addition, you will be able to apply information from federal guidance to K–12 case scenarios to support multilingual learners of English and their families. Finally, you will become familiar with sample ways to advocate for students and families whose first language is not English and follow a five-step process when advocating around a critical issue. Chapter 6 has three bite-sized learning opportunities:

- Know the Rights of Multilingual Learners of English and Their Families
- Application of Federal Guidance
- Advocate on Behalf of Multilingual Learners of English and Their Families

Chapter 7: Conclusion

In the Conclusion, we reiterate our purpose of providing teachers with access to the professional learning opportunities they deserve so they can feel more prepared to serve multilingual learners of English in their classrooms. We also revisit the larger overall self-assessments introduced in this book to assist you in determining if you have leveled up or grown in your perceived level of preparedness in supporting multilingual learners of English. In addition, the pre- and post-self-reflections will allow you to reflect upon where you are in your professional learning and where you want to go next. Finally, you will have an opportunity to reflect upon your next areas of learning at the individual, team, or school level.

References

Baecher, L. (2021, May 28). Why use the term "professional development" and not "training"? *TESOL Blog*. https://www.tesol.org/blog/posts/why-use-the-term-professional-development-and-not-training/

Every Student Succeeds Act, 20 U.S.C. § 6301 (2015). https://www.congress.gov/bill/114th-congress/senate-bill/1177

Gottlieb, M. (2021). *Classroom assessment in multiple languages: A handbook for teachers*. Corwin.

Huynh, T., & Skelton, B. (2023). *Long-term success for experienced multilinguals*. Corwin.

Kamali, J. (2021, July). 6 tips for successful continuous professional development. *TESOL Connections*. https://tcnewsletter.s3.amazonaws.com/newsmanager.commpartners.com/tesolc/issues/2021-07-01/index.html

TESOL International Association. (2019). *Standards for initial TESOL Pre-K–12 teacher preparation programs*. TESOL Press.

TESOL International Association. (2024a). *Common acronyms in the English language teaching field*. https://www.tesol.org/careers/career-tools/beginning-your-career/common-acronyms-in-the-english-language-teaching-profession

TESOL International Association. (2024b). *The 6 principles for exemplary teaching of English learners: Grades K–12* (2nd ed.). TESOL Press.

Chapter 1

Professional Learning for Teachers of Multilingual Learners of English

If you are picking up this book as a professional learning provider responsible for facilitating professional learning specific to multilingual learners of English, an English language development (ELD) teacher wanting to hone your practice, or perhaps a K–12 general education teacher who is serving multilingual learners of English in a classroom while not feeling prepared to do so, then we wrote this book specifically for you. In Chapter 1, we begin by sharing why there is a need for professional learning specific to multilingual learners of English. We then introduce five professional learning pathways designed for teachers supporting multilingual learners of English and professional learning opportunities that align with each pathway. Furthermore, we share additional considerations for effective professional learning and introduce pre- and post-self-assessments to support your professional learning. We conclude by sharing the structure of each professional learning chapter and providing recommendations for how you can use this book to meet your professional learning needs specific to serving multilingual learners of English.

Why Professional Learning for Teachers of Multilingual Learners of English Is Essential

There are many reasons why professional learning is essential for teachers to support instruction that includes multilingual learners of English. We would like to focus on three key reasons that might also resonate with you:

1. The K–12 multilingual learners of English student population has been steadily increasing.
2. Teachers report feeling underprepared to teach multilingual learners of English.
3. Underpreparation to teach multilingual learners of English is inequitable for teachers and students.

Steadily Increasing K–12 Multilingual Learners of English Student Population

The K–12 multilingual learners of English student population has been steadily increasing. For example, in 2017–18, approximately five million multilingual learners of English were enrolled in U.S. schools, equating to 10.2% or one in every 10 K–12 students (National Center for Education Statistics (NCES 2021a, 2021b). In addition, the National Education Association (NEA; 2020) shared that by 2025, one out of four children in U.S. classrooms will be multilingual learners of English. By 2050, there are estimates that multilingual learners of English will make up 40% of the U.S. public school enrollment (Weyer, 2018).

Increasing enrollment of K–12 multilingual learners of English in the United States highlights a growing probability that many teachers are serving (or will eventually be serving) multilingual students learning English. Suppose teachers have gaps in preservice coursework or in-service professional learning in serving language learners. In that case, these enrollment trends strongly highlight the need for ongoing professional learning specific to multilingual learners of English.

Teachers Report Not Feeling Prepared to Teach Multilingual Learners of English

A second reason professional learning specific to multilingual learners of English is essential stems from a long history of teachers reporting they feel underprepared to serve their students learning English. The following mini-timeline captures a sampling of research and reports related to this issue:

- 2004: A district-level survey revealed that the majority of 729 teachers with a recent influx of immigrant and refugee students in a midwestern suburb of the United States reported feeling confident in their overall teaching ability but not in their ability to teach multilingual learners of English (Karabenick & Clemens Noda, 2004).
- 2006: In the southeastern United States, 81.7% of a 279-subject sample of general education teachers felt they did not have adequate training to work with multilingual learners of English (Reeves, 2006).
- 2016: In a midwestern U.S. study, the majority of general education teacher participants self-reported feeling underprepared to teach multilingual learners of English in their classrooms (Hiatt, 2016; Hiatt & Fairbairn, 2018). Findings from this study further revealed that general education teachers would benefit from continued professional learning opportunities related to language, culture, instruction, and assessment, "with additional priority given to the areas in which teachers felt least prepared" (Hiatt & Fairbairn, 2018, p. 239).
- 2021: In a similar Virginia study with administrators whose schools had enrolled multilingual learners of English, participants self-reported being only somewhat prepared to support professional development efforts specific to multilingual learners of English, which impacted their ability to assist teachers who serve multilingual learners of English in their schools (Russ, 2021).
- 2020–2022: Furthermore, during pandemic learning, from approximately 2020 to 2022, reports from the U.S. Government Accountability Office found that general education teachers not having adequate preparation to support multilingual learners of English further exacerbated academic struggles for these learners (U.S. Government Accountability Office, 2020, 2022; Mitchell, 2020; Najarro, 2022).

Following, read on to learn about two factors contributing to teachers needing more preparation to teach multilingual learners of English: limited access to professional learning opportunities and few professional learning requirements related to multilingual learners of English.

Two Factors Contributing to Teachers Not Feeling Prepared to Teach Multilingual Learners of English

1. **Limited Access to Professional Learning Opportunities Specific to Multilingual Learners of English:** Many teachers working with multilingual learners of English need help accessing professional learning specific to multilingual learners of English. According to data from the 2011–12 School and Staffing Survey, only 24% of K–12 teachers in the United States reported participating in professional development specifically focused on multilingual learners of English (Goldring et al., 2013, as cited in National Academies of Sciences, Engineering, and Medicine, 2017, pp. 12–17). Another national survey revealed that only 12.5% of U.S. teacher respondents reported receiving 8 or more hours of professional development related to multilingual learners of English (National Center for Education Statistics, 2002). In a recent *Education Week* special report, Mitchell (2019) highlighted the prevailing feelings that teachers needed more professional learning to teach multilingual learners of English. In this report, Mitchell further emphasized that schools should include professional learning specific to multilingual learners of English for both general education teachers and administrators, regardless of prior preservice training.

2. **Few Requirements for Professional Learning Specific to Multilingual Learners of English:** In addition to the limited opportunities mentioned in the first factor, there are often few requirements for professional learning specific to multilingual learners of English to recertify. For example, the National Education Association (NEA; 2015) reported that only 20 U.S. states required some training in working with multilingual learners of English, and those requirements varied significantly from state to state. Duggan et al. (2020) also found that most U.S. states did not require general education teachers to undergo any professional development specific to multilingual learners of English to renew their general education certification. Specifically, they observed that only four states (Colorado, Massachusetts, Minnesota, and New York) required some type of professional development specific to multilingual learners of English for recertification. Considering the growing multilingual learner of English student population, Duggan et al. recommended that all general education teachers have some type of professional development specific to multilingual learners of English as part of their recertification process.

If you feel underprepared to teach multilingual learners of English and have limited opportunities for professional learning specific to language learners, rest assured that you are not alone. There remains a persistent and historical need for teachers to receive professional learning to support instruction for their growing multilingual learners of English student populations. This book aims to assist teachers in accessing professional learning opportunities specific to multilingual learners of English to help ensure they feel adequately prepared to support language learners in their daily classroom practice.

Underpreparation Impacts Equity for Both Teachers and Students

Equity is the third reason teachers serving multilingual learners of English would benefit from professional learning to support their instruction. Being underprepared to serve multilingual learners of English is inequitable for both teachers, who deserve to feel adequately prepared (NEA, 2015), and their students, who would ultimately benefit from that preparation.

Equity for Teachers

A general education teacher is responsible for teaching multilingual learners of English for most of the instructional day. In addition, there remains a shortage of certified teachers who have specialized in working with multilingual learners of English, further amplifying the responsibility of general education teachers to meet the needs of a growing multilingual learners of English population (Cross, 2016; TESOL International Association, 2022; U.S. Department of Education, Office of English Language Acquisition, 2023). If general education teachers feel underprepared to serve multilingual learners of English, it can lead to an equity issue for themselves and their students. The NEA (2015) shared, "lack of preparation is not only unfair to students, it's unfair to the teachers who are expected to serve them" (p. 20). As a result, the NEA has called on advocates to prioritize professional learning opportunities for teachers serving multilingual learners of English so they can receive the ongoing learning they need and deserve. We hope this book provides that form of advocacy.

Equity for Student Learning

An underprepared teacher of multilingual learners of English is also inequitable for students. Experts have long argued that prepared teachers can increase student achievement (Bos et al., 2012; Darling-Hammond, 2000; Hattie, 2003). Specific to the multilingual learners of English student population, Harper et al. (2008) explain that prepared teachers are critical for the academic achievement of multilingual students learning English. They stress the importance of providing teachers with additional preparation at the preservice or in-service levels to ensure they effectively address language development and the cultural, linguistic, and academic needs of multilingual learners of English.

This book prioritizes professional learning for teachers of multilingual learners of English. We seek to reduce some inequities for teachers by increasing access to professional learning specific to multilingual learners of English. We also seek to decrease inequities for students by increasing the preparedness of teachers of multilingual learners of English, with the goal of improving academic outcomes for students whose primary language is not English.

Professional Learning Pathways for Teachers of Multilingual Learners of English

As we reflected upon how to offer professional learning opportunities for teachers of multilingual learners of English, we turned to a globally known TESOL publication: *The 6 Principles for Exemplary Teaching of English Learners: Grades K–12* (TESOL International Association, 2024). These principles helped to provide a guiding compass for what K–12 teachers of multilingual learners of English should know and be able to do. By aligning our book content with The 6 Principles, we could also appeal to a broader audience of teachers serving multilingual learners of English in primary and secondary schools. In addition, when applicable, we aligned our content with relevant components of the *Standards for Initial TESOL Pre-K–12 Teacher Preparation Programs* (TESOL International Association, 2019) in a way that was not too prescriptive for in-service teachers (TESOL International Association, 2012). This additional alignment further enhanced professional learning opportunities.

Professional Learning Pathways

Figure 1.1 visualizes five professional learning pathways featured in this book for teachers of multilingual learners of English inspired by TESOL's The 6 Principles and *Standards for Initial TESOL Pre-K–12 Teacher Preparation Programs*. The five pathways are (1) Sociocultural Considerations, (2) English Language Acquisition, (3) High-Quality Lesson Design, (4) Assessment and Evaluation, and (5) Professionalism and Leadership.

Figure 1.1 *Professional learning pathways for teachers of multilingual learners of English.*

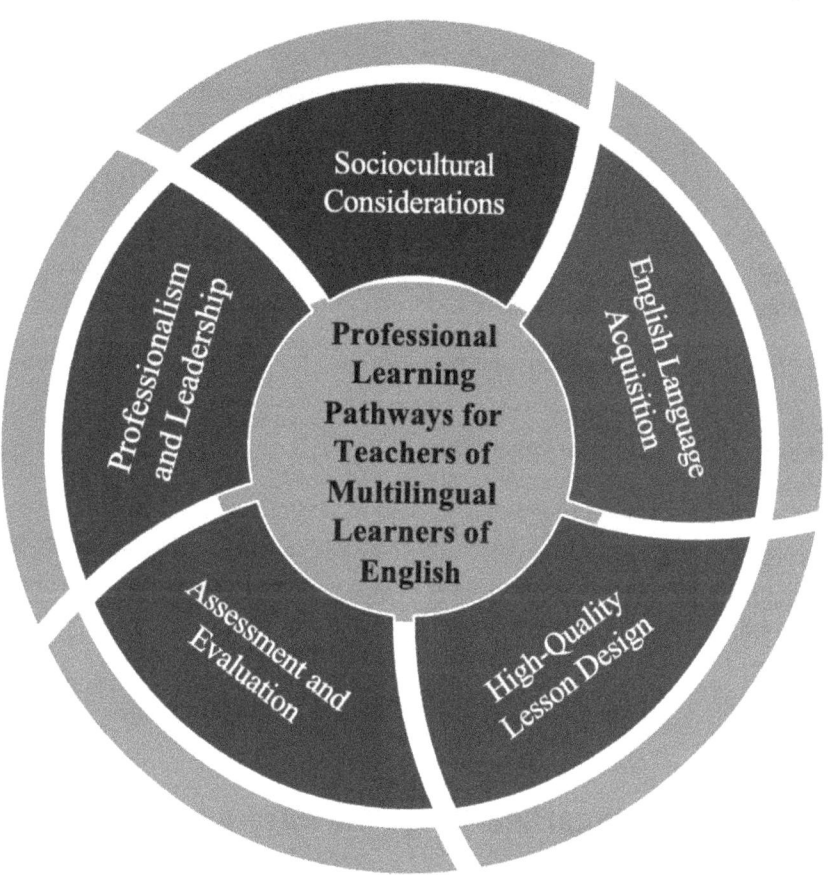

Professional Learning Opportunities

In addition, each of the five learning pathways offers a variety of professional learning opportunities that align with The 6 Principles and, when applicable, the 2019 *Standards for Initial TESOL Pre-K–12 Teacher Preparation Programs*. Table 1.1 identifies 17 professional learning opportunities for the five learning pathways.

Table 1.1 *Professional Learning Opportunities for Each Learning Pathway*

Learning Pathway	Professional Learning Opportunities
Sociocultural Considerations	1. Know Your Own Identity 2. Recognize How Culture Impacts Learning 3. Know the Backgrounds of Your Multilingual Learners of English 4. Embrace and Leverage Resources Multilingual Learners of English Bring to the Classroom 5. Create Welcoming Classroom Environments
English Language Acquisition	6. Academic Language Acquisition for Multilingual Learners of English 7. Analyze Annual Academic English Language Growth 8. Identify Barriers to Academic English Language Acquisition
High-Quality Lesson Design	9. The Equitable Content Lesson Plan for Multilingual Learners of English 10. Scaffold to Make Core Content Accessible 11. Putting It All Together
Assessment and Evaluation	12. Assessment Bias 13. Making Assessments Accessible 14. Formative Classroom Assessments
Professionalism and Leadership	15. Know the Rights of Multilingual Learners of English and Their Families 16. Application of Federal Guidance 17. Advocate on Behalf of Multilingual Learners of English and Their Families

Structure of Professional Learning Pathway Chapters

We follow a similar structure outlined in Table 1.2 to build consistency for each professional learning pathway chapter (Chapters 2 through 6).

Table 1.2 *Structure of Professional Learning Pathway Chapters*

Getting Ready to Learn	
Opening	The opening varies by chapter and may include the following: • Chapter Overview • The Why • Building Background
Preassessment	We recommend completing the preassessment before participating in each professional learning pathway to help you choose learning opportunities that best meet your learning needs.

CONTINUED

TESOL's 6 Principles (Grades K–12)	We list the principles and practices from *The 6 Principles for Exemplary Teaching of English Learners: Grades K–12* that align with each professional learning opportunity.
Standards for Initial TESOL Pre-K–12 Teacher Preparation Programs*	We also list the standards and components from the 2019 *Standards for Initial TESOL Pre-K–12 Teacher Preparation Programs* (when applicable) that align with each professional learning opportunity.
Key Learning Target(s)	The key learning target(s) represent key outcomes for the professional learning opportunities. They stem from The 6 Principles and *Standards for Initial TESOL Pre-K–12 Teacher Preparation Programs*.
Lessons and Activities	The lessons and activities allow you to reach each professional learning opportunity's learning target(s). We also provide an activity goal that supports the lesson's learning target.
Notes for Each Teacher Role	We include differentiated ideas for professional learning providers, English language development teachers, and general education teachers to consider *before* engaging in each professional learning opportunity.
Closing Questions and Suggestions for Each Teacher Role	This section includes role-specific questions and suggestions to help you reflect upon and extend your learning *after* engaging in each professional learning opportunity.

Wrapping Things Up

Postassessment	We recommend completing the postassessment after participating in each learning pathway to help inform future professional learning specific to multilingual learners of English.
Next Steps	This is an opportunity for you to consider next steps, such as: • What do you still need to know? • What are the next action steps for personal learning or professional practice? • What are your plans for advocacy to promote equity for multilingual learners of English and their teachers?
Chapter Highlights	Highlights include the following: • Closing remarks • Transition to the next chapter • Reminders of equitable education for multilingual learners of English

*We have made minor edits, with TESOL's permission, to the terminology used in these standards when referencing individuals and specific populations.

CONTINUED

| References | References specific to each chapter are included at the end of each chapter. |

Additional Considerations for Professional Learning

The U.S. Every Student Succeeds Act (ESSA) defines professional development as "sustained (not stand-alone, 1-day, or short-term workshops), intensive, collaborative, job-embedded, data-driven, and classroom-focused" (Every Student Succeeds Act, 2015, Sec 8002, no. 42).

In lines with the principles of ESSA, in this book, we offer *sustained* professional learning opportunities that teachers of multilingual learners of English can engage in for continuous improvement. They are not meant to be stand-alone or short-term. Teachers also have the option to work independently or, preferably, *collaboratively* with other colleagues when engaging in the lessons and activities to enhance their learning experiences. In addition, we encourage teachers to apply new learning to their *job-embedded* roles in schools and classrooms. To further elaborate, job-embedded "is a critical approach to supporting teachers, schools, and districts in their efforts to improve teaching and learning...[that] recognizes the importance of providing ongoing, relevant, and practical learning experiences for educators in the context of their daily work" (Yaeger, 2023). In addition, we aim to make the professional learning opportunities in this book *classroom focused* to support your students' current and changing linguistic, academic, and cultural needs (*data driven*).

Self-Assessments

We recommend that you start by determining your priorities for professional learning with the help of self-assessments included in this book. The results of the self-assessments will help you choose the learning pathways and accompanying professional learning opportunities that best meet your needs.

Overall Level of Perceived Preparedness as a Teacher of Multilingual Learners of English Self-Assessment

According to Lucas et al. (2006), a key indicator of teachers' preparedness to serve multilingual learners of English is their "own perception of the adequacy of their preparation" (p. 3). There are various ways to measure teachers' perceived preparedness to serve multilingual learners of English.

One way is to use a simple pre-and-post Likert scale, in which you indicate your beginning and changing levels of perceived preparedness. Table 1.3 functions as a pre-and-post Likert scale tool to identify your overall level of perceived preparedness as a teacher of multilingual learners of English on a 1 (low) to 10 (high) continuum. When using this tool, there are places for you to highlight a number representing your *beginning level of preparedness* as you begin professional learning; *midway*, or after engaging in a few learning opportunities; and after the *final chapter*, or when concluding your professional learning, to indicate your changing levels of preparedness. This ongoing documentation allows you to acknowledge and celebrate growth you make along the way. It also serves as a reminder that when teachers grow in their preparedness or readiness to serve multilingual learners of English, they *power up*, or become more empowered to meet their students' linguistic, academic, and cultural needs. See Table 1.3 for more details.

Table 1.3 *Overall Level of Perceived Preparedness as a Teacher of Multilingual Learners of English Self-Assessment*

Directions: This self-assessment tool allows you to indicate your overall level of perceived preparedness as a teacher of multilingual learners of English on a 1 (low) to 10 (high) continuum at the beginning, midway, and end of the book. You may complete this self-assessment when you begin your learning, midway through learning, and when concluding your professional learning to indicate your changing levels of preparedness. It is essential to acknowledge and celebrate the growth you make along the way.

Indicate your beginning, mid, and final levels of perceived preparedness by adding a symbol (e.g., date, checkmark, X, your initials) to the cell numbers representing your beginning and changing levels of preparedness.

Chapter 1 (or at the beginning of professional learning)

1	2	3	4	5	6	7	8	9	10

(Low)   (High)

Midway (or after engaging in a few professional learning opportunities)

1	2	3	4	5	6	7	8	9	10

(Low)   (High)

Final Chapter (or after concluding your professional learning)

1	2	3	4	5	6	7	8	9	10

(Low)   (High)

Note to Professional Learning Providers

Professional learning providers could adapt the Overall Level of Perceived Preparedness as a Teacher of Multilingual Learners of English Self-Assessment for a group of teachers. Figure 1.2 is an example in which a group of teachers identified their beginning levels of preparedness as teachers of multilingual learners of English with one colored dot sticker and their levels of preparedness following professional learning with a different colored dot sticker. The two different dot colors provide a pre-and-post visual representation to help teachers celebrate their growth due to professional learning specific to multilingual learners of English. Figure 1.2 highlights significant growth in perceived preparedness, with participants starting in the 1–4 range and ending in the 5–7 range over approximately one semester.

Figure 1.2 *Sample pre-and-post perceived levels of preparedness for a group of teachers of multilingual learners of English.*

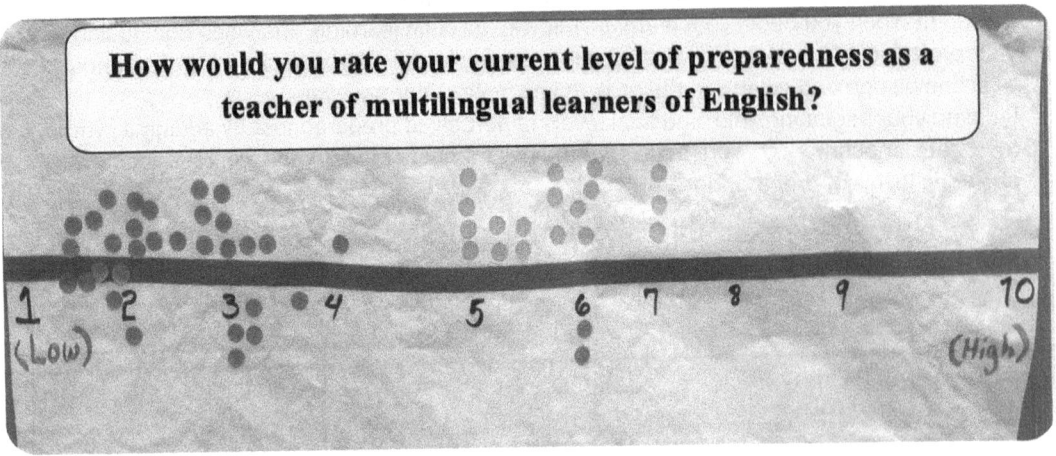

Photo by Janet Eichenberger Hiatt. Used with permission.

Five Professional Learning Pathways Self-Assessment

Each chapter also includes pre- and post-self-assessments that enable you to identify your current and changing levels of progress toward meeting learning targets for each professional learning pathway. We recommend completing a preassessment at the beginning of a pathway chapter and a postassessment at the end of a chapter. These pre- and postassessments will help you monitor and celebrate your growth and determine the next steps for learning. You may also find a compiled version of the pre- and post-self-assessments titled Five Professional Learning Pathways Self-Assessment with the Chapter 1 online resources on the companion site at www.tesol.org/ELT-power-ups. In addition, you will have an opportunity to revisit this self-assessment at the conclusion of this book.

How to Use This Book

Recommendations

If you have limited experience working with multilingual learners of English or have a lower level of perceived preparedness for serving them, we recommend reading the book from beginning to end. If you have some experience, you may pick and choose.

Potential Uses

Professional learning providers can use this book to support professional learning communities or school teams in enhancing their preparedness for selected topics or learning pathways. The book could also enhance professional learning specific to multilingual learners of English for a school or district-level faculty. In addition, teachers can engage independently in learning pathways and professional learning opportunities.

Each professional learning opportunity consists of lessons with activities. Each lesson requires approximately 30–45 minutes, or the time often allotted for a professional learning provider to conduct an activity during a faculty meeting or contribute to a professional learning community or grade-level team meeting. This timeframe would include basic housekeeping for meetings before and after professional learning activities and might vary across lessons.

Closing

In this chapter, you explored why there is a need for professional learning for K–12 teachers of multilingual learners of English by looking at increasing enrollment trends of multilingual learners of English, examining research that highlighted gaps in teacher preparedness, and becoming familiar with equity issues related to the preparation of teachers to serve multilingual learners of English. You then previewed five professional learning pathways for teachers of multilingual learners of English and professional learning opportunities that align with each pathway. In addition, you became familiar with the structure of the professional learning chapters in this book and considerations for effective professional learning. Finally, you previewed various pre- and post-self-assessments for your professional learning and considered how you might use this book to meet your learning needs specific to serving multilingual learners of English. We hope you enjoy your learning journey as you engage in professional learning specific to multilingual learners of English!

References

Bos, J., Sanchez, R., Tseng, F., Rayyes, N., Oritz, L., & Sinicrope, C. (2012). *Evaluation of quality teaching for English learners (QTEL) professional development* (NCEE 2012-4005). National Center for Education Evaluation and Regional Assistance, Institute of Education Sciences, U.S. Department of Education.

Cross, F. (2016). *Teacher shortage areas nationwide listing 1990-1991 through 2016–2017.* U.S. Department of Education, Office of Postsecondary Education. https://www2.ed.gov/about/offices/list/ope/pol/tsa.pdf

Darling-Hammond, L. (2000). Teacher quality and student achievement: A review of state policy evidence. *Education Policy Analysis Archive, 8*(1). https://www.researchgate.net/publication/240273279_Teacher_Quality_and_Student_Achievement_A_Review_of_State_Policy_Evidence

Duggan, J., Staehr Fenner, D., & Snyder, S. (2020, October). *An analysis of state recertification requirements and recommendations for all teachers of English learners.* SupportEd. https://supported.com/wp-content/uploads/State-Recertification-Requirements-and-Recommendations-for-All-Teachers-of-English-Learners-SupportEd.pdf

Every Student Succeeds Act, 20 U.S.C. § 6301 (2015). https://www.congress.gov/bill/114th-congress/senate-bill/1177

Harper, C. A., de Jong, E. J., & Platt, E. J. (2008). Marginalizing English as a second language teacher expertise: The exclusionary consequences of No Child Left Behind. *Language Policy, 7*(3), 267–284.

Hattie, J. (2003, October). *Teachers make a difference: What is the research evidence?* [Paper presentation]. Australian Council for Educational Research Annual Conference on Building Teacher Quality, Melbourne, Victoria, Australia.

Hiatt, J. E. (2016). *Quality teachers of English language learners: Exploring the use of a standards framework to improve the focus of professional development for practicing classroom and content teachers* (UMI Publication No. 10110197) [Doctoral dissertation, Drake University]. ProQuest Dissertations and Theses Global.

Hiatt, J. E., & Fairbairn, S. (2018). Improving the focus of English learner professional development for in-service teachers. *NASSP Bulletin, 102*(3), 228–263.

Hiatt, J. E., & Jones-Vo, S. (2017-2018). *In-service educator of English learners' certificate program.* University of Iowa Baker Teacher Leader Center.

Karabenick, S. A., & Clemens Noda, P. A. (2004). Professional development implications of teachers' beliefs and attitudes toward English language learners. *Bilingual Research, 28*(1), 55–75.

Lucas, T., Villegas, A. M., & Reznitskaya, A. (2006, April). *Exploring the preparedness of regular classroom teachers to teach English language learners* [Paper presentation]. Annual Meeting of the American Research Association Conference, San Francisco, CA, United States.

Mitchell, C. (2019, May 14). *Overlooked: How teacher training falls short for English-learners and students with IEPs. Blind Spots in Professional Development* [Special Report]. Education Week. https://www.edweek. org/leadership/blind-spots-in-teacher-professional-development

Mitchell, C. (2020, November 19). Schools struggled to serve students with disabilities, English-learners during shutdowns. *Education Week.* https://www.edweek.org/teaching-learning/schools-struggled-to-serve-students-with-disabilities-english-learners-during-shutdowns/2020/11

Najarro, I. (2022, June 3). Virtual learning made persistent problems worse for English learners. *Education Week.* https://www.edweek.org/teaching-learning/virtual-learning-made-persistent-problems-worse-for-english-learners/2022/06

National Academies of Sciences, Engineering, and Medicine. (2017). *Promoting the educational success of children and youth learning English: Promising futures.* The National Academies Press. https://doi.org/10.17226/24677

National Center for Education Statistics. (2002). *School and staffing survey, 1999–2000: Overview of the data for public, private, public charter and bureau of Indian affairs elementary and secondary schools.* U.S. Department of Education. http://nces.ed.gov/pubs2002/2002313.pdf

National Center for Education Statistics. (2021a). The condition of education 2021 at a glance. *Condition of Education.* U.S. Department of Education, Institute of Education Sciences. https://nces.ed.gov/programs/coe/ataglance

National Center for Education Statistics. (2021b). *English language learners in public schools. Condition of Education.* U.S. Department of Education, Institute of Education Sciences. https://nces.ed.gov/programs/coe/indicator/cgf

National Education Association. (2015). *All in! How educators can advocate for English language learners.* https://www.nea.org/sites/default/files/2020-07/ALL%20IN_%20NEA%20ELL_AdvocacyGuide2015_v7.pdf

National Education Association. (2020). *Resource library toolkit: English language learners.* https://www.nea.org/resource-library/english-language-learners

Reeves, J. (2006). Secondary teacher attitudes toward including English-language learners in mainstream classrooms. *Journal of Educational Research, 99*(3), 131–142.

Russ, B. J. (2021). *Principals' and assistant principals' self-reported levels of preparedness to assist instructional staff who work with English learners in two school districts in Virginia* [Unpublished doctoral dissertation]. Virginia Polytechnic Institute and State University. https://vtechworks.lib.vt.edu/handle/10919/102580

TESOL International Association. (2012). *Preparing effective teachers of English language learners: Practical applications for the TESOL P–12 professional teaching standards.* TESOL Press.

TESOL International Association. (2019). *Standards for initial TESOL Pre-K–12 teacher preparation programs.* TESOL Press.

TESOL International Association. (2022). Take action for English language teachers! *TESOL Advocacy Action Center.* https://www.tesol.org/advocacy/advocacy-action-center/

TESOL International Association. (2024). *The 6 principles for exemplary teaching of English learners: Grades K–12* (2nd ed.). TESOL Press.

U.S. Department of Education, Office of English Language Acquisition. (2023). *Educators of English learners: Availability, projected need, and teacher preparation* [Infographic]. https://ncela.ed.gov/sites/default/files/2023-06/ELsTeachers-Infographic-20230616-508.pdf?utm_source=nexus_newsletter&utm_medium=email&utm_campaign=el_teachers_infographic

U.S. Government Accountability Office. (2020, November). *Distance learning: Challenges providing services to K–12 English learners and students with disabilities during COVID-19* (GAO-21-43). https://www.gao.gov/assets/gao-21-43.pdf

U.S. Government Accountability Office. (2022, May). *Pandemic learning: Teachers reported obstacles for high-poverty students and English learners as well as some mitigating strategies* (GAO-22-105815). https://www.gao.gov/assets/gao-22-105815.pdf

Weyer, M. (2018, January 2). *Dual- and English-language learners.* National Conference of State Legislatures.

Yaeger, J. (2023, October 27). 11 job-embedded PD focus areas for ed leaders to consider. *Teaching Channel With Learners Edge.* https://www.teachingchannel.com/k12-hub/blog/11-job-embedded-pd-focus-areas-for-ed-leaders-to-consider

Chapter 2

Sociocultural Considerations

Image Source: MFHiatt Photography. (2022). *Lao Buddhist Temple Wat Phothisomphan.* www.mfhiattphotography.com. Used with permission.

Getting Ready to Learn

A professional learning provider for teachers of multilingual learners of English wrote the following reflection after engaging in a *cultural other* experience or an experience in a culture that was different from her own:

> I attended the open house at Lao Buddhist Temple Wat Phothisomphan...in conjunction with Meet My Religious Neighbor (Comparison Project, n.d.), a monthly open house series which allows people the chance to visit and experience a different religious community they may not have visited before. Entering the temple, I was swept into a swirling beehive of activity. Tables were set up just inside the doorway, with vendors selling a variety of goods. Families visited and ate, milling about carrying various pots and bowls. In the background, I heard a man's voice on a loudspeaker, announcing nonstop in Lao.

Looking into the temple, I saw dazzling colors: rugs, women with beautiful, bright dresses and sashes, single beds with gaudy spreads and pillows lined up along both sides, dollar bills hanging from fake trees, people with baskets full of various foods and bottled water. The background loudspeaker never ceased and never got any quieter.

I removed my shoes and placed them with what seemed like hundreds of other pairs, all jammed into the entrance of the temple. Trying not to step on or trip over any, I made my way to an empty folding chair along the wall. A few other [non-Lao] people were sitting there, too. I simply gazed all around myself. I had no idea what was happening, or what any of what I saw meant. A man walked by and offered me a bottle of water. He had a big smile on his face.

Many people were kneeling or sitting on the rugs toward the front of the temple. Older people seemed to be sitting on folding chairs toward the back.

After observing for a while, I noticed one of my classmates was there, too. Relief! Someone I could talk to! She sat next to me, and we wondered together about what we were seeing and experiencing.

A [non-Lao] man in a suit addressed our little group. He introduced us to a woman [who] would become our guide for the next few hours. This would have been a more confusing and a less enlightened experience without [our guide]. She was an engaging guide who was eager to share her culture. She led us to the front of the temple, where we sat at the feet of an American monk. (Wyatt, 2017)

The professional learning provider in the preceding reflection was exploring aspects of her own culture and that of her students and chose to immerse herself in a cultural other experience, or an "experience of *being* 'the other', 'the outsider, or the minority student'" (McBrien, 2009, p. 334). As you might see from the reflection, the professional learning provider was able to experience "firsthand the confusion, fear, and emotions of being the outsider" (McBrien, 2009, p. 337). She also realized how fellow peers and a trusting guide helped welcome and support her in navigating a new culture where she did not know the language or traditions. Most importantly, this experience helped the professional learning provider learn about her own culture and appreciate the culture of her district's students even more. Gardner (2019) shares that for many teachers, "it is really kind of hard to reflect on your own culture until you're removed from it."

In this chapter, there are opportunities to engage in a cultural other field trip experience to help deepen your understanding of your own identity by experiencing the cultures of one or more of your multilingual learners of English. You will also implement a method to collect and organize information about the individual, family, academic, and experiential backgrounds of your multilingual learners of English to support instruction and assessment. In addition, you will embrace and leverage the resources that multilingual learners of English bring to the classroom to enhance learning. Finally, there will be an opportunity to identify a few action steps to promote a welcoming classroom for your multilingual learners and families.

Preassessment

Before participating in the professional learning opportunities for this chapter, we recommend that you complete the Preassessment for Sociocultural Considerations shown in Table 2.1. For this preassessment, you indicate with a date or other symbol your perceived level of progress toward meeting learning targets on a 1–5 continuum. The continuum starts with *1-Emerging* (little to no understanding), moves to *3-Developing* (somewhat familiar but still need information to take action), and ends with *5-Proficient* (I feel confident that I understand and can take action on this learning target). The survey results will help determine your priorities for professional learning opportunities for the Sociocultural Considerations pathway. You may also compare your progress toward meeting the learning targets before and after participating in this chapter's learning opportunities.

Professional Learning Opportunities

This chapter has five professional learning opportunities. You may engage in those that best meet your learning needs. Before beginning your professional learning opportunities, we encourage you to reflect on your preassessment responses (see Table 2.1) and pursue one or all options that best fit your current learning needs. The five professional learning opportunities in this chapter are as follows:

- Know Your Own Identity
- Recognize How Culture Impacts Learning
- Know the Backgrounds of Your Multilingual Learners of English
- Embrace and Leverage Resources Multilingual Learners of English Bring to the Classroom
- Create Welcoming Classroom Environments

Professional Learning Opportunity #1: Know Your Own Identity

The first sociocultural professional learning opportunity helps you recognize dimensions of your own identity to increase your understanding of the identities of your multilingual learners of English. Knowing and understanding the dimensions of your identity indirectly helps you gain information about your multilingual learners of English (TESOL Principle 1, Practice 1a). Hollins-Alexander and Law (2022) state, "when we cultivate an understanding of the dimensions of identity we not only become more self-aware, but we increase our understanding and appreciation of others' identities" (p. 19). This understanding is essential because it can impact teachers' interpretations of the strengths and needs of their multilingual learners (Standard 2, Component 2e of the *Standards for Initial TESOL Pre-K–12 Teacher Preparation Programs*). The Know Your Own Identity box on page 36 shows the components of the first professional learning opportunity.

Lesson 1: Know Your Own Identity

Identity has many dimensions, including race, ethnicity, socioeconomic status, level of education, gender, and many more considerations (Hollins-Alexander & Law, 2022). Sometimes, teachers forget they have a unique cultural and personal identity, especially if they come from a dominant culture. Staehr Fenner (2014) explains, "many educators may not realize that even if they have lived in one country or locale all their lives and are monolingual speakers of English, they already possess a culture and worldview that influences who they are as educators" (p. 38). To understand and appreciate the identities of others, we first need to recognize that we each have a unique identity.

In the Dimensions of My Identity activity, you will identify dimensions of your identity as one way to better understand yourself and your multilingual learners of English. You will first reflect upon the dimensions of your identity and then write about those that impact your identity most. For example, one of the authors is a mom of adult children in a two-parent

Table 2.1 *Preassessment for Sociocultural Considerations*

Sociocultural Considerations Professional Learning Opportunities #1–5		1 Emerging
#1 Know Your Own Identity	1. I can identify dimensions of my own identity as one way to better understand the identities of my multilingual learners of English.	
#2 Recognize How Culture Impacts Learning	2. I can recognize the impact of culture on the education of multilingual learners of English.	
#3 Know the Backgrounds of Your Multilingual Learners of English	3. I can implement a method to collect and organize information about the individual, family, language, academic, and experiential backgrounds of multilingual learners of English to support instruction and assessment.	
#4 Embrace and Leverage Resources Multilingual Learners of English Bring to the Classroom	4. I can rely on an assets-based perspective when working with multilingual learners of English and their families.	
	5. I can embrace and leverage resources that multilingual learners of English bring to the classroom to enhance learning.	
#5 Create Welcoming Classroom Environments	6. I can promote a welcoming classroom environment for my multilingual learners of English and their families.	

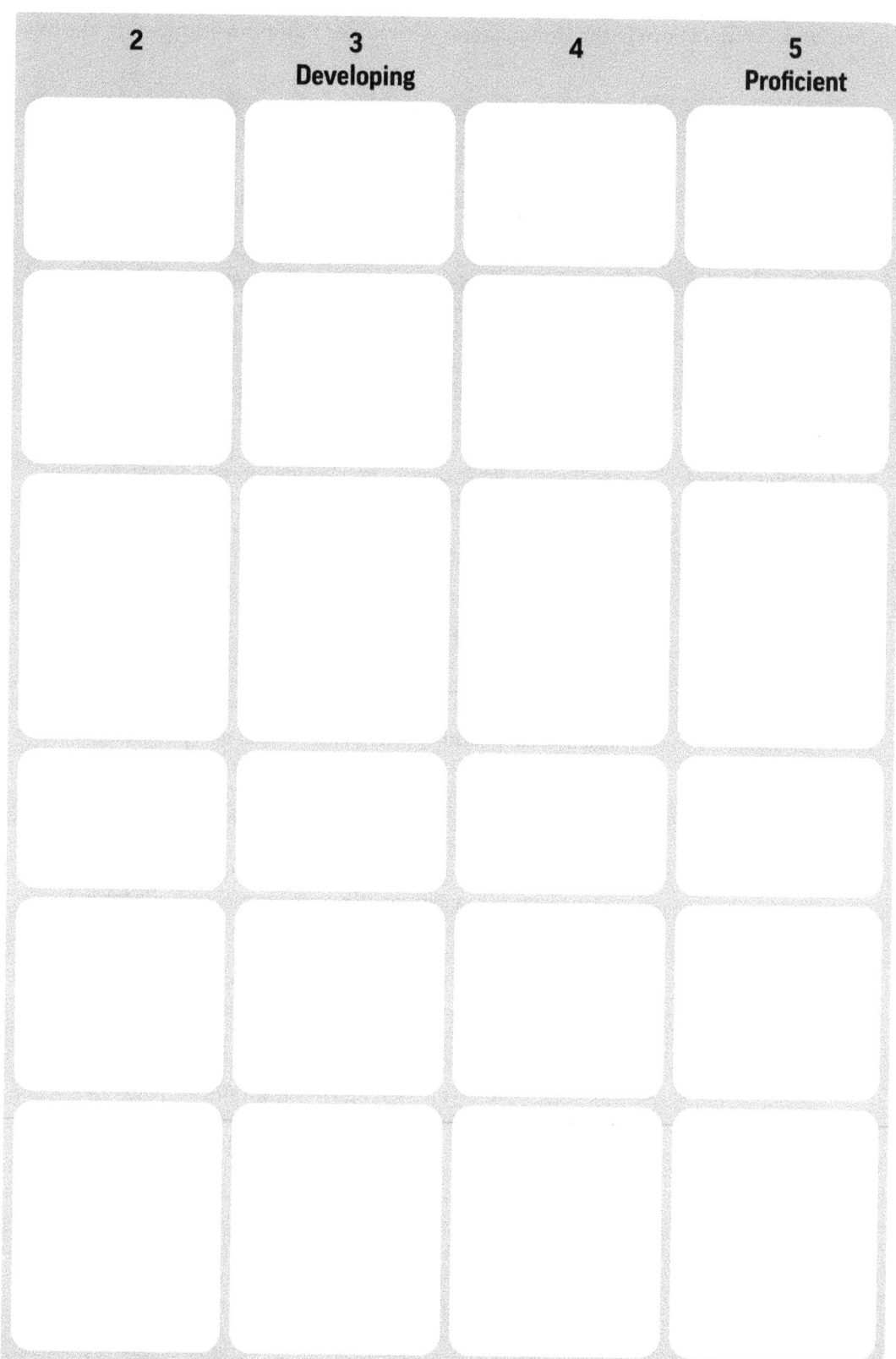

family, a Midwesterner who has lived in both rural and urban settings, a first-generation doctoral recipient, a teacher, a lifelong learner, an advocate for multilingual learners of English, and a woman born in the United States with mixed European ethnicity. In the final

Know Your Own Identity

TESOL's 6 Principles (Grades K–12)	**Principle 1. Know Your Learners** **Practice 1a.** Teachers gain information about their learners.
Standards for Initial TESOL Pre-K–12 Teacher Preparation Programs	**Standard 2: ELLs in the Sociocultural Context** **Component 2e.** Teachers identify and describe the impact of their identity, role, cultural understandings, and personal biases and conscious knowledge of U.S. culture on their interpretation of the educational strengths and needs of individual multilingual learners of English and multilingual learners of English in general.
Key Learning Target	I can identify dimensions of my own identity as one way to better understand the identities of my multilingual learners of English.
Lessons and Activities	**Lesson 1: Know Your Own Identity** **Activity** 1. Dimensions of My Identity **Lesson 2: The Cultural Other** **Activity** 2. Cultural Other Field Trip Experience
Notes for Each Teacher Role	**Professional Learning Providers:** You can easily facilitate Lesson 1: Know Your Own Identity in an approximately 30-minute whole-group staff meeting or professional learning community. Lesson 2: The Cultural Other occurs outside the school as a mini-field trip experience on another day of professional learning or on teachers' time. You can access many online resources in this chapter on the companion site for this book and may choose to print or create electronic versions for your professional learning sessions with teachers. **English Language Development Teachers:** You may find the lessons in this professional learning opportunity helpful in reminding you that you also have a unique personal and cultural identity. You can also reflect upon any dimensions of your identity that afford privileges (especially if you come from a dominant culture) and consider dimensions of identity that might be empowering or marginalizing for your multilingual learners of English. Identifying dimensions of identity for yourself and your multilingual learners of English is essential for your role as an advocate for your students and their families. **General Education Teachers:** Besides the notes for English language development teachers, you can consider how identity might impact your interpretation of the strengths and needs of your multilingual learners of English.

step of this activity, you will write a brief reflection about how recognizing dimensions of your identity might help you increase your understanding of the identities of your multilingual learners of English. For example, we realize we should welcome and celebrate all identities in our classrooms. We also recognize that some dimensions of identity can empower and afford privileges while others can be marginalizing (Center for Teaching, Learning & Mentoring, 2022/2023; Crenshaw, 1989). Because multilingual learners of English may sometimes feel marginalized because of dimensions of identity such as citizenship, race, ethnicity, language, and socioeconomic status, we encourage teachers to support multilingual learners of English in feeling empowered because of their unique linguistic and cultural backgrounds.

Activity Dimensions of My Identity

Key Learning Target: I can identify dimensions of my own identity as one way to better understand the identities of my multilingual learners of English.

Activity Goal: Reflect upon and write about dimensions of your personal identity.

Step 1: Reflect upon the sample dimensions of identity and consider those that shape your identity. You may refer to the questions and examples below each dimension to help guide your reflection. You may also jot down notes directly on the document.

Family Role/Structure

- What is your family role (e.g., parent, grandparent, son/ daughter, in-law, guardian)?
- How does being part of a family impact your identity?
- Who is part of your family?

Locale/Geography

- Do you live in a rural/ suburban/urban area?
- In which region of the world do you live?
- What is your nation of origin?
- Has your locality changed?

Special (Dis)Abilities or Interests

- Do you have any athletic/physical talents or interests?
- Do you have a mental interest or excel in an academic area?
- Do you have an artistic interest or hobby?
- Does a disability shape your identity?

Occupation

- Do you identify with your occupation? If so, why?

Political Beliefs/Affiliations

- Do your political beliefs shape your identity (e.g., Democrat, Republican, Independent, Socialist)?

Race

- Does your race impact your identity (e.g., Black, white, biracial, Native American, Latin, Asian, Pacific Islander)?

CONTINUED

Ethnicity

- Do you identify with any particular ethnic group (e.g., Irish, Mexican, Guatemalan, Sudanese, Karen)?

Socioeconomic Status

- Does socioeconomic status impact your identity (e.g., poor, middle class, upper class, wealthy)?
- Has your socioeconomic status changed over time?
- Does your level of wealth impact where you live and your housing?

Gender Identity/Sexual Orientation

- How might your gender affect your identity (e.g., male, female, cisgender, intersex, transgender)?
- Does your sexual orientation shape your identity (e.g., heterosexual, gay, lesbian, bisexual)?

Religious Beliefs

- Do your religious beliefs help shape your identity (e.g., Christian, Muslim, Jewish, Buddhist, agnostic)?

Language

- Are you monolingual, bilingual, or multilingual?
- Did you ever participate in an English language development program?

Age

- How might your age impact your identity (e.g., young, middle-aged, elderly)?
- To what generation do you belong, and how does it impact your cultural identity (e.g., Baby Boomer, Generation X, Millennial, Generation Z)?

Formal Education

- How does your level of education impact your identity?

Citizenship

- Does citizenship (or lack of citizenship) impact your identity? How so?

Health

- How might your health or the health of those close to you impact your identity?

Step 2: First, write your name. Then, referring to Step 1 of the My Identity activity, select and record five or more dimensions that impact your identity the most. You may also consider other aspects of identity not mentioned in Step 1.

CONTINUED

Name

Dimensions That Impact Your Identity

1. _____ 2. _____ 3. _____ 4. _____ 5. _____

Step 3: Next, write a few sentences that help describe your identity. The sentence starters and frames might prompt some ideas.

- I am _____.
- I identify with _____.
- A dimension of my identity that people might not know without asking is _____.
- _____ has a strong effect on my self-perception.
- _____ has a strong effect on how others perceive me.
- My ancestors came from _____.
- I am proud to identify as _____.
- I have found it to be challenging to identify _____
- I am _____, but I am/do not _____.
- I would pass on/not pass on _____.
- I am interested in _____.
- I value _____. I believe _____.

Step 4: Finally, write a brief reflection on this activity. The following questions might support your reflection:

- Which dimensions of your identity are apparent, and which are more hidden from others?
- Which dimensions of your identity might afford privilege, and which may be more marginalizing for you? For ideas, see the Wheel of Privilege and Power (Center for Teaching, Learning and Mentoring, 2022/2023, kb.wisc.edu/instructional-resources/page.php?id=119380).
- Which dimensions of identity might afford privilege, and which may be more marginalizing for your multilingual learners of English?
- How does identifying unique dimensions of your identity help you increase your understanding of the identities of your multilingual learners of English?
- How might dimensions of your identity impact how you interpret the strengths and needs of your multilingual learners of English?

The Dimensions of My Identity activity was inspired by Arriaga (2016), Center for Teaching, Learning & Mentoring (2022/2023), Gorski (2015), Hiatt and Jones-Vo (2017–2018), Hollins-Alexander and Law (2022), Lindahl (2022), Staehr Fenner and Snyder (2017), and Zion and Kozleski (2005).

Lesson 2: The Cultural Other

As mentioned in the Getting Ready to Learn section, the cultural other experience is an "experience of *being* 'the other', 'the outsider, or the minority student" (McBrien, 2009, p. 334). In Lesson 2, you have an opportunity to experience being a cultural other through a mini-immersion field trip in your community. This experience will help you learn about the culture of one or more of your multilingual learners of English "and most importantly, learn about [your] own culture" (Gardner, 2019).

Cultural Other Field Trip Experience

Key Learning Target: I can identify dimensions of my own identity as one way to better understand the identities of my multilingual learners of English.

Activity Goal: Engage in a cultural other mini-immersion field trip to learn about the culture of one or more of your multilingual learners of English and indirectly learn more about your own culture.

Background Information

For the cultural other field trip experience, you will be able to deepen your understanding of your own culture and the culture of your students and families by engaging in a mini-immersion field trip experience within your community. This will allow you to experience another culture without leaving your community.

Steps to Follow If You Choose This Activity

1. Engage in a cultural exploration of a place or event in your community that represents a culture different from your own. It should be a place or event that you are unfamiliar with and represents one or more of your multilingual learners of English and their families. You might go with a peer or, if feasible, engage in this activity by yourself. Examples might include:
   a. Place of worship (e.g., a place of worship that is different from your religion or service in another language)
   b. Business (e.g., grocery store, restaurant)
   c. Event (e.g., holiday festival)
   d. Home visit of one of your multilingual learners of English
2. Visit one or more locales or attend a cultural event to experience what it is like to be the cultural other.
3. If possible, take a photo and collect an artifact of interest to share with your colleagues.
4. Write a brief reflection on your experience and your new learning. For example, what did you learn about the culture of your multilingual learners and their families? What did you learn about your own culture? Did you have any aha moments about potential implications for your teaching? In addition, you may debrief with other colleagues if you are working collaboratively.
5. You may see the excerpt at the beginning of this chapter for a sample reflection from a cultural other field trip experience.

The Cultural Other Field Trip Experience was inspired by Hiatt and Jones-Vo (2017–2018), Gardner (2019), and McBrien (2009).

Closing Questions and Suggestions for Each Teacher Role

In the first professional learning opportunity, Know Your Own Identity, you reflected upon dimensions of your identity to better understand the identities of your multilingual learners of English. You also had an opportunity to experience being the cultural other to deepen your understanding of your own culture and that of your multilingual learners of English. The following chart offers some role-specific questions and suggestions to help you reflect upon and extend your learning after engaging in this first professional learning opportunity.

Closing Questions and Suggestions for Each Teacher Role

Directions: Take a moment to write and reflect on your learning from Professional Learning Opportunity #1, Know Your Own Identity. We have included a few role-specific questions and suggestions to prompt your thinking.

Professional Learning Providers

Closing Questions
- Which lessons and activities did you choose to facilitate?
- What went well?
- What might you want to improve?
- How might you follow up?

Suggestions for This Role
A suggestion to get started is to have your teachers debrief in small groups about Lessons 1 and 2 to determine classroom-level and schoolwide implications for instruction and family engagement.

English Language Development Teachers

Closing Questions
- What were your key takeaways from this professional learning opportunity?
- What impact did the lessons have on your work with your students and other teachers in your context?

Suggestions for This Role
You might share your personal reflections from the Dimensions of My Identity activity in a professional learning community or grade-level meeting. You could also share about a cultural other experience you have had. Being the first to share can inspire others to share as well.

General Education Teachers

Closing Questions
- How did this go?
- What went well?
- What were your key takeaways?
- How might dimensions of your personal identity impact your interpretations of the strengths and needs of your multilingual learners of English?

Suggestions for This Role
You might choose to share your personal reflections from the Dimensions of My Identity activity and what you learned from your cultural other experience with colleagues in your school. Independently or as a team, you might consider implications for instruction with your multilingual learners of English.

Professional Learning Opportunity #2: Recognize How Culture Impacts Learning

The second professional learning opportunity's key outcome is recognizing how culture can impact the education of multilingual learners of English. In doing so, you will gain information about your multilingual learners of English (TESOL Principle 1, Practice 1a) by exploring aspects of culture at the surface and deeper levels. You will also have the opportunity to identify cultural explanations for cross-cultural misunderstandings based on your cultural interpretations and the cultural perspectives of multilingual learners of English (Standard 2: Component 2e of the *Standards for Initial TESOL Pre-K–12 Teacher Preparation Programs*). The Recognize How Culture Impacts Learning box provides an overview of the second professional learning opportunity.

Recognize How Culture Impacts Learning

TESOL's 6 Principles (Grades K–12)	**Principle 1. Know Your Learners** **Practice 1a.** Teachers gain information about their learners.
Standards for Initial TESOL Pre-K–12 Teacher Preparation Programs	**Standard 2: ELLs in the Sociocultural Context** **Component 2e.** Teachers identify and describe the impact of their identity, role, cultural understandings, and personal biases and conscious knowledge of U.S. culture on their interpretation of the educational strengths and needs of individual multilingual learners of English and multilingual learners of English in general.
Key Learning Target	I can recognize the impact of culture on the education of multilingual learners of English.
Lessons and Activities	**Background Reading: What Is Culture?** **Lesson 1: Looking Below the Surface** **Activity** 1. Cultural Differences Lying Beneath the Surface **Lesson 2: Cross-Cultural Scenarios** **Activities** 1. Sample Cross-Cultural Scenarios 2. Cross-Cultural Scenarios in Your Teaching Context
Notes for Each Teacher Role	**Professional Learning Providers:** You can have participants independently read What Is Culture? to build background for Lessons 1 and 2. It is then possible to review the meaning of culture and facilitate Lessons 1 and 2 in approximately 30–45 minutes. You can access many online resources in this chapter on the companion site for this book and may choose to print or create electronic versions for your professional learning sessions with teachers. **English Language Development Teachers:** As you engage in the lessons, try to identify dimensions of your identity that might impact your instruction with multilingual learners of English. You can also review and refine your understanding of how deeper levels of culture impact learning for multilingual learners of English. **General Education Teachers**: As you begin to consider how culture impacts learning, it is essential to remember that you also have a unique cultural identity. In addition, consider some cultural differences that are important for teachers to know that might impact your teaching.

Background Reading: What Is Culture?

Defining Culture

There are many ways to define culture. Zion and Kozleski (2005) define culture as "a system of shared beliefs, values, customs, behaviors, and artifacts with which the members of society use to understand their world and one another" (p. 1). Hammond (2015) sees culture as "the way every brain makes sense of the world...or the software for the brain's hardware" (p. 22). In addition, others acknowledge that culture is dynamic or changes over time and with new experiences (Hammond, 2015; Staehr Fenner & Snyder, 2017). Notably, our work with multilingual learners of English shows that the cultural experiences of second-generation language learners might differ from those of first-generation learners from a similar cultural background. Moreover, "there is great variability of cultures within social groups" (Staehr Fenner & Snyder, 2017, p. 31), such as variability among multilingual learners of English who originate from the same country or area of the world.

Three Layers of Culture

Hammond (2015) visualizes three layers of culture (surface, shallow, and deep) as a "Culture Tree" (p. 24). In this representation, the tree's leaves represent *surface culture*, the trunk and branches depict *shallow culture*, and the roots signify *deep culture*. Hammond also emphasizes that, like a tree, surface and shallow culture change over time and "with the seasons," whereas deep culture grounds individuals and is more static. Figure 2.1 visually represents these three layers of culture.

Figure 2.1 *Three layers of culture.*

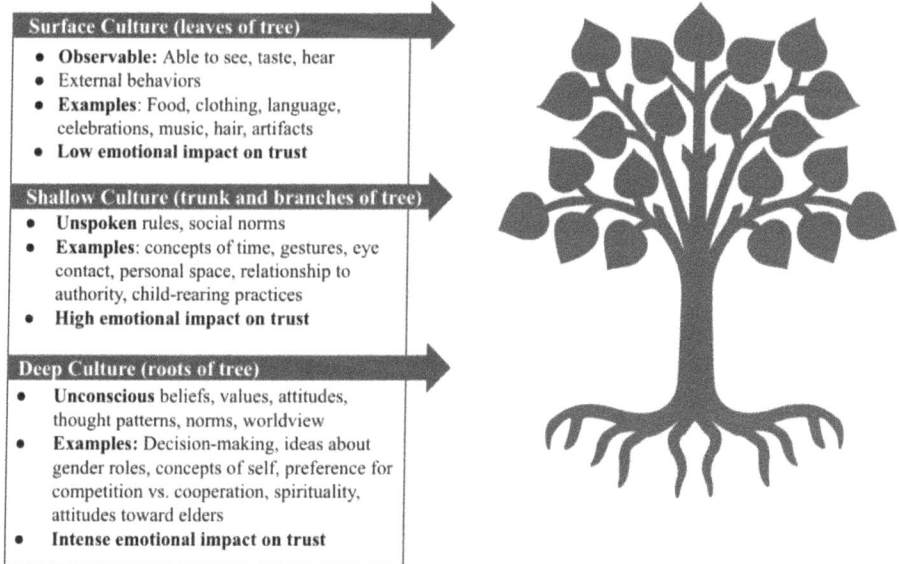

Based on Frank (2013), Hall (1976), Hammond (2015), and Ting-Toomey (1999). The concept of the Culture Tree is based on Hammond (2015).

Surface culture is the most observable and includes aspects of cultural behavior such as food, clothing, language, multicultural celebrations, music, artifacts, and other aspects of culture that can be seen, heard, or tasted. Surface culture is how people often think of culture and carries a lower emotional load (Hall, 1976; Hammond, 2015; Staehr Fenner & Snyder, 2017; Zion & Kozleski, 2005).

The *shallow* layer of culture includes unspoken rules and social norms (Frank, 2013; Hammond, 2015). Examples include beliefs about time, nonverbal communication (e.g., gestures, eye contact), sense of personal space, relationship to authority, and child-rearing practices (Frank, 2013; Hammond, 2015). Shallow culture has a higher emotional impact on trust when cultural misunderstandings occur.

The *deep* layer of culture consists of unconscious beliefs, attitudes, thought patterns, and social norms. Examples include decision-making processes, ideas about gender roles, preferences for competition or collaboration, spirituality, and attitudes toward elders (Frank, 2013; Hammond, 2015; Indiana Department of Education Office of English Language Learning & Migrant Education, n.d.; Staehr Fenner & Snyder, 2017). This layer has an intense emotional impact on trust because it is an integral part of an individual's worldview.

Surface culture is a starting point or the first layer of culture. Starting with surface culture is an acceptable approach; however, teachers sometimes focus on tangible surface culture and neglect the deeper layers of culture, which may lead to more cross-cultural confusion and different perceptions of education (Staehr Fenner & Snyder, 2017). To truly understand a culture, we must also understand shallow and deep cultures (Hammond, 2015; Ting-Toomey & Chung, 2012). Ting-Toomey and Chung (2012) explain that deeper layers of culture represent "the underlying set of cultural beliefs and values that drives people's thinking, reactions, and behaviors" (p. 16). Hall (1976) adds that shallow and deep cultures are initially hidden from view and primarily out of awareness; however, the greater our engagement with diverse cultures, the more mindful we become of varying underlying beliefs, values, and thought patterns.

Lesson 1: Looking Below the Surface

Teachers of multilingual learners of English need to be aware of some fundamental cultural differences between their own culture and the cultures of language learners and how those differences can influence different perspectives on education. In Lesson 1: Looking Below the Surface, you will take a closer look at some critical cultural differences beneath the surface layer of culture that are important for teachers of multilingual learners of English to know.

It is important to note that there is no right or wrong when it comes to cultural differences, and even within the same culture, there are variances. It is essential, however, for teachers to be aware of differences and their impact on instruction. In addition, teachers can support multilingual learners in becoming familiar with cultural practices or expectations in a new culture while helping them maintain their unique cultural identities.

Additional Resource

If you would like to see where sample countries fall on the individualism continuum and power distance continua, reviewing Hofstede's (n.d.) *Country Comparison* graphs is helpful (geerthofstede.com/country-comparison-graphs/).

Lesson 2: Cross-Cultural Scenarios

In Lesson 2: Cross-Cultural Scenarios, you will have the opportunity to apply what you have learned about shallow and deep layers of culture to help explain cross-cultural misunderstandings. This lesson has two activities: Sample Cross-Cultural Scenarios and Cross-Cultural Scenarios in Your Teaching Context.

Key Learning Target: I can recognize the impact of culture on the education of multilingual learners of English.

Activity Goal: Review cultural differences that lie beneath the surface layer of culture, specific to teachers of multilingual learners of English, and consider which cultural differences are more typical of your culture and the cultures of your multilingual learners of English.

Step 1: Review the characteristics of sample cultural differences that lie beneath the surface layer of culture that might be helpful to you as a teacher of multilingual learners of English.

Who Matters Most (Palls, 2010)	In **individualist cultures**, the individual matters most. These cultures value competition, success, and personal goals. (Rothstein-Fisch & Trumbull, 2008; Staehr Fenner & Snyder, 2017)	In **collectivist cultures,** the group matters most. These cultures prioritize the group's needs and value cooperation and group success. (Palls, 2010; Staehr Fenner & Snyder, 2017)
Relationship to Authority	In **low-power-distance cultures,** the teacher is an equal power, and students are encouraged to ask questions, state opinions, and disagree. (Rothstein-Fisch & Trumbull, 2008)	In **high-power-distance cultures,** the teacher has higher power than the students, and students are not encouraged to ask questions or state opinions and tend to show respect for authority. (Al-Issa, 2005; Rothstein-Fisch & Trumbull, 2008)
Context Expected	In **low-context cultures**, teachers and students are more direct and explicit, use details, are rule-governed, and focus more on the written word. (Palls, 2010)	In **high-context cultures**, students are more indirect, implicit, or vague when asked a question or discussing an issue in class (Al-Issa, 2005), and "much common knowledge is assumed" (Palls, 2010, p. 307).

CONTINUED

Concepts About Time	In **monochronic cultures,** punctuality matters, and being late is rude. Time is not to be wasted, and there is a tendency to get down to business right away before developing trust and relationships. (Ariza, 2006; Palls, 2010; Staehr Fenner & Snyder, 2017) 	In **polychronic cultures,** arriving late is not considered impolite, and "there is ample time to develop trust" (Palls, 2010, p. 307) before doing business. 
Eye Contact	In some cultures, having **direct eye contact** when speaking with an adult is polite. (Ariza, 2006; Staehr Fenner & Snyder, 2017)	In contrast, looking an adult in the eye is considered impolite in many other cultures, and **limited direct eye contact** is more of the norm. (Ariza, 2006; Staehr Fenner & Snyder, 2017)
Personal Space	In some cultures, people have an **unspoken personal space** around their bodies and tend to back up if others invade their personal space. (Ariza, 2006)	Other cultures prefer **closer proximity** between people, and some teachers may erroneously perceive students as crowding around them. (Ariza, 2006)

Step 2: Referring to the chart in Step 1, answer the following reflection questions about key cultural differences beneath the surface.

- Which column of the chart is more typical of the region of the world in which you currently teach?
- Which column of the chart might be more typical of your multilingual learners and their families?
- Which characteristics of culture represent your personal cultural beliefs and expectations?
- How might cultural differences impact instruction with your multilingual learners of English?

Chart based on Palls (2010).

Sample Cross-Cultural Scenarios

Key Learning Target: I can recognize the impact of culture on the education of multilingual learners of English.

Activity Goal: Determine cultural explanations for cross-cultural misunderstandings in school settings.

Directions: Read the sample cross-cultural scenarios and respond to the discussion questions while considering how shallow and deep cultures may influence different educational perceptions. You may refer to the Cultural Differences Lying Beneath the Surface activity to assist you.

Scenario 1

"A female European American teacher reports to an immigrant Latino father that his daughter is doing well in class—speaking out, expressing herself, taking an active role—he looks down at his lap and does not respond. Thinking that perhaps he has not understood, the teacher again praises his daughter's ability to speak out in class and explains that it is very important for children to participate orally. Looking even more uncomfortable, the father changes the subject. The teacher gets the impression that this parent is not interested in his daughter's school success, and she feels frustrated and a bit resentful. Toward the end of the conference, the father asks, with evident concern, 'How is she doing? She talking too much?' The teacher is confused." (Excerpt from Trumbull et al., 2000, p. 1)

Discussion
- Does this parent care whether his daughter is doing well?
- Why does the father change the subject?
- What aspect of shallow or deep culture might the teacher be enacting?
- What aspect of shallow or deep culture might the father be enacting?

Scenario 2

A fifth-grade teacher is upset when the family of his multilingual learner of English student does not show up on time for parent-teacher conferences. When arriving 2 hours after their scheduled appointment, the teacher lets the family know he will meet with them when conferences finish. He also noticed the extended family arrive for the conference, which is confusing because the school invited only the parents or guardians to attend. When the conference finally starts, the teacher gets right down to business because it has been a long night. The family feels confused as well.

Discussion
- What does the teacher think about the family?
- Where did he learn to think that way?
- What might the family be thinking?
- What aspects of shallow or deep culture might the family be enacting?
- What implications might this have for the teacher?

Activity drawn from Hiatt and Jones-Vo (2017–2018) and Trumbull et al. (2000).

For Scenario 1, the difference in relationship to authority helps to explain the cross-cultural misunderstanding. The father in the first scenario most likely comes from a high-power-distance culture in which teachers have higher power and students are not encouraged to ask questions or speak up in class (Al-Issa, 2005; Rothstein-Fisch & Trumbull, 2008). He is concerned about his child's behavior and asks if she talks too much.

In Scenario 2, concepts about time and who matters most help to explain the cross-cultural misunderstanding. The family is most likely from a culture in which arriving late is not considered impolite, while the teacher values punctuality. The family might also prefer to build a family-teacher relationship before discussing grades and academic achievement. In addition, the family is most likely from a collectivist culture since they arrive with an extended family and seem to value including a larger family unit.

When working with multilingual learners and their families, it is important to recognize cultural explanations for behaviors. It is also vital to view the cultures of multilingual learners of English as assets and to support students in bridging their existing knowledge with school expectations while preserving their personal cultural identities.

Activity   Cross-Cultural Scenario in Your Teaching Context

Key Learning Target: I can recognize the impact of culture on the education of multilingual learners of English.

Activity Goal: Identify a cross-cultural scenario in your teaching context that might have led to a misunderstanding and then identify a potential cultural explanation for that misunderstanding.

Directions
1. In the space provided, describe a cross-cultural misunderstanding you have experienced when working with multilingual learners of English that might have had a cultural explanation.
2. Then, write a reflection about this experience. In your reflection, consider how shallow and deep cultures may have influenced different educational perceptions. For ideas, you can refer the Cultural Differences Lying Beneath the Surface activity.
3. Share your experience and explanation with colleagues.

Cross-Cultural Misunderstanding

Reflection

Closing Questions and Suggestions for Each Teacher Role

The second professional learning opportunity, Recognize How Culture Impacts Learning, was intended to help you recognize the impact of culture on the education of multilingual learners of English. The following chart offers some role-specific questions and suggestions to help you reflect upon and extend your learning after engaging in this learning opportunity.

Closing Questions and Suggestions for Each Teacher Role

Directions: Take a moment to write and reflect on your learning from Professional Learning Opportunity #2, Recognize How Culture Impacts Learning. We have included a few role-specific questions and suggestions to prompt your thinking.

Professional Learning Providers

Closing Questions
- What went well in facilitating professional learning?
- What might you want to improve?

Suggestions for This Role
You might encourage your participants to share their responses from Lessons 1 and 2 in small groups. You can also consider cross-cultural differences for your school and implications for instruction and family engagement.

English Language Development Teachers

Closing Questions
- What were some aha moments for you related to how culture can impact learning?
- How did this learning inform how you design classroom instruction for your multilingual learners of English?

Suggestions for This Role
You might assist general education teachers in navigating cross-cultural differences by reminding them of the differences that exist in shallow and deep cultures and how those differences can impact perspectives on education.

General Education Teachers

Closing Questions
- What were your key takeaways?
- How will this professional learning opportunity impact how you design classroom instruction for your multilingual learners of English?
- How might it impact interactions you have with families of your multilingual learners of English?

Suggestions for This Role
For classroom instruction, you might create structured cooperative learning activities for students from a collectivistic culture. In addition, you could help bridge cultural differences by discussing how the cultures of the school and home are similar and different (and how both ways have value).

Professional Learning Opportunity #3: Know the Backgrounds of Your Multilingual Learners of English

For the third professional learning opportunity, you will identify various types of background information that are important to know about your multilingual learners of English (TESOL Principle 1, Practice 1a). You will also become familiar with tools to gather that background information and have an opportunity to implement a tool for one of your students whose first language is not English (Standard 2: Component 2c and 2d of the *Standards for Initial TESOL Pre-K–12 Teacher Preparation Programs*). The Know the Backgrounds of Your Multilingual Learners of English box shows the components of the third professional learning opportunity.

Know the Backgrounds of Your Multilingual Learners of English

TESOL's 6 Principles (Grades K–12)	**Principle 1. Know Your Learners** **Practice 1A.** Teachers gain information about their learners.
Standards for Initial TESOL Pre-K–12 Teacher Preparation Programs	**Standard 2: ELLs in the Sociocultural Context** **Component 2c.** Teachers devise and implement methods to understand the characteristics, including background knowledge, educational history, and current performance data of each multilingual learner of English, to develop effective, individualized instructional and assessment practices for their multilingual learners of English. **Component 2d**. Teachers devise and implement methods to learn about personal characteristics of the individual multilingual learners of English (e.g., interests, motivations, strengths, needs) and their families (e.g., language use, literacy practices, circumstances) to develop effective instructional practices.
Key Learning Target	I can implement a method to collect and organize information about the individual, family, language, academic, and experiential backgrounds of multilingual learners of English to support instruction and assessment.
Lessons and Activities	**Lesson 1: What Teachers Should Know About Their Multilingual Learners of English** **Activity** 1. Building Background **Lesson 2: Tools to Organize Background Information for Your Multilingual Learners of English** **Activities** 1. Know the Backgrounds of Your Multilingual Learners of English Sample Tool 2. Know the Backgrounds of Your Multilingual Learners of English: Moises Example 3. Application Activity for Know the Backgrounds of Your Multilingual Learners of English 4. Additional Tools

CONTINUED

Notes for Each Teacher Role	**Professional Learning Providers:** The Building Background activity can be facilitated in one session with a whole or small group in about 30 minutes. The first two activities of Lesson 2 can be combined and require approximately 30 minutes when facilitated back-to-back. The third activity of Lesson 2, Application for Know the Backgrounds of Your Multilingual Learners of English, can be assigned for independent work and shared in professional learning communities. The fourth activity of Lesson 2 requires approximately 15 minutes. You can access many online resources in this chapter on the companion site for this book and may choose to print or create electronic versions for your professional learning sessions with teachers.
	English Language Development Teachers: It is very likely that you already have a system to gather and document background information on your multilingual learners of English. As you engage in this professional learning opportunity, consider additional ideas you can add to your toolbox to ensure you and general education teachers have access to relevant background information for the multilingual learners of English in your school or district.
	General Education Teachers: As you engage in this learning opportunity, consider what background information is essential to know about your multilingual learners of English to support instruction and assessment. Also, reflect on how you might be able to locate and organize relevant information to support your multilingual learners of English.

Lesson 1: What Teachers Should Know About Their Multilingual Learners of English

In this first lesson, you will begin to identify different types of background information teachers should know about their multilingual learners of English. To gather ideas for what you should know, you will watch a brief video, explore TESOL's recommendations, and read an article.

Activity Building Background

Key Learning Target: I can implement a method to collect and organize information about the individual, family, language, academic, and experiential backgrounds of multilingual learners of English to support instruction and assessment.

Activity Goal: Build background for types of information teachers should know about their multilingual learners of English.

Step 1: Warm-Up Video 🎥

1. **Watch** the first 40 seconds of a video titled *Advice for New Populations* (Colorín Colorado, 2013, www.youtube.com/watch?v=qXWG279kodE).

CONTINUED

2. **Listen** for three types of basic background information that Paula Markus, the former ESL coordinator for the Toronto School Board, recommends teachers should know about their multilingual learners of English.
3. **Turn and talk** to a colleague if working together or write down what you heard if working alone.

Please note that the term *school board* in Canada is the same as that of *school district* in the United States.

Postviewing Note: You might have heard Paula Markus mention that teachers of multilingual learners of English should be aware of their students' home countries, home language(s), and prior experiences.

Step 2: TESOL's Recommendations

Review the following recommendations.
Principle 1, Know Your Learners, of TESOL's 6 Principles expands on the recommendations of Paula Markus. For example, Principle 1 (TESOL International Association, 2024) recommends K–12 teachers know the following essential characteristics of their multilingual learners of English:

- **Cultural background information** such as home country, cultural knowledge, the sociopolitical context of the home country, and life experiences
- **Home language background,** including oral proficiency and literacy levels
- **English language background** that includes levels of proficiency in the four English domains (listening, speaking, reading, and writing)
- **Educational background** considerations such as prior educational experiences, special needs, learning preferences, and access to supportive resources
- **Personal background,** such as the student's interests, gifts and talents, life goals, and socioemotional background

Furthermore, the *Standards for Initial TESOL Pre-K–12 Teacher Preparation Programs* (TESOL International Association, 2019) recommends that teachers of multilingual learners of English should know or learn **basic background information about the families** of multilingual learners of English, including their countries of origin, family member representation, assets (or strengths they bring to school), and other information related to their circumstances.

Step 3: Reading

Breiseth (2019) shares 10 things teachers need to know about the assets, challenges, and prior experiences of multilingual learners of English. Read the article entitled *10 Things You Need to Learn About Your English Language Learners* to continue to build background for this topic (www.colorincolorado.org/article/10-things-you-need-learn-about-your-english-language-learners).

Lesson 2: Tools to Organize Background Information for Your Multilingual Learners of English

TESOL's Principle 1, Practice 1a (TESOL International Association, 2024) recommends that teachers gather and organize background information on multilingual learners of English and make that information available to all teachers serving those students. Furthermore, the *Standards for Initial TESOL Pre-K–12 Teacher Preparation Programs* (TESOL International Association, 2019) recommends that teachers of multilingual learners of English should know or learn basic background information about the families of multilingual learners of English, including their countries of origin, family member representation, assets (or strengths they bring to school), and other information related to their circumstances.

There are many ways to organize background information for multilingual learners of English. One way is to record information on a print or electronic document that is customizable for teachers to add to and make available to current and future teachers. Inspired by our work with teachers of multilingual learners of English, for this book, we share a sample tool called Know the Backgrounds of Your Multilingual Learners of English that incorporates the recommendations of Paula Markus (Colorín Colorado, 2013), TESOL International Association (2019, 2024), and Lydia Breiseth (2019). The tool includes places to record information about the cultural, family, language, academic, and personal background of an individual multilingual learner of English. In addition, there is a section to record yearly updates. In the first activity, you will familiarize yourself with two versions of the tool as one way to gather and organize basic background information for the multilingual learners of English you serve.

Activity   Know the Backgrounds of Your Multilingual Learners of English Sample Tool

Key Learning Target: I can implement a method for collecting and organizing information about the individual, family, language, academic, and experiential backgrounds of multilingual learners of English to support instruction and assessment.

Activity Goal: Become familiar with a sample tool to gather and organize basic background information for an individual multilingual learner you serve.

Directions
1. Familiarize yourself with the components of the sample tool.
2. In addition, familiarize yourself with different versions of this tool. There are two versions without guiding questions and one version that includes guiding questions for each section. All versions are available on the companion site for this book.
3. Discuss which components of the different versions of the tool would be helpful in your context to gather background information on your multilingual learners of English.

Tool Description: This tool will help you gather and organize relevant background information for an individual multilingual learner of English. Teachers can complete this tool collaboratively among the ELD teacher and other significant educators involved in the student's day. In addition, the student and family can provide helpful background information. This tool should be available to all teachers supporting the multilingual learner of English to help inform instruction and assessment. Teachers can also build upon the tool in subsequent years in the Yearly Updates section of the tool.

Student Information

Picture of Student (optional)	• Student Name: • Preferred Name: • How to Pronounce Name: • School: • Date Form Started: • Age: • Grade:

CONTINUED

Cultural and Family Background

Home Country (consider the student's country and the family's country or countries of origin)	
Family Member Supports	
Family Strengths	
Other (prior/current experiences, trauma, family literacy practices, other circumstances)	

Student Language Background

Home Language(s)	**Language(s) Spoken in Home** (home language survey can be helpful): **Oral Proficiency in Home Language(s):** **Literate in Home Language(s)** (Yes/No):
English	Years of English Language Development Instruction: **Overall English Language Proficiency** (e.g., beginning, intermediate, advanced; emerging, progressing, proficient; beginning, emerging, developing, expanding, bridging, reaching): **Domain Levels:** • Listening: • Speaking: • Reading: • Writing: • Date of most recent language assessment:

Student Academic Background

Prior Educational Experiences	
Former Schools Attended	
Academic Strengths	

CONTINUED

Academic Challenges	
Special Needs	

Student Personal Background

Interests/Likes/ Motivations	
Dislikes	
Goals/Aspirations	
Personal Strengths/Talents	
Personal Challenges	

Yearly Updates

Directions: This section of the tool can be used to provide yearly updates of what worked each year and suggestions for subsequent years. This tool should be available to all teachers supporting the multilingual learner of English.

Summary of Current Grade/ School Year	Grade/School Year: What Worked: Suggestions for Next Year:

Each section of the tool is described in more detail here:

- Student Information: In this section, you record a student's name, age, grade, school, and the date you started the form. There is also a place to jot down how to pronounce the student's name correctly.
- Cultural and Family Background: This part of the tool is for recording background information about the student and family's country of birth, family members, family strengths, and other information. Knowing prior experiences that would support the student academically, culturally, and socioemotionally is helpful.
- Student Language Background: It is essential to know the language(s) spoken in the home and if a student is literate or orally proficient in the home language(s). In addition, it is important to know if multilingual learners of English have had prior ELD instruction and their overall English language proficiency levels. Use this section to collect information about the language background of your multilingual learners of English in both the home language(s) and English.
- Student Academic Background: This part of the tool allows you to gather and organize information about prior educational experiences, former schools attended, academic strengths, academic challenges, and any special needs the multilingual learner of English might have.

- Student Personal Background: This section is for recording the interests, dislikes, goals, personal strengths, and challenges of a multilingual learner of English.
- Yearly Updates: The final section of the tool can be used to document yearly updates of what worked each year and provide suggestions for subsequent years. This tool should be available to all teachers supporting a multilingual learner of English.

How to Gather All This Information

You might also be asking how gathering all of this information is possible. One way is to check the student's cumulative folder, which often has a student's home language survey (HLS). The HLS provides official documentation of languages spoken in the home. In addition, the cumulative folder often includes transcripts and grade reports from prior schools. We also recommend asking the ELD teacher or other teachers, bilingual/multilingual staff, family, community members, and the students themselves to gather relevant background information (Breiseth, n.d.). Finally, it is important to recognize that this information can be slowly gathered over time versus all at once.

It is often helpful to see a model for completing a tool. In the next activity, you will review a completed tool called Know the Backgrounds of Your Multilingual Learners of English: Moises Example. We based the completed tool on a student named Moises from a short fiction film, *Immersion* (Levien, 2020; Media That Matters, 2009, www.youtube.com/watch?v=I6YOHAjLKYI), a frequently watched video in the multilingual learner of English world. What follows are the directions for this activity.

Activity Know the Backgrounds of Your Multilingual Learners of English: Moises Example

Key Learning Target: I can implement a method to collect and organize information about the individual, family, language, academic, and experiential backgrounds of multilingual learners of English to support instruction and assessment.

Activity Goal: Become familiar with a completed sample tool to gather and organize basic background information for the multilingual learners of English you serve.

Background for This Activity: The Moises example provides a model for completing the Know the Backgrounds of Your Multilingual Learners of English Sample Tool. We completed the tool based on information from the short fiction film *Immersion* (Media That Matters, 2009, www.youtube.com/watch?v=I6YOHAjLKYI) and other hyperlinked resources.

Directions
1. Locate the Know the Backgrounds of Your Multilingual Learners of English: Moises Example on the companion site for this book.
2. Watch the short film *Immersion* (Media That Matters, 2009, www.youtube.com/watch?v=I6YOHAjLKYI).
3. Review the completed Know the Backgrounds of Your Multilingual Learners of English: Moises Example on pages 2–4 of the activity.
4. Answer two reflection questions on page 4 after watching the film and reviewing the completed form.
5. Finally, compare your responses to sample responses provided on page 5 of the Moises activity. Please note there are other possible responses for completing the Moises background tool, and answers may vary for follow-up reflection section questions.
Also, an *Immersion* trailer is available with additional information at vimeo.com/470775537?embedded=true&source=vimeo_logo&owner=737258 (Levien, 2020).

Application Activity for Know the Backgrounds of Your Multilingual Learners of English

Key Learning Target: I can implement a method to collect and organize information about the individual, family, language, academic, and experiential backgrounds of multilingual learners of English to support instruction and assessment.

Activity Goal: Implement a method to collect and organize information about the individual, family, academic, and experiential backgrounds of one of your multilingual learners of English to support instruction and assessment.

Directions

1. **Think** of at least one multilingual learner of English.
2. **Choose** one of the three versions of the Know the Backgrounds of Your Multilingual Learners of English Sample Tool (available for download with the Chapter 2 online resources) to **document** the individual, family, academic, and experiential backgrounds of one of your multilingual learners of English to support instruction and assessment.
3. **Consult** with others as needed as you complete your background information tool (e.g., the student, student's family, English language development teacher, colleagues, bilingual/multilingual staff, and community members).
4. **Reflect** upon the information you gathered for your multilingual learner of English by responding to the following two questions:
   a. How does collecting and organizing individual, family, academic, and experiential background information impact instruction and assessment for your multilingual learner of English?
   b. Why would it be important to know some background information about your multilingual learner of English soon after enrollment?

Additional Suggestions for Completing This Activity

- You may refer to the Know the Backgrounds of Your Multilingual Learners of English: Moises Example for a sample of how to complete this tool and answer reflection questions.
- You can also consider how you might differentiate based on your student's English language proficiency level, home language literacy level, amount of prior schooling, potential trauma, and so on. In addition, you can build on your student's assets, such as being multilingual and multicultural, having a supportive family, or being able to see the world from multiple perspectives. In addition, you can consider any potential gaps in learning based on interrupted schooling.

The Know the Backgrounds of Your Multilingual Learners of English Sample Tool is only one example of collecting and organizing background information on your multilingual learners of English. In the following activity, you will explore two additional examples to gather multilingual learner of English–specific background information.

Key Learning Target: I can implement a method to collect and organize information about the individual, family, language, academic, and experiential backgrounds of multilingual learners of English to support instruction and assessment.

Activity Goal: Explore additional sample tools to collect and organize essential background information on your multilingual learners of English.

Directions: Explore two additional sample tools to collect and organize essential background information on your multilingual learners of English.

1. **Virtual Tool:** SupportEd offers a free virtual template called *Virtual Tool: What I Know About My Multilingual Learner (ML) Google Slide Template* (Staehr Fenner, 2020; supported.com/knowyourel/?mc_cid=ea693e3a7b&mc_eid=52fb1d2443). This tool allows you to record information about your students' home languages, English proficiency levels, educational experiences, family background, student interests, and student plans and goals.
2. **Classroom Chart:** Benegas and Stolpestad (2024; www.tesol.org/media/ dmdfltfg/14144-chapter-4_getting-to-know-the-els-in-your-classroom. pdf?sfvrsn=2203f8dc_2) offer the handout *Getting to Know the ELs in Your Classroom* on the companion site for the book *Teacher Leadership for School-Wide English Learning* (Benegas & Stolpestad, 2020). The tool allows teachers to document background information for several multilingual learners of English on one document. Benegas and Stolpestad based the tool on six Colorín Colorado recommendations (Breiseth, n.d.) for what teachers need to know about their multilingual learners of English:
   a. Where was my student born?
   b. What brought my student and/or my student's family here?
   c. What should I know about my student's family?
   d. What language(s) does my student speak?
   e. What kind of schooling has my student had?
   f. What are my student's interests?

In addition to using the tools we shared in this book, consider creating different formats of the tools that have been shared (e.g., spreadsheet formats, slides) or designing your own tool to gather multilingual learner of English–specific background information. Whatever tool you choose, sharing and building upon collected information with other colleagues serving the same multilingual learners of English is essential for the exchange of best practices and resources to meet the student's needs.

Closing Questions and Suggestions for Each Teacher Role

In Professional Learning Opportunity #3, Know the Backgrounds of Your Multilingual Learners of English, you became familiar with various types of background information that are important to know about your multilingual learners of English and tools to help gather this essential information. The following chart offers some role-specific questions and suggestions to help you reflect upon and extend your learning after engaging in the third professional learning opportunity.

Closing Questions and Suggestions for Each Teacher Role

Directions: Take a moment to write and reflect on your learning from Professional Learning Opportunity #3, Know the Background of Your Multilingual Learner of English. We have included a few role-specific questions and suggestions to prompt your thinking.

Professional Learning Providers

Closing Questions
- What went well in facilitating professional learning?
- What might you want to improve?
- What are your teachers' plans for gathering and documenting background information for multilingual learners of English as they move forward?

Suggestions for This Role
Consider having your teachers identify a standard form to gather background information for multilingual learners of English to share electronically or place in students' cumulative files. Remind your teachers of the importance of updating these forms annually and ensuring forms are passed on year to year so teachers can access the background information on the multilingual learners of English they support.

English Language Development Teachers

Closing Questions
- What role did you play in helping to gather background information on your multilingual learners of English?
- What is your English language development program plan for ensuring background information is shared with all teachers serving multilingual learners of English?

Suggestions for This Role
As language specialists in the building, you might want to lead a school-wide initiative to gather background information on your multilingual learners of English that can be used for the current year and future years.

Geneal Education Teachers

Closing Questions
- How did this professional learning opportunity go?
- What went well? What will you continue?
- How will this professional learning opportunity impact your instruction with multilingual learners of English?

Suggestions for This Role
Consider which of your multilingual learners of English could benefit from a differentiated approach to access content based on the information you gathered about their backgrounds. You can also promote an assets-based perspective for your students based on all the knowledge and experiences they bring to the classroom.

Professional Learning Opportunity #4: Embrace and Leverage Resources Multilingual Learners of English Bring to the Classroom

For the fourth professional learning opportunity in the Sociocultural Considerations pathway, you will be encouraged to embrace and leverage resources that multilingual learners of English and their families bring to the classroom to enhance learning (TESOL Principle 1, Practice 1b). In addition, you will become familiar with the concepts of relying on an assets-based perspective and how to incorporate the assets of multilingual learners of English into instruction (Standard 2, Components 2a and 2b of the *Standards for Initial TESOL Pre-K–12 Teacher Preparation Programs*). The Embrace and Leverage Resources Multilingual Learners of English Bring to the Classroom box shows the components of the fourth professional learning opportunity.

Embrace and Leverage Resources Multilingual Learners of English Bring to the Classroom

TESOL's 6 Principles (Grades K–12)	**Principle 1. Know Your Learners** **Practice 1b.** Teachers embrace and leverage the resources that learners bring to the classroom to enhance learning.
Standards for Initial TESOL Pre-K–12 Teacher Preparation Programs	**Standard 2: ELLs in the Sociocultural Context** **Component 2a.** Teachers demonstrate knowledge of how dynamic academic, personal, familial, cultural, and social contexts, including sociopolitical factors, impact the education of multilingual learners of English. **Component 2b.** Teachers demonstrate knowledge of research and theories of cultural and linguistic diversity and equity that promote academic and social language learning for multilingual learners of English.
Key Learning Targets	I can rely on an assets-based perspective when working with multilingual learners of English and their families. I can embrace and leverage the resources that multilingual learners of English bring to the classroom to enhance learning.
Lessons, Activities, and Application Task	**Lesson 1: An Assets-Based Perspective**
	Activities 1. Your Piece of the Puzzle 2. Word Associations
	Lesson 2: Funds of Knowledge
	Activities 1. Funds of Knowledge Matrix 2. Application of Funds of Knowledge Matrix

CONTINUED

Notes for Each Teacher Role	**Professional Learning Providers:** Considering the time allotted for a staff meeting or professional learning community, allow approximately 30 minutes to facilitate Lesson 1. The first activity of Lesson 2 requires approximately 10–15 minutes. The Lesson 2 application activity can be assigned for independent work and shared in professional learning communities. You can access many online resources in this chapter on the companion site for this book and may choose to print or create electronic versions for your professional learning sessions with teachers.
	English Language Development Teachers: As language specialists, this professional learning opportunity may remind you of the importance of having an assets-based perspective and supporting other teachers to see the assets multilingual learners of English and families bring to a school setting. In addition, you will be invaluable in supporting your general education teachers in identifying funds of knowledge (Moll et al., 1992) and ways to incorporate those assets into instruction.
	General Education Teachers: As you engage in these lessons and activities, consider how you can identify the assets your multilingual learners of English bring to the classroom and how you can incorporate those assets into your instruction and assessment.

Lesson 1: An Assets-Based Perspective

With an *assets-based perspective,* teachers consider the strengths students bring to learning, such as being multilingual, being multicultural, and having a wealth of prior experiences and global perspectives (Snyder & Staehr Fenner, 2021). In addition, teachers also consider how they can build upon students' assets in classrooms, the school environment, and family engagement partnerships (Gonzalez, 2018; Snyder & Staehr Fenner, 2021).

In contrast, when relying on a *deficits-based perspective*, students, families, home languages, and cultures are often seen as the causes of school limitations (Snyder & Staehr Fenner, 2021). For example, with a deficits-based perspective, (1) students are often identified by what they are lacking (e.g., not on grade level, not proficient in English, not familiar with the new school culture, or lacking prior schooling), (2) families are expected to change or conform to school expectations versus the school affirming and building upon the assets they bring to learning, and (3) home languages and cultures are not valued or incorporated into instruction (Snyder & Staehr Fenner, 2021).

We encourage you to have an assets-based or glass-half-full approach when working with multilingual learners of English. Lesson 1: An Assets-Based Perspective includes two activities: Your Piece of the Puzzle and Word Associations.

Key Learning Target: I can rely on an assets-based perspective when working with multilingual learners of English and their families.

Activity Goal: Reflect upon the personal and professional assets you bring to teaching multilingual learners of English.

Directions: In this activity, you will be able to consider your personal and professional assets. Follow the steps below to complete this activity.

1. **Reflect** upon the cultural, linguistic, and experiential assets you bring to teaching multilingual learners of English or your piece of the puzzle. For example:
   a. Perhaps you have traveled or studied in another country?
   b. Studied another language?
   c. Have experience or interest in diversity?
   d. Worked with diverse student populations?
   e. Have participated in preservice coursework or in-service professional learning focused on multilingual learners of English?
   f. Or are just beginning to develop personal and professional assets in teaching multilingual learners of English?
2. **Jot down** one or more ideas and share them with a colleague.
3. **As a variation for professional learning providers** (if you are working with a group), have every group member create a puzzle piece highlighting an asset they bring to teaching multilingual learners of English. Then, compile all the pieces into a puzzle to celebrate the many assets the group can draw upon when teaching multilingual learners of English.
   a. Please note that craft stores often sell do-it-yourself blank puzzles. See the photo below for one example:

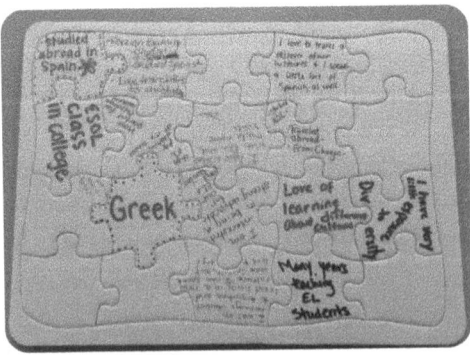

   b. If participants use deficits-based language, help them reframe it to be more assets-based. For example, one respondent in the group puzzle said, "I have little exposure to diversity." A professional learning provider could encourage that participant to reframe the statement to "I am open to learning about diversity."
4. **Celebrate** the assets you and your group bring to instruction.

The Your Piece of the Puzzle activity is based on Hiatt and Jones-Vo (2017–2018), with special thanks to Stephaney Jones-Vo.

Puzzle photo from Janet Eichenberger Hiatt, 2017. Used with permission.

Activity Word Associations

Key Learning Target: I can rely on an assets-based perspective when working with multilingual learners of English and their families.

Activity Goal: Reflect upon and categorize words or phrases that come to mind when you think of your multilingual learners of English.

Note: This activity is designed for a small or large group but can also be completed independently.

Step 1

1. Think of words and phrases that come to mind when hearing the term *multilingual learners of English*.
2. Then, locate some sticky notes and write one word or phrase per sticky note to reflect your thinking.

Step 2

1. Review the words and phrases you wrote on your sticky notes for Step 1.
2. Consider which words and phrases have more of an assets-based perspective (label with A) or a deficits-based perspective (label with D).
3. Sort them into two groups and consider how to reframe the deficits to make them more assets-based. For example, you might change "They do not know English" to "They are multilingual."
4. Alternatively, you can dispose of the deficit sticky notes and rely on your assets-based language.

The Word Associations activity is based on Hiatt and Jones-Vo (2017–2018) and inspired by Stephaney Jones-Vo.

Lesson 2: Funds of Knowledge

In the second lesson, you will become familiar with the concept of funds of knowledge (Moll et al., 1992) as an additional way to embrace and leverage the resources that multilingual learners of English bring to the classroom. You will also become familiar with identifying types of funds of knowledge and how to incorporate these assets into classroom instruction.

Defining Funds of Knowledge

From an educational perspective, *funds of knowledge* refer to a student's "academic and personal background, accumulated life experiences, skills and knowledge used to navigate everyday social contexts, and world views structured by broader historically and politically influenced social forces" (Washington Office of Superintendent of Public Instruction, n.d.). Funds of knowledge "are useful tools to help [multilingual learners of English] navigate back and forth among their schools and their communities' valuable resources...[and] should be embedded within curriculum, instruction, and assessment" (Council of Chief State Officers, 2014, p. 1).

To learn more about the meaning of funds of knowledge from the perspective of families, watch the video *Funds of Knowledge* (usgovACF, 2015; www.youtube.com/watch?v=aWSOYBpGkkE) featuring Luis Moll, a professor at the University of Arizona.

Identifying Funds of Knowledge

You might be wondering how it is possible to identify funds of knowledge. The Washington Office of Superintendent of Public Instruction (n.d.) recommends identifying funds of knowledge both *inside* and *outside* the classroom. *Inside the classroom*, students can share funds of knowledge through written essays, oral presentations, interviews, or family heritage projects. Teachers and students can also engage in informal conversations to tap into "life experiences, skills, and background knowledge" (Washington Office of Superintendent of Public Instruction, n.d., p. 1). *Outside the classroom* or school, it is possible to identify funds of knowledge through home and community visits (Washington Office of Superintendent of Public Instruction, n.d.). These visits can help teachers gather assets that students and families bring to learning.

Incorporating Funds of Knowledge Into Instruction

After identifying funds of knowledge, the next and often overlooked step is determining how to incorporate that knowledge into instruction and assessment. The Washington Office of Superintendent of Public Instruction (n.d.) explains the importance of incorporating funds of knowledge into instruction:

> The fundamental premise here is that most school-based practices, curricula, and behaviors are based on mainstream, middle-class norms and perspectives. By integrating learning patterns, knowing, and doing that are familiar to culturally and economically diverse students, academic content becomes easier to connect to their lives and is understood on a deeper level. This approach is especially relevant for English Language Learners. (p. 1)

In the Funds of Knowledge Matrix activity, you will have an opportunity to identify and determine ways to incorporate funds of knowledge into instruction.

Activity   Funds of Knowledge Matrix

Key Learning Target: I can embrace and leverage the resources that multilingual learners of English bring to the classroom to enhance learning.

Activity Goal: Review and discuss a complete sample Funds of Knowledge Matrix.

Background for Matrix: The Washington Office of Superintendent of Public Instruction (n.d.) created a Funds of Knowledge Matrix to support teachers in documenting funds of knowledge information. The matrix lists common categories of funds of knowledge and areas to record home/community practices and potential classroom applications based on those categories.

Directions

1. Review the following sample application of the Washington Office of Superintendent of Public Instruction (n.d.) matrix.
2. Discuss with a colleague (if working with a small or large group) or write (if working independently) responses to the following questions:
   a. What stood out to you as examples of funds of knowledge from the Home/Community Practice column?
   b. What stood out to you as possible classroom applications to incorporate assets into instruction and assessment from the Classroom Application column?

CONTINUED

Funds of Knowledge	Image	Home/Community Practice	Classroom Application
Art		Many multilingual learners of English and their families have artistic skills. For example, Hmong families practice the tradition of creating *story cloths*.	For Hmong students, build upon their visual sense of storytelling by incorporating a similar story structure into language arts activities.
Agriculture		Many multilingual learners of English and their families come from agricultural backgrounds or are familiar with gardening and farming.	Teachers could incorporate this knowledge into science units.
Childcare		Many older multilingual learners of English are responsible for helping with childcare while their parents or other family members work.	Teachers could build upon the leadership and organizational skills required to care for younger children.
Cooking		The families of multilingual learners of English are familiar with various ways to cook worldwide.	Teachers could incorporate the genre of recipes into language arts and math units.
Economics		Some families might own stores or restaurants or have experience selling goods at markets.	A sample classroom application might incorporate some products from a family's store or restaurant into a math unit on pricing or weights.
Entertainment		Multilingual learners of English enjoy games and other forms of entertainment that vary across cultures.	Teachers could incorporate knowledge of games played in other cultures into free time or content-based activities.

CONTINUED

Geography		Multilingual learners of English and their families often come from various countries and regions of the world.	Some classroom applications might include embedding information about landforms and weather patterns from students' countries into the curriculum, incorporating a unit on immigration or migration into social studies, or inviting family members to be guest speakers.
Health		Families might practice different health treatments. For example, in some cultures, cupping is a technique used as a part of healing.	A classroom application could be to compare cupping practices to contemporary occurrences, such as the cupping practice used by Michael Phelps in the Olympics.
Language		Multilingual learners of English and their families speak multiple languages.	Classroom applications could incorporate texts in students' home languages or words and phrases from their home languages. Students could also use their home languages to promote a deeper understanding of content material.
Politics		Multilingual learners of English and their families have background knowledge about the rights within a country.	This knowledge might have applications in social studies. For example, when studying a country's rights, the teacher could incorporate examples from multiple countries, such as the United States (the Constitution and Bill of Rights), Mexico (Individual Guarantees, Fundamental Rights), India (the Consitution), the Philippines (Bill of Rights), and the Republic of the Marshall Islands (National Day). (Blinken, 2022; Hamayan et al., 2013)

CONTINUED

Religion		Multilingual learners of English and their families often have funds of knowledge in religion and spirituality. A home/community practice is that families observe different religious holidays.	A classroom application could build awareness of special days in the world calendar.
Sports		Many multilingual learners of English are familiar with soccer or other sports.	Students could be encouraged to play familiar sports as an extracurricular activity in their schools. They could also build upon this interest in reading and writing.
Technology		Many families have technology in the home, such as computers, cell phones, and televisions.	A sample classroom application could be using computers and cell phones to enhance communication with the family.

Based on the Washington Office of Superintendent of Public Instruction (n.d.).

Referring to the sample matrix, we find that multilingual learners of English and their families often have rich backgrounds in the arts, agriculture, childcare, cooking, economics, entertainment, geography, health, language, politics, religion, sports, and technology. In the final column, we have also identified several sample ways to incorporate these funds of knowledge into instruction and assessment.

Key Learning Target: I can embrace and leverage the resources that multilingual learners of English bring to the classroom to enhance learning.

Activity Goal: Apply what you have learned about funds of knowledge to your context by completing a blank Funds of Knowledge Matrix for one or more of your multilingual learners of English. This task will allow you to recognize and subsequently incorporate funds of knowledge into instruction and assessment for your multilingual learners of English.

Directions

1. **Locate** the Application of Funds of Knowledge Matrix activity (blank template) on the companion site for this book.
2. **Then**, individually or collaboratively, complete the Funds of Knowledge Matrix (blank template) for one or more of your multilingual learners of English and their families:
   a. As you identify funds of knowledge, record examples in the matrix's Home/Community Practice column.
   b. Then, consider possible classroom applications to incorporate these assets into instruction and record them in the Classroom Application column.
   c. Add an optional image in the Image column.
3. **If working collaboratively, discuss** the following questions with a colleague. If working independently, reflect on how you would respond to the questions. Then **write** your responses to the questions on page 3 of the Application of Funds of Knowledge Matrix activity.
   a. What stood out to you as funds of knowledge for your multilingual learners of English and their families from the Home/Community Practice column?
   b. What stood out to you as classroom applications to incorporate the assets of your multilingual learners of English into instruction from the Classroom Application column?

Note: You can continue to add to this matrix over time as you learn more about your students and their families' funds of knowledge.

Closing Questions and Suggestions for Each Role

In the fourth professional learning opportunity, Embrace and Leverage Resources Multilingual Learners of English Bring to the Classroom, you built familiarity with relying on an assets-based perspective. You also embraced and leveraged the resources multilingual learners of English bring to the classroom by becoming familiar with identifying and incorporating their funds of knowledge into instruction. The following chart offers some role-specific questions and suggestions to help you reflect upon and extend your learning after engaging in the fourth professional learning opportunity.

Closing Questions and Suggestions for Each Teacher Role

Directions: Take a moment to write and reflect on your learning from Professional Learning Opportunity #4, Embrace and Leverage Resources Multilingual Learners of English Bring to the Classroom. We have included a few role-specific questions and suggestions to prompt your thinking.

CONTINUED

Professional Learning Providers

Closing Questions
- What went well in facilitating professional learning?
- What might you want to improve?
- How will you support teachers in incorporating students' funds of knowledge into classroom practices?

Suggestions for This Role
Continue to remind your teachers of the assets they bring to teaching multilingual learners of English. Also, support teachers in connecting the funds of knowledge that multilingual learners bring to classroom instruction and assessment.

English Language Development Teachers

Closing Questions
- What did you notice while engaging in lessons and activities for this professional learning opportunity?
- What were your key takeaways?
- How might you share your learning with general education teachers?

Suggestions for This Role
To help general education teachers get started, you might share a completed Funds of Knowledge Matrix with your colleagues and discuss how they might use that information to help inform instruction.

General Education Teachers

Closing Questions
- What were your key takeaways?
- How will having an assets-based perspective and embracing and leveraging funds of knowledge impact your instruction with multilingual learners of English?

Suggestions for This Role
One example to get started is to promote languages as assets. To do so, you might incorporate texts in students' home languages or allow multilingual learners of English to discuss content concepts in their home languages.

Professional Learning Opportunity #5: Create Welcoming Classroom Environments

In the fifth professional learning opportunity, you will evaluate considerations for creating a welcoming classroom environment and identify a few action steps to promote one for your multilingual learners of English and their families. This will help you promote an emotionally positive and organized classroom, with attention to reducing students' anxiety and developing trust (TESOL Principle 3, Practice 2a). The Create Welcoming Classroom Environments box highlights the components of the fifth professional learning opportunity.

Create Welcoming Classroom Environments

TESOL's 6 Principles (Grades K–12)	**Principle 2. Create Conditions for Language Learning** **Practice 2a.** Teachers promote an emotionally positive and organized classroom.
Key Learning Target	I can promote a welcoming classroom environment for my multilingual learners of English and their families.
Lessons and Activities	**Lesson 1: Considerations for Creating a Welcoming Classroom Environment**
	Activities 1. Quick Write 2. Eight Considerations
	Lesson 2: Promoting a Welcoming Classroom Environment
	Activity 1. Creating a Welcoming Classroom Environment for Multilingual Learners of English and Their Families Self-Assessment
Notes for Each Teacher Role	**Professional Learning Providers:** For Lesson 1, you can have participants begin by engaging in the Quick Write activity. Then you might jigsaw the Eight Considerations and have small groups report what they learned. Participants can then complete the self-assessment from Lesson 2. When combined, Lessons 1 and 2 require approximately 45 minutes. You can access many online resources in this chapter on the companion site for this book and may choose to print or create electronic versions for your professional learning sessions with teachers. **English Language Development Teachers:** As you review how to create a welcoming environment, consider serving as a role model for your general education teachers so they can see what a welcoming classroom looks and feels like. You could have them spot examples of how you create one in your classroom so they can try something similar in their classrooms. **General Education Teachers:** Consider how you can continue to create a welcoming classroom environment for your multilingual learners of English. Celebrate considerations you have already implemented and continue to foster a welcoming classroom environment with considerations that might be new to you.

Lesson 1: Considerations for Creating a Welcoming Classroom Environment

In Lesson 1, you will become familiar with eight considerations for creating a welcoming classroom environment where multilingual learners of English and their families feel welcomed and see their cultural and linguistic identities reflected.

Key Learning Target: I can promote a welcoming classroom environment for my multilingual learners of English and their families.

Activity Goal: Consider what you would like to see or hear to create a welcoming classroom environment.

Directions: Read the prompt and answer the question on a piece of paper or digitally.

Image Source: Empty Classroom by https://www.flickr.com/photos/cgc/10128594. "Imagine that you have arrived in a new country where you don't speak the language" (Breiseth et al., 2011, p. 9). The school staff directs you and your child to an empty room that feels strange and unfamiliar (much like the photograph). What types of things would you like to see or hear to help reduce your anxiety and make you feel more welcome?

Based on Breiseth et al. (2011, p. 9) and Hiatt and Jones-Vo (2017–2018).

Your response might have been that you would like to see signs in multiple languages, student work posted on walls, maps and flags of students' countries, books representing students' languages and cultures, desks in groups to support collaboration, charts with visuals, and greeters or mentors that welcome you with a smile. These and other potential responses help promote a welcoming classroom environment for multilingual learners and families.

Key Learning Target: I can promote a welcoming classroom environment for my multilingual learners of English and their families.

Activity Goal: Build background for eight considerations for creating a welcoming classroom environment where multilingual learners of English and their families see their cultural and linguistic identities reflected, conditions are met, and teachers foster language development.

Directions
1. **Read** information (following this chart) about eight considerations for creating a welcoming classroom environment for multilingual learners and their families:
   - Create welcoming first impressions.
   - Know your students' names (and how to pronounce them correctly).
   - Build awareness of home languages.
   - Build awareness of home cultures.
   - Showcase culturally and linguistically relevant materials.
   - Display student work.
   - Invite bilingual and multilingual staff and volunteers to support your multilingual learners of English and their families.
   - Organize the physical environment to foster language learning.
2. In the spaces provided, **take notes** on any key points that stood out to you while reading about each consideration.
3. **Explore the electronic links** and other resources referenced for the eight considerations.

1. **Create welcoming first impressions.**
   - **Notes:**

2. **Know your students' names (and how to pronounce them correctly).**
   - **Notes:**
   - **Resources to Explore**
     - Getting It Right: Reference Guides for Registering Students With Non-English Names (Greenberg et al., 2017; ies.ed.gov/ncee/rel/Products/Publication/3740)
     - PronounceNames.com (n.d.; www.pronouncenames.com)
     - What Is Your Name Story? My Name, My Identity Initiative (Santa Clara Office of Education, 2018; www.youtube.com/watch?v=AqyR9Ke8Ebg)

3. **Build awareness of home languages.**
   - **Notes:**
   - **Resources to Explore**
     - The Languages of New York State: A CUNY-NYSIEB Guide for Educators (CUNY-NYSIEB, 2012; www.cuny-nysieb.org/wp-content/uploads/2016/05/NYSLanguageProfiles.pdf)
     - Omniglot: The Online Encyclopedia of Writing Systems and Languages (Omniglot, 2024; www.omniglot.com/language/phrases/phraseindex.htm)
     - Phonemic Inventories and Cultural and Linguistic Information Across Languages (American Speech-Language-Hearing Association, n.d.; www.asha.org/practice/multicultural/Phono)

CONTINUED

4. **Build awareness of home cultures.**
   - **Notes:**
   - **Resources to Explore**
     - About Refugee Populations: Backgrounders (Cultural Orientation Resource Center, n.d.; coresourceexchange.org/refugee-populations)
     - Culture Crossing Guide: A Community Built Resource for Cross-Cultural Etiquette and Understanding (Culture Crossing, 2017; guide.culturecrossing.net)
     - World Culture Encyclopedia (Countries and Their Cultures, 2022; www.everyculture.com)

5. **Showcase culturally and linguistically relevant materials.**
   - **Notes:**

6. **Display student work.**
   - **Notes:**

7. **Invite bilingual and multilingual staff and volunteers to support your multilingual learners of English and their families.**
   - **Notes:**
   - **Resource to Explore**
     - Helping Immigrant Students Adjust to New Schools, New Lives (Education Week, 2016; www.youtube.com/watch?v=A5gkQ4_aAeY)

8. **Organize the physical environment to foster language learning.**
   - **Notes:**

Create Welcoming First Impressions

TESOL's Principle 2, Create Conditions for Language Learning, Practice 2a recommends that "teachers ensure that new students receive a warm welcome from classmates" (TESOL International Association, 2024, p. 56). Teachers can send a warm welcome through a smile and other inviting facial gestures (Colorín Colorado, 2019b). Teachers can also assign mentors to new students to assist them with schedules and other classroom routines (TESOL International Association, 2024).

In addition, teachers can decorate their classrooms with flags and maps of students' home countries, multicultural signs/posters/photographs representing the cultures of multilingual learners of English and their families, and signs in multiple languages (Breiseth et al., 2011; Short & Boyson, 2012; U.S. Department of Education, Office of English Language Acquisition, 2015). All these strategies are what Howard (2016) refers to as creating welcoming "front porches" for students and their families so they feel like their cultural and linguistic identities are welcomed in the classroom.

Dr. Deborah Short, director of academic language research and training, shares that creating welcoming environments contributes to student success and helps multilingual learners of English and their families belong (U.S. Department of Education, Office of English Language Acquisition, 2015). She gently reminds teachers that "you only get one chance to make a first impression" and that welcoming environments are essential for making good first impressions (U.S. Department of Education, Office of English Language Acquisition, 2015).

Know Your Students' Names

One easy way to help multilingual learners of English feel welcome and see their identities reflected is by knowing their names and saying them correctly (Arriaga, 2016). Arriaga (2017) states, "the most important word in any language is one's own name."

My Name My Identity is a national project created by the Santa Clara County Office of Education and the National Association for Bilingual Education that advocates for knowing your students' names (Santa Clara County Office of Education, n.d.). You can watch a brief video clip called *What Is Your Name Story? My Name My Identity Initiative* to hear students share why knowing their names is so critical to their identities (Santa Clara County Office of Education, 2018; www.youtube.com/watch?v=AqyR9Ke8Ebg&t=2s). Greenberg et al. (2017, ies.ed.gov/ncee/rel/Products/Region/northwest/Publication/3740) also offer helpful suggestions for getting names right when registering students in their publication *Getting It Right: Reference Guide for Registering Students with Non-English Names*. They share naming conventions for students with 11 different language backgrounds.

In addition to knowing students' names, knowing how to pronounce them correctly is crucial (Mitchell, 2016). Colorín Colorado (2019a; www.colorincolorado.org/teaching-ells/creating-welcoming-classroom/getting-students-names-right) notes, "one of the most important steps in building a positive relationship with [multilingual learners of English] is to learn to pronounce students' and families' names correctly." The student or family can assist with correct pronunciation. In addition, various websites offer guidance on hearing correct pronunciations, such as *PronounceNames.com* (PronounceNames.com, n.d.; www.pronouncenames.com). Of course, websites do not guarantee 100% accuracy, so it is also essential to cross-check with the student or family.

Build Awareness of Home Languages

As part of creating a welcoming environment, teachers should also attempt to learn a few words and phrases in their students' home languages (Snyder & Staehr Fenner, 2021) and some basic phonemic and linguistic information about those languages.

- **To learn some words and phrases in your students' home languages,** we encourage you to explore *Omniglot: Useful Foreign Phrases* (Omniglot, 2024; www.omniglot.com/language/phrases/phraseindex.htm).
- **To learn some basic information about students' home languages,** we recommend exploring *Phonemic Inventories and Cultural and Linguistic Information Across Languages* (American Speech-Language-Hearing Association, n.d.; www.asha.org/practice/multicultural/Phono) and *The Languages of New York State: A CUNY-NYSIEB Guide for Educators* (CUNY-NYSIEB, 2012; www.cuny-nysieb.org/wp-content/uploads/2016/05/NYSLanguageProfiles.pdf).

Build Awareness of Home Cultures

Teachers can also create welcoming classrooms by learning basic information about the home countries of their students. This awareness is essential for incorporating cultural backgrounds into the classroom environment and instruction.

- **To help you research various countries and cultures,** we encourage you to explore three websites: *Culture Crossing Guide: A Community Built Resource for Cross-Cultural Etiquette and Understanding* (Culture Crossing, 2017; guide.culturecrossing.net), *Refugee Backgrounders* (Cultural Orientation Resource Center, 2022; culturalorientation.net/learning/backgrounders), and *World Culture Encyclopedia* (Countries and Their Cultures, 2022; www.everyculture.com).

Showcase Culturally and Linguistically Relevant Materials

A fifth consideration for promoting a welcoming classroom environment is to showcase culturally and linguistically relevant materials. Teachers can display books in their students' home languages or have books depicting the diverse cultures and backgrounds of multilingual learners of English and their families (Breiseth et al., 2011; Short & Boyson, 2012; TESOL International Association, 2024; U.S. Department of Education, Office of English Language Acquisition, 2015).

Showcasing home languages sends an invitation to students and families to "[keep] home languages alive" (McGarvey, 2018). Maintaining home languages improves cultural and linguistic identities and has positive educational, cognitive, sociocultural, and economic benefits for students and families (Kapela, 2022; McGarvey, 2018; U.S. Department of Education, Office of English Language Acquisition, 2020). Showcasing culturally and linguistically relevant materials that depict the backgrounds and experiences of multilingual learners of English also increases student and family sense of belonging (Breiseth et al., 2011; Short & Boyson, 2012). Freeman and Freeman (2008) offer the following explanation: "Books are easier to understand when readers have background knowledge about the setting, the characters, and the events" (p. 49). Additionally, culturally and linguistically relevant materials increase both reading comprehension and motivation to read (Freeman & Freeman, 2008).

Display Student Work

Instead of blank walls, Deborah Short shares, "If you look at the corridors and the hallways, there will be student work displayed, and it will be all different kinds of students" (U.S. Department of Education, Office of English Language Acquisition, 2015). This same statement extends to the walls of individual classrooms.

Invite Bilingual and Multilingual Staff and Volunteers to Support Your Multilingual Learners of English and Their Families

To illustrate the importance of first-person voices who know the language and cultures of students and families, view the video *Helping Immigrant Students Adjust to New Schools, New Lives* (Education Week, 2016; www.youtube.com/watch?v=A5gkQ4_aAeY). In this video, you meet two bilingual communication support specialists hired by St. Cloud, Minnesota, Public Schools to support a growing Somali immigrant student population. As you listen to the video, consider how the bilingual staff made a difference.

Some possible responses may include the bilingual communication support specialists: (1) understood the languages and cultures of multilingual learners of English and their families, (2) helped bridge the gap of cultural differences between home and community, (3) had skills to interpret (oral) and translate (written), (4) helped the school staff mirror the community, (5) helped to build relationships, (6) valued the language, culture, and perspectives of students, and (7) helped to create a safe and welcoming environment.

Organize the Physical Environment to Foster Language Learning

One way to foster language development in the physical environment is to arrange furniture for cooperative grouping or collaborative conversations (Teich, 2022; TESOL International Association, 2024). This arrangement involves grouping desks in pods versus placing them in rows. Teachers can also use the walls, bulletin boards, and whiteboards to promote language development by posting anchor charts, labels, schedules with visual icons, word walls, language and content objectives, and sentence stems and starters, all of which scaffold language development (Gonzalez, 2017; Teich, 2022; TESOL International Association, 2024).

Activity	Creating a Welcoming Classroom Environment for Multilingual Learners of English and Their Families Self-Assessment

Key Learning Target: I can promote a welcoming classroom environment for my multilingual learners of English and their families.

Activity Goals: Reflect on the degree to which you currently promote a welcoming classroom environment based on the Eight Considerations activity from Lesson 1. Also, identify your strengths, areas of growth, and a few action steps you would like to take to create an even more welcoming classroom environment.

Step 1: Read each classroom strategy statement about creating a welcoming classroom environment for your multilingual learners of English and their families. Determine to what extent you agree or disagree with each statement. Indicate your level of agreement or disagreement on the Strongly Disagree to Strongly Agree continuum with an X or other symbol.

Consideration	Classroom Strategy	Strongly Disagree	Disagree	Neutral	Agree	Strongly Agree
1. Create Welcoming First Impressions	**a.** I welcome my language learners with a smile or inviting facial gestures.					
	b. I assign my new students a mentor to assist with schedules and other classroom routines. When possible, this peer helper speaks the new student's home language.					
	c. I display maps and flags of students' home countries.					
	d. I decorate with multicultural signs/posters/photographs representing the cultures of multilingual learners of English and their families.					
	e. I have signs in multiple languages.					
2. Know Your Students' Names	**a.** I know my students' names and am learning to pronounce them correctly.					

CONTINUED

3. Build Awareness of Home Languages	**a.** I attempt to learn some common words and phrases in the home languages of my multilingual learners of English and their families.					
4. Build Awareness of Home Cultures	**a.** I know some key information about the cultures of my multilingual learners of English and their families.					
5. Showcase Culturally and Linguistically Relevant Materials	**a.** I showcase books in the home languages of students in my classroom.					
	b. I showcase books representing the cultures and experiences of students in my classrooms.					
6. Display Student Work	**a.** I display student work and photos on the wall.					
7. Invite Bilingual and Multilingual Staff and Volunteers to Support Multilingual Learners of English and Families	**a.** I have bilingual and multilingual staff and volunteers in my classrooms who speak the language(s) of my multilingual learners of English and their families. Alternatively, I know how to access interpreters/translators who can help multilingual learners of English and families feel more at ease and have meaningful access to school information.					
8. Organize a Physical Environment to Foster Language Learning	**a.** I arrange my furniture for cooperative groups or collaborative conversations.					
	b. I scaffold language development by using the walls and bulletin/whiteboards to post scaffolds such as anchor charts, labels, schedules with visual icons, word walls, language and content objectives, and sentence stems and starters.					

In summation of the eight considerations for creating a welcoming classroom environment, Breiseth et al. (2011) state:

> Another way to think of this is to keep your [multilingual learners of English] visible. [They] are often treated as an invisible minority, but [multilingual learners of English] and their families should "see themselves" throughout the school:
>
> - On the walls, through student work and photos
> - In the classroom, with books and lessons that incorporate their experiences and traditions
> - In school-wide cultural activities
> - In the faces of staff and volunteers who come from similar backgrounds. (p. 9)

Lesson 2: Promoting a Welcoming Classroom Environment

In Lesson 2, you will determine the degree to which you currently create a welcoming classroom environment based on the eight considerations from Lesson 1 by completing a Creating a Welcoming Classroom Environment for Multilingual Learners of English and Their Families Self-Assessment. You will also identify your *glows* (areas you do well), your *grows* (areas you would like to improve), and the next steps you would like to follow to create an even more welcoming classroom environment.

Step 2: Next, review your answers to identify your *glows*, or what you do well, and *grows*, or where you might improve. In addition, identify a few action steps you would like to take to create an even more welcoming classroom environment.

1. What are your *glows*, or what are you doing well, to promote a welcoming classroom environment for your multilingual learners of English and their families?
2. What are your *grows*, or what could you improve, in promoting a welcoming classroom environment?
3. What action steps would you like to take to create a more welcoming classroom environment for your multilingual learners of English and their families?

Steps 1 and 2 of this self-assessment activity are based on SupportEd's (2023) schoolwide-level tool: *Creating a Welcoming Environment for Multilingual Learners and Their Families Checklist*. It is also inspired by Breiseth et al. (2011), Colorín Colorado (2019b), Gonzalez (2017), Short and Boyson (2012), Teich (2022), TESOL International Association (2024), and the U.S. Department of Education, Office of English Language Acquisition (2015).

Closing Questions and Suggestions for Each Teacher Role

In this chapter's final professional learning opportunity, you evaluated considerations for creating a welcoming classroom environment and identified a few action steps to promote a welcoming classroom for your multilingual learners of English and their families. The following chart offers some role-specific questions and suggestions to help you reflect upon and extend your learning after engaging in the fifth professional learning opportunity, Create Welcoming Classroom Environments.

Closing Questions and Suggestions for Each Teacher Role

Directions: Take a moment to write and reflect on your learning from Professional Learning Opportunity #5, Create Welcoming Classroom Environments. We have included a few role-specific questions and suggestions to prompt your thinking.

Professional Learning Providers

Closing Questions
- How did this go?
- What went well?
- What might you have done differently?
- What changes did you notice in the classrooms of teachers who participated in your professional learning?

Suggestions for This Role
You could consider having your teachers complete the Creating a Welcoming Classroom Environment for Multilingual Learners of English and Their Families Self-Assessment as a pre- and postassessment to document changes over time in creating welcoming classroom environments for language learners in your school or district. You could also assist your teachers in identifying grade-level or schoolwide action steps to take to help create a more welcoming environment for your multilingual learners of English and their families.

English Language Development Teachers

Closing Questions
- Did you change your classroom to make it even more welcoming? If so, what did you change?
- How might you support the general education teachers in your building to create welcoming classroom environments?

Suggestions for This Role
To help generate ideas for general education teachers, you might show them examples from your classroom and your colleagues' classes for creating a welcoming classroom environment for multilingual learners of English and their families.

General Education Teachers

Closing Questions
- What were your key takeaways?
- What refinements (if any) did you make to your classroom to make it even more welcoming for your multilingual learners of English?

Suggestions for This Role
It's important to take small action steps. For example, you might begin by learning how to pronounce your students' names correctly or learning a few words or phrases in your students' languages. You could also decorate your room with a few artifacts representing the languages and cultures of your multilingual learners of English and their families.

Table 2.2 *Postassessment for Sociocultural Considerations*

Sociocultural Considerations Professional Learning Opportunities #1–5		1 Emerging
#1 Know Your Own Identity	1. I can identify dimensions of my own identity as one way to better understand the identities of my multilingual learners of English.	
#2 Recognize How Culture Impacts Learning	2. I can recognize the impact of culture on the education of multilingual learners of English.	
#3 Know the Backgrounds of Your Multilingual Learners of English	3. I can implement a method to collect and organize information about the individual, family, language, academic, and experiential backgrounds of multilingual learners of English to support instruction and assessment.	
#4 Embrace and Leverage Resources Multilingual Learners of English Bring to the Classroom	4. I can rely on an assets-based perspective when working with multilingual learners of English and their families.	
	5. I can embrace and leverage resources that multilingual learners of English bring to the classroom to enhance learning.	
#5 Create Welcoming Classroom Environments	6. I can promote a welcoming classroom environment for my multilingual learners of English and their families.	

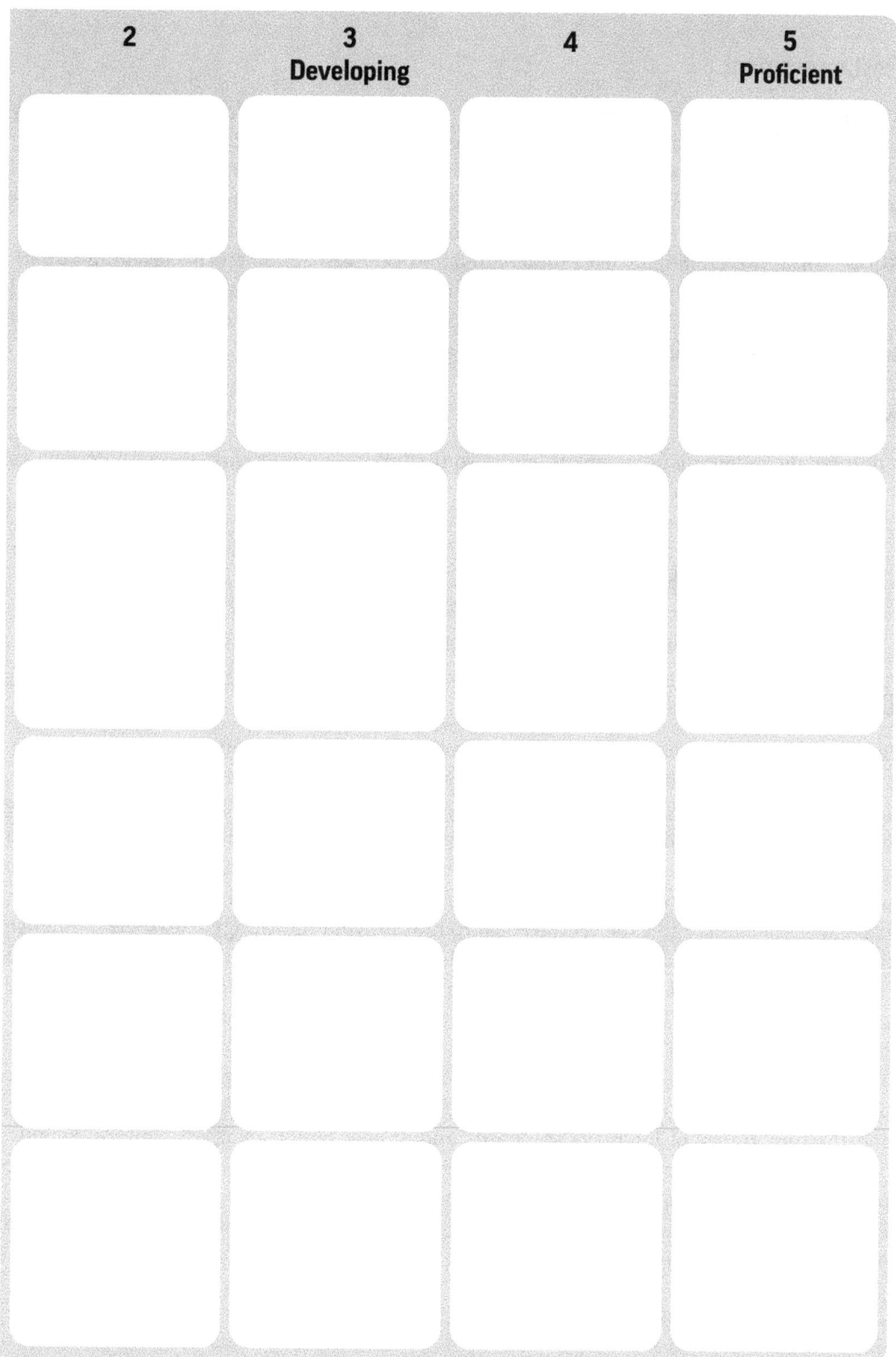

2	3 Developing	4	5 Proficient

Wrapping Things Up

Postassessment

Complete the Postassessment for Sociocultural Considerations found in Table 2.2 by indicating with a date or other symbol your new perceived level of progress toward meeting learning targets for the sociocultural context learning pathway on a 1–5 continuum. As you may recall, the continuum starts with *1-Emerging* (little to no understanding), moves to *3-Developing* (somewhat familiar but still need information to take action), and ends in *5-Proficient* (I feel confident that I understand and can take action on this learning target). You can then compare your postassessment results to your preassessment to monitor and celebrate your growth. The postassessment could also guide future continued professional learning choices specific to multilingual learners of English.

Next Steps

Consider the following questions to guide your thinking around what you will do next to inform your future continued learning for the sociocultural considerations pathway.

1. What do I still need to know about this topic?
2. What are my next action steps for personal continued learning or professional practice related to sociocultural considerations?
3. To promote equity for multilingual learners of English and their teachers, how could I extend my learning around this learning pathway to my colleagues?

Chapter Highlights

Based on your individual needs and the professional learning opportunities you chose, Chapter 2 provided many opportunities to recognize and apply sociocultural considerations to your teaching contexts with multilingual learners of English. We hope that by reflecting upon your unique cultural identity and analyzing some of the hidden aspects of culture, you gained a new appreciation for seeking cultural explanations for cross-cultural communication patterns. We also encourage ongoing gathering and documenting of individual, family, language, academic, and experiential backgrounds for your multilingual learners of English to support instruction and assessment. Finally, we hope we have supported you in ways to incorporate the many assets and funds of knowledge multilingual learners of English and their families bring to learning and have provided some ideas for promoting a welcoming classroom environment.

In the next chapter, you will explore academic English language acquisition, the role of academic language in the language acquisition process for students learning English, and the importance of language standards and annual language assessments to support content instruction for multilingual learners of English. Furthermore, you will learn how to record and monitor language growth to guide your instructional practices and identify and evaluate potential barriers to academic English language development. Enjoy your continued professional learning journey!

References

Al-Issa, A. (2005). When the west teaches the east: Analyzing intercultural conflict in the classroom. *Intercultural Communication Studies, 14*(4), 149–168.

American Speech-Language-Hearing Association. (n.d.). *Phonemic inventories and cultural and linguistic information across languages.* https://www.asha.org/practice/multicultural/Phono

Ariza, E. N. (2006). *Not for ESOL teachers: What every classroom teacher needs to know about the linguistically, culturally, and ethnically diverse student* (2nd ed.). Allyn & Bacon.

Arriaga, T. (2016, August 18). *Escorting students through open doors* [Presentation]. Corwin Equity and Academic Language Institute, Whittier College, Whittier, CA, United States.

Arriaga, T. (2017, June 13). *Opening doors for diversity, equity, and access* [Presentation]. Our Kids Summer Institute, Waukee High School, Waukee, IA, United States.

Benegas, M., & Stolpestad, A. (2020). *Teacher leadership for school-wide English learning.* TESOL Press.

Benegas, M., & Stolpestad, A. (2024). *Getting to know the ELs in your classroom* [Handout]. TESOL International Association. https://www.tesol.org/media/dmdfltfg/14144-chapter-4_getting-to-know-the-els-in-your-classroom.pdf?sfvrsn=2203f8dc_2

Blinken, A. J. (2022, April 29). *Republic of the Marshall Islands, National day* [Press statement]. U.S. Department of State. https://www.state.gov/republic-of-the-marshall-islands-national-day

Breiseth, L. (n.d). *Getting to know your ELLs: Six steps for success.* Colorín Colorado. https://www.colorincolorado.org/article/getting-know-your-ells-six-steps-success

Breiseth, L. (2019). *10 things you need to learn about your English language learners.* Colorín Colorado. https://www.colorincolorado.org/article/10-things-you-need-learn-about-your-english-language-learners

Breiseth, L., Robertson, K., & Lafond, S. (2011). *A guide for engaging ELL families: Twenty strategies for school leaders.* Colorín Colorado. http://www.colorincolorado.org/sites/default/files/Engaging_ELL_Families_FINAL.pdf

Center for Teaching, Learning & Mentoring. (2022/2023). *Wheel of privilege and power.* University of Wisconsin-Madison, Division for Teaching and Learning. https://kb.wisc.edu/instructional-resources/page.php?id=119380

Colorín Colorado. (2013, January 8). *Advice for new populations* [Video]. YouTube. https://www.youtube.com/watch?v=qXWG279kodE

Colorín Colorado. (2019a). *Getting students' names right.* WETA Public Broadcasting. https://www.colorincolorado.org/teaching-ells/creating-welcoming-classroom/getting-students-names-right

Colorín Colorado. (2019b). *How to create a welcoming classroom environment for ELLs.* WETA Public Broadcasting. https://www.colorincolorado.org/article/how-create-welcoming-classroom-environment

Comparison Project. (n.d.). *Events archive.* Drake University. https://comparisonproject.wp.drake.edu/events-archive-2

Council of Chief State School Officers. (2014). *English language proficiency (ELP) standards with correspondences to K–12 English language arts (ELA), mathematics, and science practices, K–12 ELA standards, and 6-12 literacy standards.* https://ccsso.org/sites/default/files/2017-11/Final%204_30%20ELPA21%20Standards%281%29.pdf

Countries and Their Cultures. (2022). *World culture encyclopedia.* Advameg. https://www.everyculture.com

Crenshaw, K. (1989). Demarginalizing the intersection of race and sex: A black feminist critique of antidiscrimination doctrine, feminist theory and antiracist politics. *University of Chicago Legal Forum, 1989*(1). https://chicagounbound.uchicago.edu/cgi/viewcontent.cgi?article=1052&context=uclf

Cultural Orientation Resource Center. (n.d.). *About refugee populations: Backgrounders.* https://coresourceexchange.org/refugee-populations

Culture Crossing. (2017). *Culture crossing guide: A community built resource for cross-cultural etiquette and understanding.* http://guide.culturecrossing.net

CUNY-NYSIEB. (2012). *The languages of New York State: A CUNY-NYSIEB guide for educators.* CUNY-NYSIEB, Graduate Center, City University of New York. https://www.cuny-nysieb.org/wp-content/uploads/2016/05/NYSLanguageProfiles.pdf

Education Week. (2016, March 16). *Helping immigrant students adjust to new schools, new lives* [Video]. YouTube. https://www.youtube.com/watch?v=A5gkQ4_aAeY

Frank, J. (2013). Raising cultural awareness in the English language classroom. *English Teaching Forum, 51*(4), 2–35. https://americanenglish.state.gov/files/ae/resource_files/51_4_2_frank.pdf

Freeman, Y. S., & Freeman, D. E. (2008). English language learners: Who are they? How can teachers support them? In Y. S. Freeman, D. E. Freeman, & R. Ramírez (Eds.), *Diverse learners in the mainstream classroom: Strategies for Supporting ALL students across content areas* (pp. 31–58). Heinemann.

Gardner, L. (Guest). (2019, January 30). Building relationships with immigrant communities through local cultural immersion (No. S2/E2) [Audio podcast episode]. In *Highest Aspirations.* Ellevation. https://open.spotify.com/episode/7lQ7EwK1OISmOr7txPWN1z?si=XHslrBDdQWqQyDhypxyhnA

Gonzalez, V. (2017, March 25). *ELL friendly classrooms: What to notice* [Video]. YouTube. https://www.youtube.com/watch?v=_2sFbuA6OMc

Gonzalez, V. (2018, October 7). Making students' assets our #1 teaching priority. *MiddleWeb Blog.* https://www.middleweb.com/38853/making-students-assets-our-1-teaching-priority/

Gorski, P. (2015). *Circles of my multicultural self* [Handout]. Critical Multicultural Pavilion Awareness Activities [an EdChange Project]. http://www.edchange.org/multicultural/activities/circlesofself_handout.html

Greenberg, M. J., Jaffery, Z., Hagen, A., & Yoon, S. Y. (2017). *Getting it right: Reference guides for registering students with non-English names,* (2nd ed., REL 2016-158 v2). U.S. Department of Education, Institute of Education Sciences, National Center for Education Evaluation and Regional Assistance, Regional Educational Laboratory Northwest. https://ies.ed.gov/ncee/rel/Products/Publication/3740

Hall, E. T. (1976). *Beyond culture.* Doubleday.

Hamayan, E., Marler, B., Sánchez-López, C., & Damico, J. (2013). *Special education considerations for English language learners: A continuum of services* (2nd ed.). Caslon.

Hammond, Z. (2015). *Culturally responsive teaching and the brain: Promoting authentic engagement and rigor among culturally and linguistically diverse students.* Corwin.

Hiatt, J. E., & Jones-Vo, S. (2017-2018). *In-service educator of ELs certificate program.* University of Iowa Baker Teacher Leader Center.

Hofstede, G. (n.d.). *Country comparison* [Graph]. https://geerthofstede.com/country-comparison-graphs/

Hollins-Alexander, S., & Law, N. (2022). *Collective equity: A movement for creating communities where we can all breathe.* Corwin.

Howard, G. (2016, November 1). *Deep equity: Working together for inclusion, equity, and excellence* [Workshop]. Heartland Area Education Agency, Johnston, IA, United States.

Indiana Department of Education Office of English Language Learning & Migrant Education. (n.d) *The iceberg concept of culture* [Infographic]. https://www.nrpa.org/contentassets/5c83d14700ae40e4825f54482530bbb6/iceberg-concept-of-culture.pdf

Kapela, K. (2022, June 29). Bilingual speakers face heartbreak of losing fluency in their mother language. *Columbia Chronicle*. https://columbiachronicle.com/bilingual-speakers-face-heartbreak-of-losing-fluency-in-their-mother-language

Levien, R. (2020, October 21). *Immersion* [Trailer]. Vimeo. https://vimeo.com/470775537?embedded=true&source=vimeo_logo&owner=737258

Lindahl, K. (2022, July). Teacher professional development as identity work: 2 activities [Special issue]. *TESOL Connections*. https://tcnewsletter.s3.amazonaws.com/newsmanager.commpartners.com/tesolc/issues/2022-07-01/index.html

McBrien, J. L. (2009). Soy la otra. *Phi Delta Kappan, 90*(5), 333–337.

McGarvey, D. (2018, October 29). *Keeping home languages alive key to English success for new comer kids*. CBC News. https://www.cbc.ca/news/canada/calgary/newcomers-language-english-calgary-success-1.4880207

Media That Matters. (2009, June 16). *Immersion* [Video]. YouTube. https://www.youtube.com/watch?v=I6Y0HAjLKYI

Mitchell, C. (2016, May 10). Mispronouncing students' names: A slight that can cut deep. *Education Week*. https://www.edweek.org/leadership/mispronouncing-students-names-a-slight-that-can-cut-deep/2016/05?cmp=eml-contshr-shr

Moll, L. C., Amanti, C., Neff, D., & Gonzalez, N. (1992). Funds of knowledge for teaching. Using a qualitative approach to connect homes and classrooms. *Theory Into Practice, 31*(2), 132–141. https://education.ucsc.edu/ellisa/pdfs/Moll_Amanti_1992_Funds_of_Knowledge.pdf

Omniglot. (2024). *Omniglot: The online encyclopedia of writing systems and languages*. https://www.omniglot.com/language/phrases/phraseindex.htm

Palls, B. P. (2010). *Cultural portraits: A synoptic guide* (2nd ed.). B&B Educational Consultants.

PronounceNames.com. (n.d.). *Pronounce names*. https://www.pronouncenames.com/

Rothstein-Fisch, C., & Trumbull, E. (2008). *Managing diverse classrooms: How to build on students' cultural strengths*. Association for Supervision and Curriculum Development.

Santa Clara County Office of Education. (2018, December 3). *What is your name story? My name, my identity initiative* [Video]. YouTube. https://www.youtube.com/watch?v=AqyR9Ke8Ebg

Santa Clara County Office of Education. (n.d.). *My name, my identity: A declaration of self*. Santa Clara County Office of Education and National Association of Bilingual Education. https://www.mynamemyidentity.org

Short, D. J., & Boyson, B. A. (2012). *Helping newcomer students succeed in secondary schools and beyond*. Center for Applied Linguistics. https://www.carnegie.org/publications/helping-newcomer-students-succeed-in-secondary-schools-and-beyond/

Snyder, S., & Staehr Fenner, D. (2021). *Culturally responsive teaching for multilingual learners: Tools for equity*. Corwin.

Staehr Fenner, D. (2014). *Advocating for English learners: A guide for educators*. Corwin.

Staehr Fenner, D. (2020, October 7). *Virtual tool: What I know about my multilingual learner (ML) template for Google slides* [Google slides]. SupportEd Blog. https://supported.com/knowyourel/?mc_cid=ea693e3a7b&mc_eid=52fb1d2443

Staehr Fenner, D., & Snyder, S. (2017). *Unlocking English learners' potential: Strategies for making content accessible*. Corwin.

SupportEd. (2023). *Creating a welcoming environment for multilingual learners and their families checklist*. https://supported.com/wp-content/uploads/2023/11/Welcoming_Environment_Checklist.pdf

Teich, M. (2022, August 12). Setting up your classroom to foster a language learning environment for MLs. *SupportEd*. https://supported.com/setting-up-your-classroom-to-foster-a-language-learning-environment-for-mls/?mc_cid=f9ceb1ea1c&mc_eid=52fb1d2443

TESOL International Association. (2019). *Standards for initial TESOL Pre-K–12 teacher preparation programs*. TESOL Press.

TESOL International Association. (2024). *The 6 principles for exemplary teaching of English learners: Grades K–12* (2nd ed.). TESOL Press.

Ting-Toomey, S. (1999). *Communicating across cultures*. Guilford Press.

Ting-Toomey, S., & Chung, L. C. (2012). *Understanding intercultural communication* (2nd ed.). Oxford University Press.

Trumbull, E., Rothstein-Fisch, C., & Greenfield, P. M. (2000). *Bridging cultures in our schools: New approaches that work* [Knowledge brief]. WestEd. https://www.wested.org/wp-content/uploads/2023/07/lcd-99-01.pdf

U.S. Department of Education, Office of English Language Acquisition. (2015). *Webinar #2: Creating welcoming schools* [Webinar]. Office of English Language Acquisition, White House Task Force on New Americans Educational and Linguistic Integration Webinar Series.

U.S. Department of Education, Office of English Language Acquisition. (2020). *Benefits of multilingualism* [Infographic]. https://ncela.ed.gov/files/announcements/20200805-NCELAInfographic-508.pdf

usgovACF. (2015, May 12). *Funds of knowledge* [Video]. YouTube. https://www.youtube.com/watch?v=aWS0YBpGkkE

Washington Office of Superintendent of Public Instruction. (n.d.). *Funds of knowledge toolkit*. https://www.k12.wa.us/sites/default/files/public/migrantbilingual/pubdocs/Funds_of_Knowledge_Toolkit.pdf

Wyatt, L. (2017). *Refection for cultural other field trip experience*. In-Service Educator of English Learners' Certificate Program. University of Iowa Baker Teacher Leader Center.

Zion, S., & Kozleski, E. B. (2005). *Module 1: Understanding culture and cultural responsiveness. Academy 1: Appreciating culture and cultural responsiveness* [Facilitator's manual]. National Center for Culturally Responsive Educational Systems.

Chapter 3

English Language Acquisition

Getting Ready to Learn

English language acquisition in academic settings is a beautifully complex area of education. We use the term *complex* because intrinsic and extrinsic factors influence language acquisition. From the student's home language and culture to the language learning environment in a community or school, English language acquisition can be a journey unique to each student.

Communicating in a language means knowing what to say, when to say it, to whom it should be said, and under what circumstances it is appropriate (Hymes, 1972). In K–12 education, our goal is to support students as they develop the academic language necessary to access grade-level content and produce evidence of their learning toward grade-level academic content standards. This chapter focuses on the learning of teachers who may not have previously considered how students acquire academic English language.

In this chapter on language acquisition, we offer three professional learning opportunities that explore how multilingual learners of English access and develop their academic language in the K–12 academic setting. First, we explore how students are selected to receive academic English support and how teachers can use the stages of language acquisition and information about student backgrounds to plan their initial work in planning language support for every student. Next, we define language standards and assessments to help teachers understand how English language proficiency is defined and measured. We will also learn to record and monitor language growth to guide our instructional practices with multilingual learners of English. Finally, we identify and evaluate potential barriers to English language acquisition and consider which barriers may be most relevant for the students in our classrooms and schools.

Preassessment

Before we begin our learning around English language acquisition, please take a moment to consider your current level of understanding of each of the key learning targets by completing the Preassessment for English Language Acquisition shown in Table 3.1. For this preassessment, indicate with a date or other symbol your perceived level of progress toward meeting learning targets on a 1–5 continuum. As you complete the preassessment, reflect on your knowledge of each key learning target and consider where you would place your current ability to meet this target in your classroom.

Table 3.1 *Preassessment for English Language Acquisition*

English Language Acquisition Professional Learning Opportunities #6–8		1 Emerging
#6 Academic Language Acquisition for Multilingual Learners of English	1. I can identify each student's home language and compare home language(s) with English to better support my student's acquisition of English.	
	2. I can identify newcomers, SLIFE (students with limited or interrupted formal education), and progressing multilingual learners of English in my classes.	
	3. I can analyze instructional plans for academic terms and concepts that may need explicit instruction and language support.	
#7 Analyze Annual Academic English Language Growth	4. I can locate the language standards and accompanying supports used in our state or region for multilingual learners of English.	
	5. I can forecast (predict) ways my multilingual learners of English may use current language skills to demonstrate their content knowledge and skills.	
	6. I can analyze the language development of multilingual learners of English over time in four language domains.	
#8 Identify Barriers to Academic English Language Acquisition	7. I can utilize proficiency level descriptors to describe what multilingual learners of English can do with their current academic English skills.	
	8. I can identify potential barriers that may impact English language acquisition.	

2	3 Developing	4	5 Proficient

We have provided a continuum that ranges from *1-Emerging* (no current understanding), to *3-Developing* (somewhat familiar but still needs information to take action), and ends with *5-Proficient* (able to understand and take action on this learning target). After you have rated your level of understanding and skill on each learning target, consider how your results might inform which professional learning opportunities you would like to explore first in this chapter.

Professional Learning Opportunities

In this chapter, we offer three new professional learning opportunities that introduce learning about language acquisition for multilingual learners of English in Grades K–12. You may engage in those learning opportunities that best meet your learning needs. Before you begin, we encourage you to reflect on your preassessment responses in Table 3.1 and pursue one or all options that best fit your current learning needs. The three professional learning opportunities are:

- Academic Language Acquisition for Multilingual Learners of English
- Analyze Annual Academic English Language Growth
- Identify Barriers to Academic English Language Acquisition

Professional Learning Opportunity #6: Academic Language Acquisition for Multilingual Learners of English

This initial professional learning opportunity in the academic English acquisition chapter offers a general overview of how schools identify students as multilingual learners of English. The lessons guide you in understanding the various categories of multilingual learners of English in your classroom, allowing informed decisions about the support each student may require. Gathering information about students' home language and previous English language learning experiences before enrolling in your school aligns with TESOL Principle 1, Practice 1a, providing valuable insights into your multilingual learners of English. Understanding student backgrounds becomes particularly important when assessing social and academic language development. This insight better informs instruction to support student knowledge of English language structures and aligns with Standard 2, Component 2e of the *Standards for Initial TESOL Pre-K–12 Teacher Preparation Programs*. The Academic Language Acquisition for Multilingual Learners of English box shows the components of the sixth professional learning opportunity.

Academic Language Acquisition for Multilingual Learners of English

TESOL's 6 Principles (Grades K–12)	**Principle 1. Know Your Learners** **Practice 1a.** Teachers gain information about their learners.
Standards for Initial TESOL Pre-K–12 Teacher Preparation Programs	**Standard 1: Knowledge About Language** **Component 1a:** Teachers demonstrate knowledge of English language structures in different discourse contexts to promote the acquisition of reading, writing, speaking, and listening skills across content areas. Candidates serve as language models for multilingual learners of English. **Component 1b:** Teachers demonstrate knowledge of second language acquisition theory and the developmental process of language to set expectations for and facilitate language learning.
Key Learning Targets	I can identify each student's home language by locating their home language survey (HLS) in our district records. I can identify newcomers, SLIFE, and progressing multilingual learners of English in my classes. I can analyze instructional plans for academic terms and concepts that may need explicit instruction and language support.
Lessons and Activities	**Lesson 1: Home Language and English Language Connections** **Activities** 1. Home Language Survey 2. Identifying My Newcomer, SLIFE, and Progressing Students **Lesson 2: Academic Language and Multilingual Learners of English** **Activity** 1. Social and Academic Language
Notes for Each Teacher Role	**Professional Learning Providers:** Our professional learning goal in this professional learning opportunity is to help teachers understand how the language used in educational settings necessitates language support that allows their students to participate in grade-level academic work. Many teachers have yet to learn a new language, so initial learning about language acquisition may be challenging. As teachers become more proficient in identifying how multilingual learners of English develop their academic language in school, they should be able to plan instruction that makes content instruction accessible to multilingual learners of English. Both Lessons 1 and 2 should require approximately 45 minutes of professional learning time with large or small groups of teachers. You may choose to add additional activities to the information provided here and should add time to your professional learning plans accordingly. You can access many online resources in this chapter on the companion site for this book and may choose to print or create electronic versions for your professional learning sessions with teachers.

CONTINUED

English Language Development Teachers: General education teachers may not have prior experience differentiating between social and academic language and supporting academic language development so their students can participate in grade-level academic work. We recommend that all teachers focus on what multilingual learners of English can do with their English language and what language supports will help students continue to develop grade-level academic knowledge and skills.

General Education Teachers: The objectives in this professional learning opportunity target academic language development and how this may look different for multilingual learners of English with various home languages and varying levels of English language proficiency. As you become familiar with identifying academic language demands for each student, you will design classroom instruction that makes content accessible to your multilingual learners of English.

Lesson 1: Home Language and English Language Connections

Effective English language support has a significant impact on the academic success of students who are newcomers to the U.S. education system. For this reason, schools must identify students needing English language support at enrollment or soon after. The home language survey (HLS) is a questionnaire given to parents or guardians that helps schools know which newly enrolled students may benefit from language support based on their early exposure and experiences with languages other than English in the home (U.S. Department of Education, Office of English Language Acquisition, 2017). While some families or teachers may perceive screening students for English proficiency as discrimination, the intent of the HLS is to ensure that every student and family has access to language services that support academic progress similar to those of their peers who are not learning English.

Figure 3.1 outlines the general steps in identifying students for language assistance programs. The HLS varies from state to state, but generally the survey includes three questions about what language(s) the student first learned, understands, uses, and hears, and in what contexts languages are used in the home and by the student (U.S. Department of Education, Office of English Language Acquisition, 2017). HLS information guides the decision to administer a language screener, determining whether a student would benefit from an English language assistance program placement. Language assistance programs may vary between districts and states and include but are not limited to bilingual or dual language programs and English language development (ELD) programs. Once a student's current level of academic language proficiency is measured, schools determine the appropriate language supports that will help each student develop their academic English language proficiency.

Figure 3.1 *Identification of potential multilingual learners of English.*

```
All families who enroll     Students who may           Student is proficient in
in a district complete a    potentially benefit        academic English: not
home language survey        from English language      identified as a multilingual
                            instruction take the       learner of English
                            state's approved
                            language screener          Student is not proficient
                                                       in academic English:
                                                       identified as a multilingual
                                                       learner of English
```

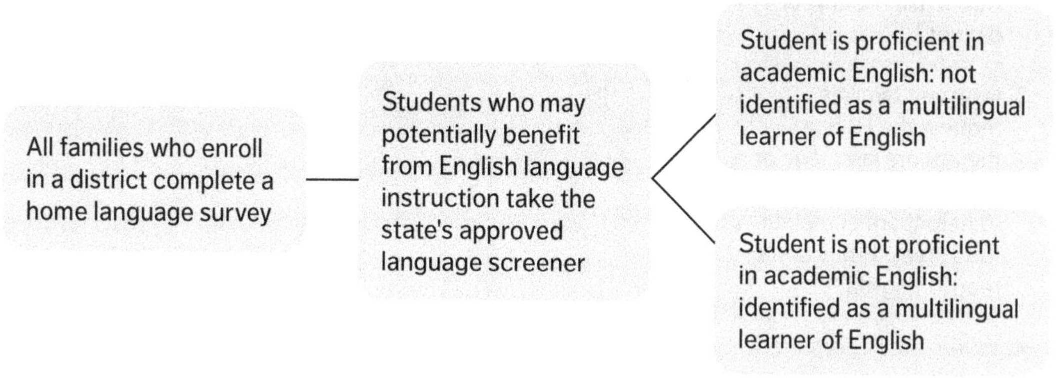

This may be the first time you have heard of the HLS or been aware that this is the first step in identifying potential multilingual learners of English in your school district. Our first activity in Lesson 1 asks you to locate answers to initial information about the HLS, which we believe is essential knowledge for every schoolteacher. We encourage you to investigate the HLS process in your district to understand the process better and consider how you can advocate for district processes that make access to the HLS easier for families whose home language may not be English. If you are a general education teacher, we suggest working through this activity with your school's ELD specialist to gain their perspective on the process and access additional information about students in your classroom.

Activity   Home Language Survey

Key Learning Target: I can identify each student's home language and compare home language(s) with English to better support my student's acquisition of English.

Activity Goal: Locate and evaluate the HLS and how it is used in your school district.

Directions: You may print this resource from the companion site or enter the information in the spaces provided in this activity. This activity is appropriate to complete individually, with a partner or team, or as part of school professional development.

Step 1: Consider individually or discuss with colleagues the five questions in the Question column. You may choose to address additional questions specific to your school or district. Fill out the answer to each question and also note in the final column where you can find the information for your district.

Question	Answer	Where can I get this information in our district?
1. How do families fill out the HLS at initial school enrollment? Electronically? On paper? By interview? Other?		

CONTINUED

2. In what languages is the HLS available in your district?		
3. How can families request the HLS in their home language or request an interpreter to help them complete the survey if they don't read in English?		
4. Where are HLSs stored after they are completed by each family?		
5. Where can teachers access their students' HLSs to learn each student's home language?		

Step 2: As appropriate, discuss with colleagues and district leaders how initial enrollment procedures and access to the HLS might be improved for families who do not yet speak or read in English.

Step 3: Reflect on the answers you generated for each question.
- What information did you learn about where the HLS is located and how it is used in your school district?
- What might be some ways you can use this information to inform your work with students and families?
- How could you collaborate with district leaders to improve the initial enrollment procedures and accessibility of the HLS for families who are not proficient in English?

Note. HLS = home language survey.

Identifying Students for Language Support

Once students are identified through the HLS questions, they are given a language screener to determine which students will benefit from ELD instruction (U.S. Department of Education, Office of English Language Acquisition, 2017). The initial language screener used in your state will provide results that reflect each student's approximate English language proficiency in four language domains: speaking, listening, reading, and writing. This information helps schools determine the appropriate initial language support for each student.

Language proficiency scales describe predictable and sequential language development stages that help teachers describe a student's current stage of language learning in four language domains. This information contributes to instructional designs that support student progress toward the next stage of language proficiency and eventual exiting from ELD services. While different models for the stages of language acquisition are present in the K–12 education field today, Table 3.2 represents the most common stages and terms, with brief descriptors of how students use academic language at each stage of new language acquisition.

Table 3.2 *Six Stages of Academic English Language Acquisition*

Stage 1 *Preproduction*	Often referred to as the silent period, students may not speak in their new language due to the process of taking in aspects of the new language. Although students may not yet speak in their new language, they may respond to prompts using communication strategies such as pointing to an object, picture, or person; performing an action such as standing up or closing a door; using gestures, including nodding yes or shaking their head no; or responding with a simple "yes" or "no" as their listening comprehension skills develop.
Stage 2 *Early Production*	During early production, students may begin to speak in one- or two-word phrases. Students may indicate comprehension of new learning by giving short answers to simple yes/no, either/or, or wh- questions, such as who/what/when/where. Students may still be focused on the skills related to listening comprehension in their new language. It is not unusual to observe many errors in language production as students try using different forms of their new language.
Stage 3 *Speech Emergent*	Speech production increases in this stage, evidenced by more frequent speaking in the new language. Phrases and sentences become longer and more complex, often with grammatical errors that may at times interfere with clear communication. The student is still dependent on context clues and may only be able to have conversations on familiar topics. Vocabulary continues to increase, and errors decrease, especially when students can have common or repeated interactions. Students begin to use dialogue and can form and respond to simple questions.
Stage 4 *Intermediate Proficiency*	Speech is fairly fluent in social situations with minimal errors. New contexts and academic language may be challenging, and students may struggle to express themselves and access content-related vocabulary and appropriate phrases. Students begin to make complex statements, state opinions, ask for clarification, share thoughts, and speak at greater length.
Stage 5 *Advanced Intermediate*	Communication in the new language becomes more fluent, especially when using social language. The student approaches early levels of fluency in new situations or academic areas, but there may be gaps in vocabulary knowledge and some unknown expressions. Language errors decrease, and the student can demonstrate higher order thinking skills in the new language in situations such as offering an opinion or analyzing a problem. By this stage, the student has developed some specialized content-area vocabulary and can fully participate in classroom activities when provided with occasional language support as needed.

CONTINUED

Stage 6 *Advanced*	The student communicates fluently in most settings and uses each language domain successfully in a variety of contexts and when presented with new academic information. While the student is now considered fluent, their speech may retain their home language accent. The student may still confuse idioms related to their current geographic location or local culture instead of their home country or culture.

Based on Reed & Railsback (2003).

According to federal guidance (U.S. Department of Education, 2022), school districts are required to offer programs that allow multilingual learners of English to actively and equitably engage in educational activities. This means that all teachers must provide language assistance across all classrooms and programs, extending beyond the ELD classroom or group settings. General education teachers can increase their teaching and classroom support for multilingual learners of English by being informed about each student's current language development levels.

Simple labels cannot fully capture the complexity of culture and language that reflect each student's characteristics. Two students from the same country or region can reflect different academic and language backgrounds. Despite this complexity, organizing multilingual learners of English based on their screener levels of English language proficiency can be helpful in offering appropriate initial language support in both content and ELD classrooms. The three general categories of multilingual learners of English in Table 3.3 are used to represent language learning groups.

Table 3.3 *Multilingual Learners of English: Language Categories*

Language Development Category	Description
Newcomers	Students who were born outside of the United States, have recently arrived, and have enrolled in school within the past 1 to 4 years. Some states may use different ranges of arrival times to qualify as a newcomer (Gottlieb, 2021).
Newcomer Language Skills	Limited to no English language or beginning level in all language domains.
SLIFE	Students with limited and/or interrupted formal education. The term *limited* refers to an educational background in the student's previous country of residence where the learning opportunities were not as thorough or comprehensive as those available in the education system of their current country of residence. The term *interrupted* refers to the need for a student to be absent from their regular schooling for various reasons, including war, natural disaster, migration, and other factors (DeCapua et al., 2020).

CONTINUED

SLIFE Language Skills	Limited to no English language or beginning level in all language domains. They may have limited literacy in the home language.
Progressing Students	Students who have been identified as multilingual learners of English and have not yet reached English language proficiency, as determined by their state annual summative language assessment (Gottlieb, 2021).
Progressing Student Language Skills	Combination of language levels in all four language domains, ranging from beginning to proficient.

Activity · Identifying My Newcomer, SLIFE, and Progressing Students

Key Learning Target: I can identify newcomers, SLIFE, and progressing multilingual learners of English in my classes.

Activity Goal: Gather information about current language development levels for multilingual learners of English in my classroom.

Directions

1. Contact the ELD teacher in your school or district to meet and discuss current language development levels for multilingual learners of English in your classroom. If you are the ELD teacher, contact a general education teacher and invite them to meet and discuss what language development looks like for multilingual learners of English in their classroom.
2. Identify the home language of one multilingual learner of English in your classroom by exploring the family's listed home language on your district learning management system (LMS) or by accessing the home language survey for that student.
3. Working with the school ELD teacher, use Table 3.3 to identify whether each multilingual learner of English in your class is considered a newcomer, SLIFE, or progressing student.
4. Discuss with your colleague the considerations for language support for students in your classroom who are newcomers, SLIFE, or progressing.

We have listed some initial considerations for newcomers, SLIFE, and progressing students. You may also generate additional ideas with your colleague(s) on how to get started meeting the individual learning needs of multilingual learners of English in each group. Use the following space to generate ideas on how to begin providing supports for your multilingual learners of English in each category.

Newcomers	• Students new to learning English are in the process of learning the language structures of English. If you have a newcomer student in your classroom, this student may be comparing and contrasting their home language with English and, depending on their literacy skills in their home language, may benefit from translated texts and instructional resources. • • •

SLIFE	• Students may have varying literacy levels in their home language, and translated materials may not be as helpful in the classroom. Providing language support that decodes the structures of the English language helps multilingual learners of English in their English language acquisition efforts. • • •
Progressing Students	• Students have progressed beyond the initial stages of English language acquisition and may be developing language skills at different rates in each of the four language domains of listening, speaking, reading, and writing. • • •

Note. ELD = English language development; SLIFE = students with limited or interrupted formal education.

Lesson 2: Academic Language and Multilingual Learners of English

The Language of School

Academic language proficiency is often defined as constructing meaning from oral and written information and using complex strategies within various academic disciplines. Academic language may also be defined as the skills to describe complex ideas and abstract concepts within academic content areas (Cummins, 1979; Dutro & Moran, 2003; Zwiers, 2014). Students need a solid understanding of English language structures to engage in academic discussions and produce evidence of their foundational content knowledge and abstract ideas that may occur within each content area subject.

Figure 3.2 *Language structures for academic English development.*

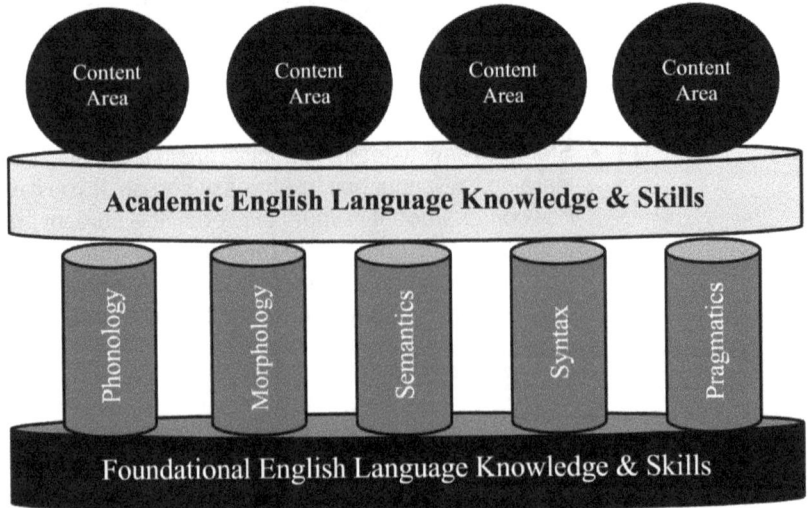

Figure 3.2 represents how academic language proficiency is based on each student's foundational language knowledge and skills in English. Language form, content, and use are constructed through five pillars of language structure: phonology, morphology, semantics, syntax, and pragmatics (Bloom & Lahey, 1978).

Phonology is related to the sounds and sound patterns that occur in a language, which in this case is English. Students need to identify and produce the sounds of English to produce speech and develop writing skills correctly. *Morphology* helps students recognize language forms by identifying the smallest units of meaning within words. *Semantics* relates to the meaning of words that extend beyond providing a definition. Semantics encompasses the context in which words are used and the words or sentences chosen to represent thoughts and ideas. *Syntax* is the way in which words and phrases are put together in a certain order to create a sentence. *Pragmatics* refers to language rules in informal or formal conversations, contexts, and settings. As students increase their ability to manipulate these English language structures, they are likely to access higher order thinking skills and the ability to comprehend abstract concepts. In other words, increased knowledge and comprehension are dependent on increased linguistic capacity.

Social and Academic Language Development

We might observe our multilingual learners of English engaging in casual conversations and demonstrating apparent proficiency in the English language. However, when we observe students in the classroom setting, these same students may struggle to express their ideas when speaking or writing. These differences can be attributed to the distinct language structures used in social communication, which differ significantly from those utilized in academic environments.

The acronyms BICS and CALP were developed by Jim Cummins (1979) to explain the difference between the two forms of language. Cummins identified *basic interpersonal communication skills* (BICS) as informal language a student might use in social conversations and *cognitive academic language proficiency* (CALP) as cognitively demanding language such as that a student might encounter and use in the content classroom. Cummins explained the role of BICS and CALP after observing teachers who assumed that multilingual learners of English were fully fluent in English because their students could converse in everyday, conversational English. These students were placed in mainstream classes without access to language support based on their social language fluency. Cummins argued that these students' subsequent lack of academic progress was due to a lack of support in developing academic English language skills rather than a lack of ability (Cummins, 1979; Zwiers, 2014).

Multilingual learners of English at all grade levels can learn English when provided evidence-based instruction and academic support appropriate to their current English language proficiency level (Cárdenas-Hagan, 2020). Many teachers find it challenging to identify the learning needs of multilingual learners of English in their classrooms because of a phenomenon that Zwiers (2014) compares to "fish describing water." Recognizing academic language challenges faced by multilingual learners of English is difficult for many teachers whose home language is English because they are surrounded by the language and context of their culture, just as fish hypothetically might be confused when asked to describe water. Only when we analyze and identify the differences between the English language and culture and those of our students can we provide the appropriate support that each student needs.

Consider the graphic shown in Figure 3.3. Depending on their previous exposure to the English language, our students learning English develop the pillars of language structure through the influence of their home language structures. They continually consciously or sometimes subconsciously compare the linguistic features of their home language with those of English. While students may be fluent in many languages, the language of instruction and influences, such as time in a monolingual instructional environment, will dominate the students' literacy development and language proficiency.

Figure 3.3 *Academic language development for multilingual learners of English.*

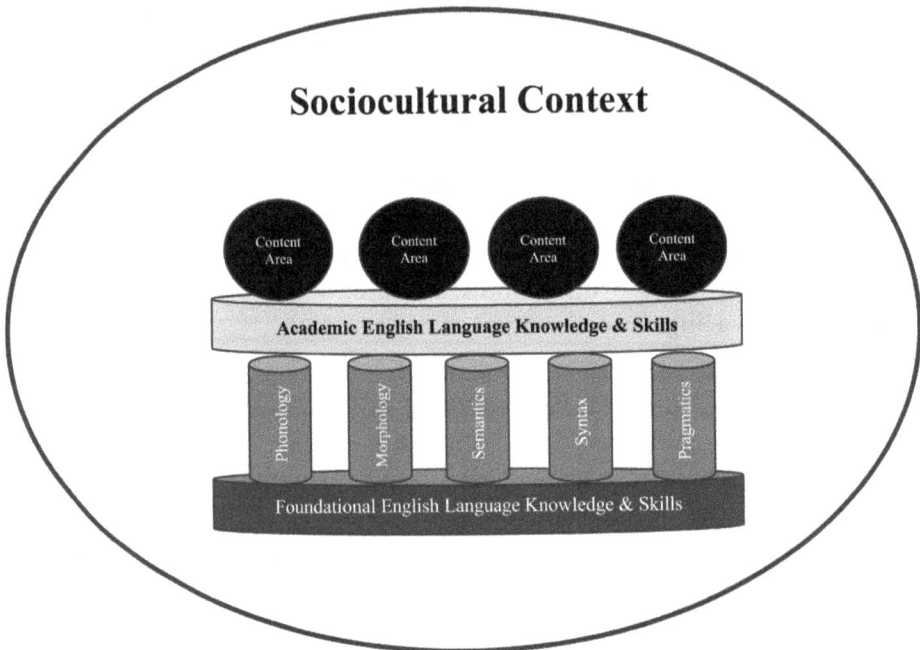

The sociocultural context of the learning environment influences each student's social and academic language development. We define the sociocultural context in education as how language develops through interconnections among teachers, learners, and tasks, resulting in learning that stems from individual interactions (Turuk, 2008). Although the language development of all students is influenced by the sociocultural context or the culture and society in which it is used, multilingual learners of English are uniquely affected by a blend of their home culture and the new culture in which both their home language and new language play a role in shaping their learning experiences.

Academic Language at the Word, Sentence, Discourse, and Conceptual Levels

Multilingual learners of English encounter academic language in many forms and formats, including but not limited to literature and informational texts, instructional and learning resources, instructions, success criteria, standards, objectives, and presentations. Many teachers draw on Zwiers's (2008) framework that compares content-specific vocabulary as the bricks of academic language and general academic terms and phrases as the mortar that connects academic concepts together. Another helpful framework presents characteristics of proficient academic language organized into word, sentence, discourse, and conceptual levels (TESOL International Association, 2024). We have adopted TESOL International Association's (2024) four-level framework because of its extension to conceptual learning. This additional level captures the importance of grade-level conceptual understanding by incorporating the language of academic standards and assessing students' abilities to demonstrate knowledge and skills in each content area.

Key Learning Target: I can analyze instructional plans for academic terms and concepts that may need explicit instruction and language support.

Activity Goal: Predict academic terms and concepts.

Directions

1. To practice identifying academic language, locate a lesson you have taught or plan to teach in your classroom.
2. Review the text or resources you plan to use during instruction and identify key academic terms that you predict may be unfamiliar to your multilingual learners of English. We provide a middle school science standard in the following example for you to observe how academic terms may be predicted.

Example
Next Generation Science Standard: MS-ESS2-5
Collect data to provide evidence for how the motions and complex interactions of air masses result in changes in weather conditions.

3. After identifying the first key terms in your lesson, practice predicting key academic terms or concepts that will need explicit instruction or language support for multilingual learners of English in your classroom.
   - In this example, the teacher initially identified four academic terms they felt should be explicitly taught to support learning toward this science standard: *weather, interaction, experiment,* and *analysis.*
   - As the lesson proceeded, they realized that many additional academic terms and concepts stemmed from the initially identified vocabulary for that lesson.

Predict Key Academic Terms
Consider the background and culture of each multilingual learner of English in your classroom. Drawing on what you know about each student's background, what concepts might require additional explanation or examples during classroom instruction or independent student work? For example, newcomers from warm climates may not be familiar with concepts related to winter weather.

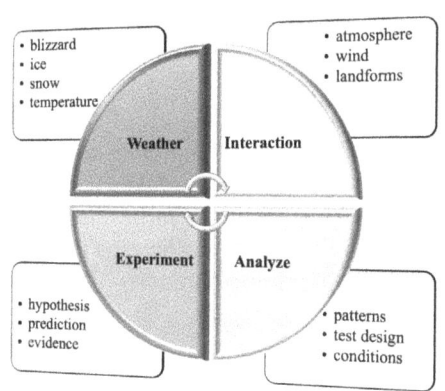

4. Work through these steps in identifying key academic terms for more than one lesson to increase your skills in identifying academic terms and concepts that may need explicit instruction for multilingual learners of English.

Teachers can plan for and assess academic language use in the classroom by considering to what extent multilingual learners of English at varying levels of English language proficiency are able to access grade-level content and provide evidence of their learning. Table 3.4 illustrates how multilingual learners of English may use four tiers of academic language skills to demonstrate knowledge and skills aligned with content standards.

Table 3.4 *Word, Sentence, Discourse, and Conceptual Levels of Academic Language*

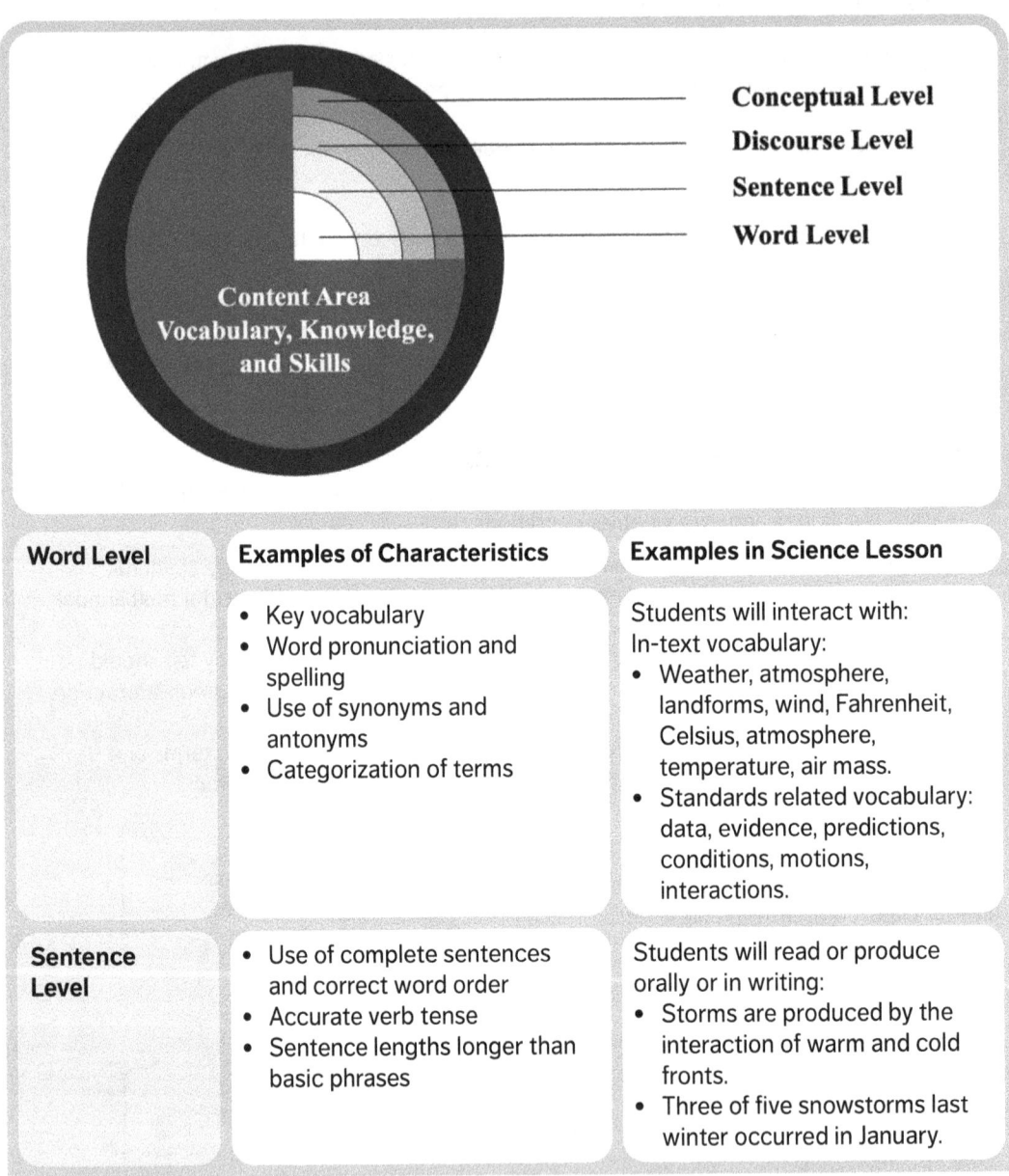

Word Level	Examples of Characteristics	Examples in Science Lesson
	• Key vocabulary • Word pronunciation and spelling • Use of synonyms and antonyms • Categorization of terms	Students will interact with: In-text vocabulary: • Weather, atmosphere, landforms, wind, Fahrenheit, Celsius, atmosphere, temperature, air mass. • Standards related vocabulary: data, evidence, predictions, conditions, motions, interactions.
Sentence Level	• Use of complete sentences and correct word order • Accurate verb tense • Sentence lengths longer than basic phrases	Students will read or produce orally or in writing: • Storms are produced by the interaction of warm and cold fronts. • Three of five snowstorms last winter occurred in January.

CONTINUED

Discourse Level	• Language is used to state a position in a discussion or written assignment • Connection of ideas that create a statement or defense • Statements follow a logical order	Students will listen to or produce orally in a discussion: • I predict that when a cold air mass catches up with a warm air mass, the cold air will slide under the warm air. • Cumulonimbus clouds often result in storms that produce heavy rain or snow. I know this is correct by using our data that compared cloud formations and measured precipitation in the past month.
Conceptual Level	• Language is used to reflect cognitive functions represented in content standards such as describing, explaining, sequencing, analyzing, evaluating, and synthesizing • Content information is used to form a conclusion • Accurate use of claims and evidence • Conclusions are based in data and/or observation	Students will demonstrate content standards–related skills such as: • Collect, identify, and discuss data. • Provide evidence for how the motions and complex interactions of air masses result in changes in weather conditions.

As we examine each level with examples depicted in Table 3.4, we should consider how we can facilitate classroom learning by focusing on the use of academic language corresponding to the current language skills of our multilingual learners of English. For example, our newcomer students may not yet be proficient in forming complete sentences, but they can engage with the vocabulary and word functions used in graphic organizers, note-taking sheets, and sentence starters and frames. Students who may not yet be able to participate in a detailed conversation or debate on academic topics may be able to represent facts and opinions, summarize academic concepts, or identify foundational information at the sentence level of academic language use.

Closing Questions and Suggestions for Each Teacher Role

In our sixth professional learning opportunity, Academic Language Development for Multilingual Learners of English, you explored how to identify multilingual learners of English and obtain information about each student's home language. You also compared social and academic language and recognized the need to support academic language development in the classroom. As we conclude this section of the chapter, consider the following questions to reflect on your learning and plan actionable steps to support your students' academic language development.

Closing Questions and Suggestions for Each Teacher Role

Directions: Take a moment to write and reflect on your learning from Professional Learning Opportunity #6, Academic Language Development for Multilingual Learners of English. We have included a few role-specific questions and suggestions to prompt your thinking.

Professional Learning Providers

Closing Questions
- Which activities did you choose to facilitate?
- What went well?
- What might you want to improve?

Suggestions for This Role
If you are new to leading professional development in your school or district, you might start by consulting with general education teachers to pinpoint their main challenges in teaching multilingual learners of English. Both their feedback and your assessment will help you best prioritize topics. Additionally, communicate with English language development teachers to identify further areas of need in your school or district based on their insight and expertise.

English Language Development Teachers

Closing Questions
- What were your key takeaways from these lessons?
- What impact did these lessons have on your work with your students?
- Which aspects of this learning opportunity would you like to bring up for discussion and collaboration with general education teachers in your school?

Suggestions for This Role
Understanding language acquisition might be unfamiliar territory for you or your colleagues. If you are a new English language development (ELD) teacher, you might feel pressured to have all the answers regarding language learning. To prepare, familiarize yourself with the supports offered by your state department of education in the United States or regional ministry of education in your country. Know where to find guidance on tasks like administering the home language survey and required language screeners. These readily available resources will enable you to assist your colleagues and quickly access information when questions arise about language acquisition and support in your school or district.

General Education Teachers

Closing Questions
- How did this go? What went well?
- What were your key takeaways?
- How did this learning inform how you design classroom instruction and make content accessible to multilingual learners of English?

Suggestions for This Role
To begin supporting multilingual learners of English in your classroom, start by better understanding the varying language proficiency levels of students and how this affects their learning access. Consult with your ELD teacher(s) to identify newcomers or students with limited and/or interrupted formal education and how previous academic experiences or lack of experiences might inform the support we can provide to fill learning gaps.

Professional Learning Opportunity #7: Analyze Annual Academic English Language Growth

Our next professional learning opportunity provides learning around analyzing annual academic English language growth for multilingual learners of English. Monitoring academic language growth helps us gain information beneficial to direct instruction and the language support needed for each student (TESOL Principle 1, Practice 1a). Teachers should also have a working knowledge of how English language proficiency assessment results are used for identification, instructional decisions, and understanding of how multilingual learners of English are determined to be proficient and reclassified as non–multilingual learners of English in your state (Standard 4, Component 4d of the *Standards for Initial TESOL Pre-K–12 Teacher Preparation Programs*). The Analyze Annual Academic English Language Growth box shows the components of the seventh professional learning opportunity.

Analyze Annual Academic English Language Growth

TESOL's 6 Principles (Grades K–12)	**Principle 1. Know Your Learners** **Practice 1a.** Teachers gain information about their learners.
Standards for Initial TESOL Pre-K–12 Teacher Preparation Programs	**Standard 4: Assessment and Evaluation** **Component 4d:** Teachers demonstrate an understanding of how English language proficiency assessment results are used for identification, placement, and reclassification.
Key Learning Targets	I can locate the language standards and accompanying supports used in our state or region for multilingual learners of English. I can forecast (predict) ways my multilingual learners of English may use current language skills to demonstrate their content knowledge and skills. I can analyze the language development of multilingual learners of English over time in four language domains.
Lessons and Activities	**Lesson 1: Identify Your Regional or State Language Standards and Summative Assessment**
	Activities 1. Locate Regional or State English Language Development Resources 2. Ways to Record Information and Notes
	Lesson 2: Measuring Skills in Four Language Domains
	Activities 1. Forecasting (Predicting) Language Use During Instruction, Activities, and Assessment 2. Analyze Student Language Development

CONTINUED

Notes for Each Teacher Role	**Professional Learning Providers:** The objectives of professional learning in this professional learning opportunity are for teachers to develop a basic understanding of how to access and discuss summative language assessment results with a colleague as well as develop skills to analyze student language development over time. As teachers develop a deeper understanding of all four language domains and the time needed for students to progress through language levels, they should increase their skills in planning instruction to meet the academic needs of students at various stages of academic English development. You can access many online resources in this chapter on the companion site for this book and may choose to print or create electronic versions for your professional learning sessions with teachers. Each activity in Lessons 1 and 2 should require approximately 45 minutes of professional learning time with large or small groups of teachers. You may choose to add additional activities to the information provided here and add time to your professional learning plans accordingly. **English Language Development Teachers:** General education teachers may not have prior experience in locating summative language assessment scores or interpreting these data for multilingual learners of English. We recommend that when working with your colleagues, you focus on building an overall picture of language skills and their growth for each student over time. It is important to keep in mind that annual language assessments are only one data point in the overall spectrum of knowledge and skills of each multilingual learner of English and serve as just one indicator of student performance on a standardized test. Daily observation of student learning following instruction is the best source of information about student language development and skills. **General Education Teachers:** Our work in this professional learning opportunity targets locating summative language assessment scores or interpreting these data for multilingual learners of English. As you develop a deeper understanding of all four language domains and the time needed for students to progress through language levels, you will increase your skills in planning instruction to meet the academic needs of students at various stages of academic English development.

Lesson 1: Identify Your Regional or State Language Standards and Summative Assessment

It's important for all teachers, not just ELD teachers, to become familiar with the English language standards and summative assessments used in their schools. For example, the U.S. Department of Education requires each state to identify English language program entrance and exit criteria, conduct an annual summative assessment, and align English language development standards with that assessment. These tools provide information that supports both multilingual learners of English and teachers alike. ELD standards outline the content knowledge and academic English skills that reflect English language proficiency at each grade level. They assist general education teachers in understanding what tasks their multilingual learners of English can accomplish in the classroom based on their current levels of academic English proficiency.

Meaningful Participation in K–12 Education

In the United States, the Civil Rights Act (1964) and the Equal Educational Opportunities Act (1974) advanced multilingual student access to a fair and equitable education by making learning accessible to *all* students and ensuring that multilingual learners of English can participate meaningfully and equally in their educational programs (U.S. Department of Education, 2022).

In 2015, new federal legislation under Title III of the Elementary and Secondary Education Act (1965), as amended by the Every Student Succeeds Act (2015), required each state to identify a language assessment screener as well as entrance and exit criteria for multilingual learners of English (U.S. Department of Education, Office of English Language Acquisition, 2017). The purpose of mandatory screening for academic English was to ensure that each student entering a school in the United States had full access to every advantage and entitlement under the law (Straubhaar & Portes, 2022). Because of this legislation, schools are required to annually measure and monitor levels of academic English proficiency in four language domains: speaking, listening, reading, and writing (Every Student Succeeds Act, 2015). Academic English language progress is measured through an annual language assessment chosen and implemented at the state level. Table 3.5 lists the English language development standards and summative assessments chosen by each state at the time of this book's publication. You may also note that the summative assessments and language standards selected by each state typically align with the assessment consortium to which the state is affiliated.

Table 3.5 *Summative Language Assessments and Standards by State in the United States*

English Language Development Standards	Summative Assessment	State(s)	Consortium
ELD Standards Framework	ACCESS	Alabama, Alaska, Colorado, Delaware, District of Columbia, Florida, Georgia, Hawaii, Idaho, Illinois, Indiana, Kansas, Kentucky, Maine, Maryland, Massachusetts, Michigan, Minnesota, Missouri, Montana, Nevada, New Hampshire, New Jersey, New Mexico, North Carolina, North Dakota, Oklahoma, Pennsylvania, Rhode Island, South Carolina, South Dakota, Tennessee, Utah, Virginia, Washington, Wisconsin, Wyoming	WIDA
ELPA21 Language Standards	ELPA21	Arkansas, Iowa, Nebraska, Ohio, Oregon, West Virginia	ELPA21

CONTINUED

AZ English Language Proficiency Standards	AZELLA	Arizona	N/A
California English Language Development Standards	ELPAC	California	N/A
CELP Standards	LAS Links	Connecticut	N/A
MS English Language Proficiency Standards	LAS Links	Mississippi	N/A
Connectors for English Learners	ELPT	Louisiana	N/A
Office of Bilingual Education and English as a New Language	NYSESLAT	New York	N/A
Texas English Language Proficiency Standards	TELPAS	Texas	N/A

Activity Locate State English Language Development Resources

Key Learning Target: I can locate the language standards and accompanying supports used in our state for multilingual learners of English.

Activity Goal: Identify your state's summative language assessment.

Directions
1. Table 3.5 lists the names of each state's English language development standards and aligned summative assessments at the time this book was published. Many states belong to a language assessment consortium, while others have developed their own assessments or adopted assessments from another source.
2. Take a moment to locate and record the name of your state's summative assessment, English language development standards, and their locations listed in Table 3.5 for future use. You may use the online version of Table 3.5 on the companion site of this book to find the links to the mentioned assessments.
3. After you locate your state's summative language assessment, meet with your English language development teacher to develop your understanding of the summative assessment process.
4. Generate questions you have about the summative assessment or the processes related to annual language testing for multilingual learners of English. We have suggested some general questions in the following section, but you will most likely develop more questions as your knowledge in this area grows.

CONTINUED

Questions for Summative Language Assessment Discussion

Questions	Answers With Notes
1. When do students take the summative language assessment in our state?	
2. When do we receive the results of that assessment?	
3. What information do we receive, and what is most important for me to understand?	
4. How will I know if the student has made sufficient progress?	
5. What should I do in my classroom after receiving the language assessment results?	
6. Where can I locate summative language assessment results for each student during the school year?	
7. How can I best collaborate with you around working with students before and after they take the summative language assessment?	
Additional Questions	
Follow-up Actions After Discussion	

It's important to remember that while annual summative language assessments offer valuable supplementary data, they represent just one data point and, in the end, are standardized tests. Summative language assessments should not be used to determine student language skills exclusively. Students may not demonstrate their true skills in different areas of language use when interacting with a computer test or with a test that asks for responses on content that has not been delivered in the context of authentic language use. While summative language assessments add one additional data point for our consideration, nothing replaces the critical role of authentic assessments and interaction with a teacher familiar with each student.

Additional English Language Supports

Each U.S. state's department of education typically houses all language assessment tools and additional resources that support academic work with multilingual learners of English. Some teachers or administrators may not be aware of these resources or access them as consistently as their ELD teachers in the district, so it is easy to forget the documents' names or locations. It is important for all teachers who work with multilingual learners of English to know where to locate information provided by your state. We suggest you use a format such as the one found in Table 3.6 to document and record the name and location of English language resources specific to your state.

Table 3.6 demonstrates how a teacher in Iowa might use this document to keep track of the names of assessments, tools, and online locations. Some school districts may choose to have teachers access resources directly through their state department of education site or, alternatively, through a district website dedicated to multilingual learners of English assessments and supporting resources.

Table 3.6 *Supports to Measure and Monitor English Language Development for Multilingual Learners of English: Iowa Example*

	Document Name	Location in Our District	Intended Use
Initial Language Screener	ELP21 Dynamic Screener	Iowa ELPA Portal	Based on home language survey results and given to determine Title III eligibility.
Annual Summative Language Assessment	ELPA21 Summative Assessment	Iowa ELPA Portal	Given annually to report academic English language development in four language domains.
English Language Standards	ELPA21 English Language Proficiency Standards	Direct link to ELPA21 English Language Proficiency Standards	Guides determining instructional learning targets and alignment to content area standards.
English Proficiency Level Descriptors	ELPA21 Proficiency Level Descriptors	Direct Link to ELPA21 Proficiency Level Descriptors	Describes academic English language descriptors by grade band in four language domains.

Additional Notes
- Must take the training online before receiving access to assessments
- Extra resources available on the ELPA Portal; test administration manuals, etc.
- Dynamic screener must be administered within 30 days of new student enrollment in the district (new to the United States)
- Check student transcripts and cumulative files for transfer students to find home language survey information and possible prior English language assessment results.

Key Learning Target: I can locate the language standards and accompanying supports used in our state for multilingual learners of English.

Activity Goal: Identify your state's language development supports.

Directions

1. Work through the example provided for Iowa in Table 3.6 and clarify the intended use and location of these supports in your state through collaboration with your English language development teachers or school leaders.
2. Note the areas of information that should be accessible to all teachers. General education teachers may not always have direct access to the results of language screeners or summative language assessments, but all teachers should utilize their state's English language standards and English proficiency level descriptors.
3. Save any questions that arise after your initial exploration of state supports for assessing language development in multilingual learners of English.

Later in this chapter, we offer additional activities and explain how to use English proficiency level descriptors in more detail. Knowing where to locate this resource in your state is sufficient for now. Consider how you would like to save the location of all four resources for future use.

Lesson 2: Measuring Skills in Four Language Domains

Summative language assessments are used to measure the growth of English language skills in four language domains. These four language domains are speaking, writing, reading, and listening and are organized by their language skill function. Generally, the term *receptive* is used to identify language skills that receive and comprehend language through listening or reading. *Productive* language skills reflect students' abilities to produce language in the form of speaking or writing. You may also see receptive skills referred to in various resources as *interpretive* and productive skills as *expressive*. Though we agree these are valuable descriptors for these skills, we use the terms *productive* and *receptive* skills to align with the language terms most often used in ELD education. Additionally, you may find that your state or government standards also include foundational standards that reflect learning around English language structures or integrate skills related to English grammar into the broader framework of overall language standards.

Language Reservoirs

As we see in Figure 3.4, when we first learn a language as children, we take in the sounds, words, phrases, and meanings of words and phrases, adding them to our inner conceptual reservoir of language. The potential output of our language is determined by the quantity and quality of language input we receive from our surrounding environment.

Figure 3.4 *Conceptual language reservoir.*

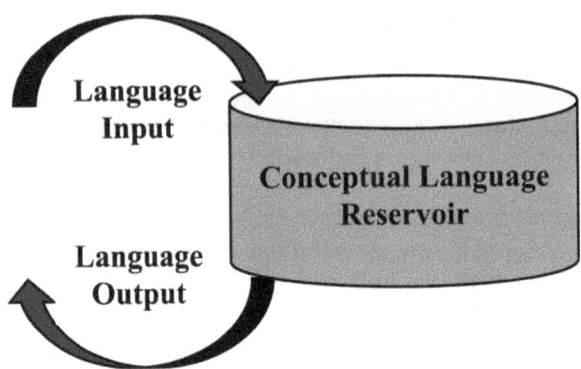

When learning a new language, we take in the sounds, words, phrases, and meanings of words and phrases of this new language, adding them to our inner conceptual reservoir, which already contains the sounds, words, phrases, and meanings of our home language. When a new language is added to our conceptual reservoir, it alters to accommodate our home and the addition of any new languages. We refer to this as the *new language reservoir* in Figure 3.5.

Figure 3.5 *The new language reservoir.*

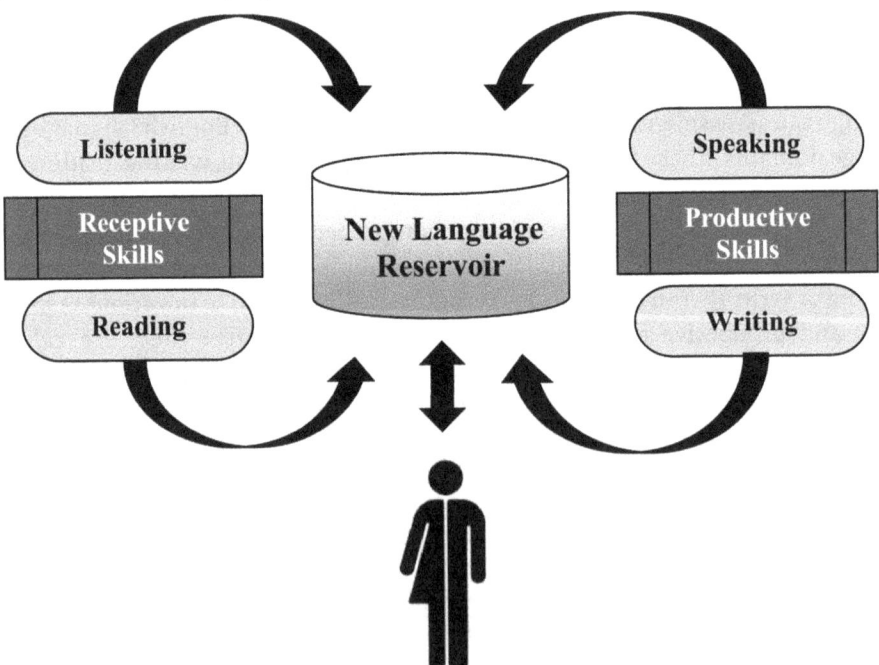

In the K–12 setting, this reservoir combines social and academic language acquisition. As students engage in experiences with a new language, they add new language knowledge and skills to their language reservoir, where they compare, contrast, and analyze new language terms and meanings with their home language(s). In short, for students to produce their new academic English language, they must have opportunities to learn the English language in meaningful ways to add it to the new language reservoir. As teachers, we must always consider that the degree to which our multilingual learners of English can produce academic language may depend on the opportunities we provide for our students to interact with and receive academic English in our classrooms.

Multilingual learners of English must have opportunities to develop their academic language skills, and some students may need more support in one language domain than another. Some students may have strong writing skills but have difficulty comprehending oral English. Other students may be eloquent speakers but unable to read a grade-level text. In our next activity, we examine resources and activities in our classroom to recognize how students use language during instruction, activities, and assessment.

Activity Forecasting (Predicting) Language Use During Instruction, Activities, and Assessment

Key Learning Target: I can forecast (predict) ways my multilingual learners of English may use current language skills to demonstrate their content knowledge and skills.

Activity Goal: Forecasting (predicting) academic language use in four language domains.

Directions
1. To begin this activity, locate a resource that guides your instruction. This might be a text, a presentation, videos, and so on. In other words, how are students receiving information during this lesson?
2. Once you have located your resource, visualize your students engaging with the information. Which language domains (speaking [s], listening [l], reading [r], writing [w]) will students draw on to access the information?
   Will they only use receptive language such as listening or reading, or will they also speak or write to gather information? Benegas and Stolpestad (2020) refer to this process as *forecasting*.
3. After you have completed forecasting your instructional resources, consider the activities you have planned for class and your method of assessing how students will provide evidence of their learning at the end of your lesson, depending on their current level of English language proficiency in each language domain.
4. We have provided an example of how you might record your information for this activity in the next section.

Resources/Student Actions	Instruction	Learning Activities	Assessment
	S L R W?	S L R W?	S L R W?
Anticipatory Set: Video		Listen to video Possibly read video captions	
Chart Your Predictions		Listen to classmates Speak ideas Write or draw predictions	

CONTINUED

Then and Now Prediction Checker		**Listen** and **speak** with classmates about accurate or corrected predictions **Write** results on the chart or **Read** the results classmates write on the chart	
Sentence Frame Exit Ticket			**Read** sentence frame and **write** responses
Newspaper Articles of Event	**Read** newspaper articles		
Text Passage of Event With Guided Notes	**Read** text passage **Write** guided notes		

English Language Development Over Time

Once we understand the purpose of language standards and where to find those used in our state or region, we can apply ourselves to learning how academic English develops over time. It is necessary to monitor English language development for our students, not only to note students' current levels of English proficiency but also to observe where each student may need additional English language support in the content area classroom. As mentioned earlier in this chapter, while summative language assessments serve as just one data point, monitoring the progress in these scores over time allows us to compare our observations of student performance in all four language domains used in our classrooms.

Many standardized assessments report two types of information: cut scores and score levels. *Cut scores* represent a range of scores the assessment designers determine to describe a specific result. In annual summative language assessments, multilingual learners of English receive a cut score in the four language domains of speaking, listening, reading, and writing. The cut score range for each language domain is unique and based on factors related to how skills in that specific language domain are tabulated by the assessment designers. The *score level* is the correlating language level assigned to each cut score range for a specific language domain. Because each language domain may develop at different rates for each student, they may have different proficiency level combinations each time they take the summative language assessment. Table 3.7 shows how cut scores and their correlating score levels may appear on a generic summative language assessment.

Table 3.7 *Example of Cut Scores and Scale Levels for All Language Domains*

Speaking	Scale Level 3	Listening	Scale Level 3
	Cut Score 570 (527–581)		Cut Score 475 (473–552)
Reading	Scale Level 3	**Writing**	Scale Level 1
	Cut Score 498 (486–533)		Cut Score (470 and below)

Example for Grades 6–8 Reading Level 3 Range of Cut Scores	
6th Grade Score Range	496–564
7th Grade Score Range	534–608
8th Grade Score Range	547–639

Understanding how to use cut scores accurately involves being familiar with the range that determines a score level. While students can make significant progress in a school year, it may seem like their language development hasn't improved if the score level remains unchanged. In Table 3.7, scores are listed within a range below each cut score. For instance, our hypothetical student in Table 3.7 achieved a reading cut score of 498, placing them at a scale level of three. This cut score falls at the lower end of the range (496–564) in sixth grade. If the student receives a cut score of 602 in their seventh-grade annual summative language assessment, it indicates the student is only a few points from moving to score level four, yet the score level for seventh grade is still reported as level three. At first glance, it might appear that the student hasn't made any reading gains, but by observing the cut scores, we can see the student has made progress and is now just a few points away from advancing to the next higher score level.

Our next activity demonstrates one possible way teachers might monitor language growth for multilingual learners of English in their school. Because standardized language assessments are administered on an annual basis, the ELD teacher, school data team, or school administrators might be the individuals to best monitor growth over time for each student.

Analyze Student Language Development

Key Learning Target: I can analyze the language development of multilingual learners of English over time in four language domains.

Activity Goal: Analyze annual language development for multilingual learners of English in all four language domains.

Directions: Working with your ELD teacher, access and record annual language assessment scores for one or all of your multilingual learners of English. If you have not looked at summative language scores before, we suggest you start by analyzing results for one student.

Step 1: Read through the sample chart that our hypothetical teacher, Mr. Sosa, created to monitor his student Aaliyah's academic language growth in all four language domains. Notice the discussion notes Mr. Sosa added after charting Aaliyah's scores from one year to the next.

Example: Score Level and Cut Score Annual Results

Student Name and Grade Level: Aaliyah P., 7th grade
General Education Teacher: 7th Grade, Language Arts, Mr. Sosa
(include this information so that ELD teachers may also have a copy and keep track of individual student progress)

Language Domain/Mode	Current Score Level	Current Cut Score	Previous Score Level	Previous Cut Score
Listening	3	475	2	422
Speaking	3	570	2	470
Reading	2	492	1	455
Writing	1	472	1	320

Discussion Notes
- The cut scores change with grade level, so Aaliyah made progress in all four language domains even though her score level remained the same in writing.
- It is essential to examine the proficiency level descriptors for seventh grade to see what skills should be targeted during instruction to help Aaliyah make continual language growth before the end of the school year.

Step 2: Now that you have worked through one example of how to record scores, practice finding the cut score and score levels for multilingual learners of English in your classroom. As you gather scores and information, note the student's scale-level score in each language domain and where that score falls in the possible score range for each language domain. Discuss with your ELD teacher how each student did or did not make progress in each area of assessed language use and how this did or did not reflect what you observed working with this student in your classroom.

Note. ELD = English language development.

Once we understand what assessment results mean and how to interpret the scores, we can analyze development rates in each language domain over time. We have stated that language domains progress differently for each student and may not all progress simultaneously. We should, however, observe gradual growth over time in every language domain. If there is insufficient progress in one or more specific language domains over time, it may suggest the need to adjust the language support plan for that particular student. It is also important not to compare cut scores between language domains. Each cut score range is determined for that specific language skill, and it would be inaccurate to compare scores between two different language domains.

Table 3.8 provides an example of how a sixth-grade teacher worked with their ELD teacher to monitor growth in each language domain for the three multilingual learners of English in her classroom. Working with the school's ELD teacher, Ms. Visser recorded a history of language development scores according to annual summative assessments. She started by recording the current year's language scores in every language domain and then worked backward, using assessment score records to see the rate of progress her students made in each area of speaking, listening, reading, and writing. She also made a note of when the students arrived as newcomers in their school so she could consider the rate of progress for her students who were new to the English language.

Table 3.8 *English Development Progress Sheet*

General Education Teacher: 6th Grade, Math, Ms. Visser
(include this information so that English language development teachers may also have a copy and keep track of individual student progress)

Student Name: Alexander	Number of Previous Years in the English Language Development Program						
	+6	+5	+4	+3	+2	+1	Current Year
	Kdg	Grade 1 Newcomer	Grade 2	Grade 3	Grade 4	Grade 5	Grade 6
Listening		2	3	4	4	5	5
Speaking		2	2	3	4	5	5
Reading		1	1	2	3	3	4
Writing		1	1	2	3	3	3
Student Name: Josephine	Number of Previous Years in the English Language Development Program						
	+6	+5	+4	+3	+2	+1	Current Year
	Kdg	Grade 1	Grade 2	Grade 3 Newcomer	Grade 4	Grade 5	Grade 6
Listening				1	2	3	3

CONTINUED

	+6	+5	+4	+3	+2	+1	Current Year
Speaking				1	2	1	1
Reading				1	1	2	2
Writing				1	2	2	3

Student Name: Serge	Number of Previous Years in the English Language Development Program						
	+6	+5	+4	+3	+2	+1	Current Year
	Kdg	Grade 1	Grade 2	Grade 3	Grade 4 Newcomer	Grade 5	Grade 6
Listening					1	2	3
Speaking					1	2	2
Reading					1	1	1
Writing					1	1	1

Notes
- Alexander appears to be making gradual growth in all language domains; he is proficient in listening and speaking and nearing proficiency in reading. Consider ways to build awareness of writing skills and Alexander's knowledge of what the writing standards are asking him to do.
- Josephine is not improving in her English speaking skills. We have seen her speaking comfortably with her friends in her home language, but she is hesitant to speak often in English. We need to learn more about why she might be reluctant to communicate using English in class.
- Serge has shown gradual growth in speaking and listening, but their reading and writing skills have not increased since their arrival as a newcomer. We should talk to other general education teachers to see if they have noticed reading struggles and meet as a grade level to discuss ways to build additional language support in our classes for Serge.

Closing Questions and Suggestions for Each Teacher Role

In the seventh professional learning opportunity, Analyze Annual Academic English Language Growth, you explored the language standards, assessments, and supports used in your state to monitor academic English language growth for multilingual learners of English. You also collaborated as ELD teachers and general education teachers to identify how academic language is used in the classroom and how your multilingual learners of English are progressing toward proficiency in each language domain of speaking, listening, reading, and writing. As we conclude this professional learning opportunity, consider the following questions to reflect on your learning and plan actionable steps to support your students' academic language development.

Closing Questions and Suggestions for Each Teacher Role

Directions: Take a moment to write and reflect on your learning from Professional Learning Opportunity #7: Analyze Annual Academic English Language Growth. We have included a few role-specific questions and suggestions to prompt your thinking.

Professional Learning Providers

Closing Questions
- Which activities did you choose to facilitate?
- What went well?
- What might you want to improve?
- In what ways do you feel teachers are now able to analyze annual academic language growth and identify areas of language support most needed by each student as a result of the learning you facilitated?

Suggestions for This Role
When educators are introduced to monitoring language development in a professional development setting, it can initially seem daunting. To facilitate their learning, you may encourage them to bring samples of student work to sessions. This allows teachers to assess how the evidence from activities and assignments reflects each student's current language proficiency across different language domains.

English Language Development Teachers

Closing Questions
- What were your key takeaways from these lessons?
- What impact did these lessons have on your work with your students?
- What points from this learning opportunity might you want to discuss and collaborate around with general education teachers in your school?

Suggestions for This Role
If you're new to teaching English language development (ELD), consider establishing a system for managing data pertaining to the language development and assessment of multilingual learners of English in your school or district. Organizing data sources with links or location notes can be beneficial for quick access when colleagues make requests.

General Education Teachers

Closing Questions
- How did this go?
- What went well?
- What were your key takeaways?
- How did this learning inform how you design classroom instruction and language supports to be accessible to multilingual learners of English?

Suggestions for This Role
Both novice and seasoned educators who teach multilingual learners of English may benefit from creating a language proficiency profile for each student at the start of the academic year. We recommend meeting with your ELD teacher(s) to identify the latest reported language proficiency levels across the four language domains either at the beginning of the school year or at the time you become aware that this information is available. As you proceed with your students, dedicate time to analyze evidence of their learning to pinpoint areas where language skills could benefit from further instruction and assistance.

Professional Learning Opportunity #8: Identify Barriers to Academic English Language Acquisition

The final professional learning opportunity in this chapter considers potential barriers to academic English language acquisition for multilingual learners of English. Teachers should embrace and leverage the resources that multilingual learners of English bring to the classroom (TESOL Principle 1, Practice 1b) and also recognize how various factors may create barriers to students making progress in their academic English proficiency (Standard 1, Component 1c of the *Standards for Initial TESOL Pre-K–12 Teacher Preparation Programs*). The Identify Barriers to Academic English Language Acquisition box shows the components of the eighth professional learning opportunity.

Identify Barriers to Academic English Language Acquisition	
TESOL's 6 Principles (Grades K–12)	**Principle 1. Know Your Learners** **Practice 1b.** Teachers embrace and leverage the resources that learners bring to the classroom to enhance learning.
Standards for Initial TESOL Pre-K–12 Teacher Preparation Programs	**Standard 1: Knowledge About Language** **Component 1c:** Teachers demonstrate knowledge of language processes (e.g., interlanguage and language progressions) to facilitate and monitor language learning in English. **Standard 2: ELLs in the Sociocultural Context** **Component 2a:** Educators demonstrate knowledge of how dynamic academic, personal, familial, cultural, and social contexts, including sociopolitical factors, impact the education of multilingual learners of English.
Key Learning Targets	I can utilize proficiency level descriptors to describe what multilingual learners of English can do with their current academic English skills. I can identify potential barriers that may impact English language acquisition.
Lessons and Activities	**Lesson 1: Time Needed to Become Proficient in Academic English** **Activity** 1. Practice Using Proficiency Level Descriptors **Lesson 2: Potential Barriers to Academic Language Development** **Activity** 1. Addressing Language Barriers for Students

CONTINUED

Notes for Each Teacher Role	**Professional Learning Providers:** The objectives of professional learning in this professional learning opportunity are for teachers to become familiar with the varying rates of academic English language acquisition. Not all multilingual learners of English have the same language learning backgrounds before arriving at their school in a new country, and not all students learn academic English in the same ways. As teachers become more proficient with recognizing how students acquire English in the classroom, they should be able to better plan instruction that makes content instruction accessible to multilingual learners of English.
	Both Lessons 1 and 2 should require approximately 45 minutes of professional learning time with large or small groups of teachers. You may choose to add additional activities to the information provided here and add time to your professional learning plans accordingly. You can access many online resources in this chapter on the companion site for this book and may choose to print or create electronic versions for your professional learning sessions with teachers.
	English Language Development Teachers: General education teachers may not have prior experience in observing different rates of academic English language acquisition among their students with various learning backgrounds. We recommend that when working with your colleagues, you focus on how student backgrounds and previous exposure to academic English may result in different rates of language growth. General education teachers may not have used proficiency level descriptors before, so this would be an opportunity to provide a tool for teachers to use in formative assessment and to also support discussions about overall academic English language acquisition.
	General Education Teachers: Our learning goals in this professional learning opportunity focus on interpreting language proficiency evidence and identifying potential barriers that may prevent multilingual learners of English from making progress in the acquisition of academic English. We will also learn how to access proficiency level descriptors to guide our instruction and evaluation of language evidence multilingual learners of English produce in our classroom. As you increase your knowledge about how academic English is acquired, consider how this may inform the ways you design classroom instruction that makes classroom instruction and content accessible to multilingual learners of English.

Lesson 1: Time Needed to Become Proficient in Academic English

Timelines for Learning Academic English

Many general education teachers are curious about how long it typically takes a multilingual learner of English to reach full academic English language proficiency. As you observed and recorded language assessment scores in our previous learning in this chapter, you may have been curious about what circumstances influenced growth in different language domains for students in your classroom(s). In this next section, we explore factors that may influence the time it takes for multilingual learners of English to become proficient in academic English.

Language researchers such as Cummins (1981, 2000), Wong-Filmore (1979), and Collier (1995) completed foundational studies that further informed the education field about expected rates of language acquisition and factors that may impact that process for multilingual learners of English. A comparison of these studies found three primary conclusions on the standard rates of English language acquisition:

1. The rate of English language acquisition may be influenced by the student's first language and literacy skills (their home language and literacy development before arrival in the new country of residence).

2. With a strong language support system in place across all academic settings, a student may approach grade-level English language proficiency within a period ranging from 5–7 years.

3. In cases with limited first language and literacy development, students may require 7–10 years to reach full academic English proficiency. This same range of 7–10 years may also apply when a student does not receive adequate English language development support in the academic setting.

Collier (1995) also noted that language development expectations change each academic year because of the increased cognitive and linguistic demands required in each subsequent grade level. In other words, teachers and schools must consider the grade level at which multilingual learners of English initially enter the U.S. education system and allow more time for secondary newcomers to reach English language proficiency than those students who arrive in primary grade levels.

Each multilingual learner of English is unique in both personality and life experiences. As teachers, we must be aware of the factors that may influence or inhibit our students' academic content and English language acquisition. Several factors may impact how each student acquires academic English, including but not limited to their personality traits, immigration experiences, access to education, and previous exposure to the English language in both social and academic settings.

As we consider the number of years required for multilingual learners of English to reach full academic English proficiency, we cannot ignore that access to a robust system of English language instruction results in more rapid growth of English language acquisition. While the purpose of this book is not to discuss ELD program models, we should note that language support is necessary across all academic settings in the school to support English language acquisition and eventual fluency.

Proficiency Level Descriptors

Proficiency level descriptors are language skill rubrics that describe what language skills multilingual learners of English may exhibit in each language domain. While each state or region may refer to proficiency level descriptors by different names, the range of language skills in proficiency level descriptors aligns with each state or region's adopted summative assessment. The levels in the proficiency level descriptors range from descriptors at the beginning levels of English acquisition to the highest level representing full English language proficiency or fluency. Table 3.9 illustrates a sample proficiency level descriptor from California. This rubric shows productive language skills across six proficiency levels. As you examine the skill development from level one to level six, you can see that the rubric describes how multilingual learners of English might use productive language through speaking, drawing, and simple writing with language supports such as drawings, charts, or graphic organizers. As students continue to develop academic English, they are able to use more developed productive language skills to show their knowledge and abilities related to task demands in the content standards.

Table 3.9 *California Proficiency Level Descriptor Example*

		English Language Development Proficiency Level Continuum Productive Language Mode
Emerging	1	Express ideas using visuals such as drawings, charts, or graphic organizers.
	2	Express ideas using information and short responses within structured contexts.
Expanding	3	Express ideas in highly structured and scaffolded academic interactions.
	4	Write and express ideas to meet most social and academic needs by recombining learned vocabulary and structures with support.
Bridging	5	Write and express ideas to meet increasingly complex academic demands for specific purposes and audiences.
	6	Write and express ideas to meet a variety of social needs and academic demands for specific purposes and audiences.

Activity Practice Using Proficiency Level Descriptors

Key Learning Target: I can utilize proficiency level descriptors to describe what multilingual learners of English can do with their current academic English skills.

Activity Goal: Locate and practice using your state's proficiency level descriptors

Directions
1. Review the California proficiency level descriptors provided in Table 3.9. California includes six levels across its proficiency level descriptors continuum, from emerging to bridging.
2. Compare the identified productive language skills for multilingual learners of English across these six proficiency levels.
   - You may notice that students must demonstrate increased skills in expressing ideas at the emerging level. Writing skills are added to the continuum during the expanding level. This continuum is an example of how proficiency level descriptors describe the degree of difficulty and the number of required tasks that multilingual learners of English must demonstrate at each level as they work toward full English language proficiency.
3. Now, locate the proficiency level descriptors used in your state. Tables 3.5 and 3.6 remind you of different language resources that should be available on your state department of education website.
4. Once you locate your state proficiency level descriptors, refer to the proficiency level descriptors for the grade level you teach.

CONTINUED

5. Choose the language domain of speaking, listening, reading, or writing, and review how language skills are represented across all language levels in your state. Typically, proficiency level descriptors will have five or six proficiency levels. Skills represented in the proficiency level descriptors are aligned with content standards and unique to each grade level or band.

We should remember that not all language domains progress predictably, linearly, or even at the same rate of progression as other language domains for every student (Lightbown & Spada, 2021.) For example, a student may progress rapidly in the listening domain but slower in the reading domain. Some language domains may progress one level every academic year, while others may take more than one year to increase one level. Each multilingual learner of English is a unique individual with different lived experiences that impact how their English language develops. As teachers, we should scaffold grade-level content for our students acquiring the English language. Proficiency level descriptors act as guideposts, providing insights into how our multilingual learners of English can utilize their existing levels of English. They also indicate the actions we may need to incorporate into our instruction to support academic growth and success for each student.

Lesson 2: Potential Barriers to Academic Language Development

Some multilingual learners of English learn a new language faster or with fewer obstacles than others (Lightbown & Spada, 2021). Teachers may find it challenging to understand why some students make rapid gains while others struggle when all students access the same language support and learning opportunities. We know from previous learning in this chapter that language learning is a unique experience, and no two multilingual learners of English will progress in the same way or at the same rate. We have previously focused on academic learning experiences in our classrooms. This lesson considers social and psychological elements in the academic and community environments that may influence or create barriers to individual students' academic language growth and development. The fields of sociolinguistics and psycholinguistics describe how some multilingual learners of English may encounter barriers while learning English.

Sociolinguistics is the study of the interaction between language, culture, society, and the social context in which language is used (Sağlam & Salı, 2013; Trudgill, 2001). We might think of the sociocultural aspects of language acquisition as how language is used in the real world and how culture influences language learning and acquisition. *Psycholinguistics* is the study of the relationship between psychological processes that occur in the brain while producing and perceiving language (Purba, 2018). Another way to describe this is how each person's psyche responds to words, language, and language learning.

As we consider potential barriers to language acquisition, we should always keep in mind the individual histories of our students to better address past and present personal experiences. The infographic in Figure 3.6 depicts intrinsic and extrinsic factors that may impact language acquisition for multilingual learners of English in your classroom or school. We define *intrinsic factors* as a student's internal motivation to learn a new language or engage with the language and culture of their current community. *Extrinsic factors* are external motivations, like academic or family pressure, social integration, or cultural expectations from the current community of residence. The infographic in Figure 3.6 represents how sociolinguistics and psycholinguistics may impact English language acquisition.

Figure 3.6 *Factors that impact language acquisition.*

Factors That Impact Language Acquisition

Motivation

Motivation can be extrinsic (how educators influence learning) or intrinsic (student attitude toward learning the new language).

Personality

Learning Styles

Cognition

Culture and Status

Perceptions of different cultures may impact different ways the majority culture interacts with new language learners. Students may also develop perceptions of their status in a new school.

Language Distance

A student's language may be similar to or significantly different from English.

Immigration Experience

The move to a new country may be planned or unexpected for families. We should always consider the possibility that a student has experienced trauma before, during, or after relocating to a new country.

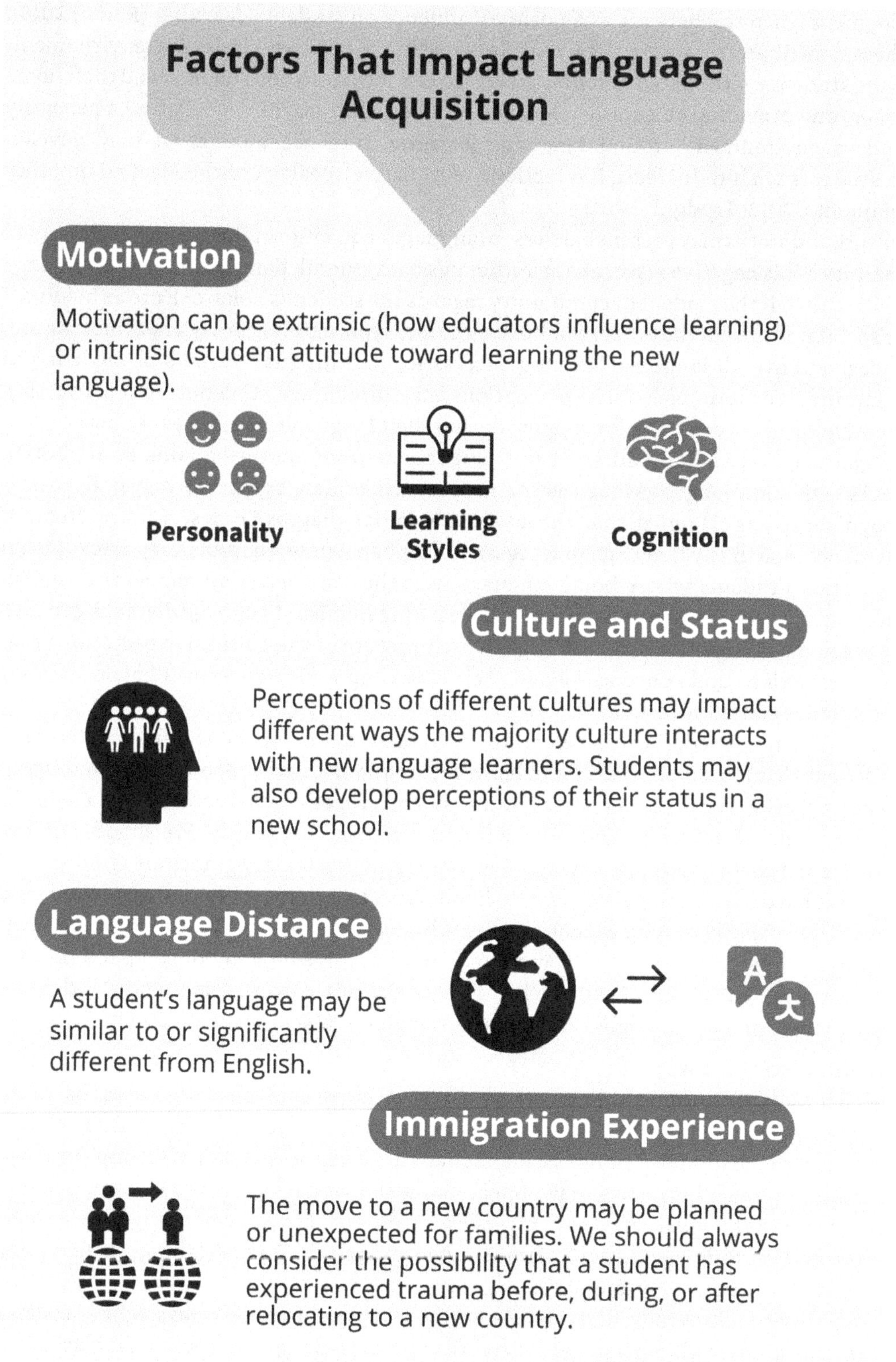

Sociolinguistic Factors

Another way to define sociolinguistics is the study of how language is formed through interactions of individuals and society. As discussed, motivation can be both extrinsic and intrinsic. In the field of sociolinguistics, extrinsic motivation may boost student language development when teachers act as a positive influence on students' learning (Purba, 2018). Teachers contribute to student learning by creating a positive classroom environment, allowing students with shared home languages to collaborate in both English and their home language, and providing culturally relevant resources, clear learning goals, and a generally supportive environment around language learning. Intrinsic motivation may develop when students wish to increase interactions with native speakers of the local community (Tagliamonte, 2012; Trudgill, 2001).

Culture and status may present barriers to language acquisition if the student or the school community holds negative views about a student's background, home culture, and language (Haynes, 2007). If the student or community regards the student's home culture as holding a lower social status than the other members of the local community, it may affect motivation, attitudes, and overall language learning success for multilingual learners of English and their families. For example, status perceptions may discourage students from conversing with native speakers or asking for support during their language learning experience.

Language distance is how different one language is from another (Llama et al., 2009). Students with home languages such as Spanish, French, Italian, or German may find it easier to recognize aspects of English than those whose home language is Chinese, Farsi, or Hebrew. The symbols used in any language to represent its alphabet or word forms vary across global communities. Students whose home language uses the same letter system as the English language may encounter fewer barriers while learning English. Language distance can also occur when multilingual learners of English are unaware of the cultural expectations that govern interactions and conversations in their new community, creating a barrier to clear and productive communication.

Immigration experiences can have lasting effects on students and their families, potentially to the extent that it becomes difficult to learn the new language in their new community of residence. Whether families relocate as immigrants or refugees, transitioning from a person's home to an unknown country and culture is daunting for most people. We should not lose sight of the fact that our students in both elementary and secondary grades are children and may not yet have the emotional capacity to handle these significant life changes. We should also not dismiss the possibility that our students have experienced trauma as a result of their immigration experience. Whether trauma may have occurred before, during, and/or after arrival in a new country, it can negatively influence student learning experiences and create barriers to their successful English language development (Zacarian et al., 2017).

Psycholinguistic Factors

Another way to define psycholinguistics is study of the psychological processes that occur when a person learns language. This chapter considers how psycholinguistics informs how students comprehend and produce academic language in the education setting. Intrinsic motivation in psycholinguistics may appear as an individual's desire to communicate in English with native English speakers. Intrinsic motivation increases when language learners have a positive attitude toward native English speakers and the English language, increasing their desire to learn this new language.

Student personalities may affect new language learning in various ways. Some students may be excited to learn a language and feel free to practice the language freely in the classroom.

In contrast, other students may feel inhibited about practicing new language skills in front of their peers. Some students may experience anxiety, worry, nervousness, or stress regularly or in particular situations and circumstances related to learning or producing their new language. Individual self-esteem, talkativeness, and other personality characteristics may also impact the rate at which students acquire their new English language.

We define *learning style* as an individual's natural and preferred way of absorbing, processing, and retaining new information and skills. Education research often discusses the differences between visual, auditory, and kinesthetic learners. These categories may also apply to your multilingual learners of English. Given the additional demands of learning a new language, multilingual learners of English may require different approaches to learning a language, such as implementing their home language(s) during learning, requiring specific language supports in each language domain, and accessing language comprehension through multiple opportunities to learn the content information. Failure to know these learning styles are unique to academic language acquisition may unintentionally create barriers to our students' English language development.

Cognition refers to individual student factors related to comprehension or cognitive processing challenges. We know that personal learning styles and ways of accessing information may serve as strengths or obstacles and present differently in different academic settings. We also know that students with significant cognitive abilities may or may not differ from true peers in their rate of language acquisition.

Activity   Addressing Language Barriers for Students

Key Learning Target: I can identify potential barriers that may impact English language acquisition.

Activity Goal: Identify potential barriers to student language acquisition.

Directions
1. Select one student with whom you work in your school or classroom to consider for identifying potential barriers to English language acquisition.
2. Reflect on the infographic in Figure 3.6 and additional information discussed in this chapter that may impact this student's overall English language acquisition.
3. Review the selected student's history of language development as indicated by their summative language assessment scores in all four language domains. You may also include information from formative assessments in all classroom environments and information you gather from direct student observation.
4. Use Table 3.10 to organize ideas from this chapter. You may choose to add additional rows or columns to capture information unique to each student.
5. As you consider solutions for each student, ask yourself what solutions to specific student language needs are within your control. How might you support students when a solution is not within your control?

The best way to become aware of potential barriers to language acquisition is to observe language growth over time and then evaluate possible factors impacting each student's gradual growth in English. While we need information about student backgrounds to identify potential barriers for students, we must be cautious not to inadvertently traumatize our students by asking sensitive questions in an attempt to learn more about their personal life, home life, or experiences before immigrating. Students and their families are entitled to their privacy, and teachers should work with the information they receive naturally through conversations and interactions with students or members of their family. Even then, observations about students' lives and possible barriers to language learning should be considered private and handled with discretion in subsequent discussions or comments in the classroom.

Table 3.10 *Analyzing Potential Barriers to Language Acquisition*

	Intrinsic Factors	Extrinsic Factors	Potential Solution(s) to Try
Motivation			
Personality			
Learning Styles			
Cognition			
Culture and Status			
Language Distance			
Immigration Experience			

Reflection Questions
- What do I know about my student's language learning development history?
- What do I know about my student's background?
- What additional information do I need to know?
- Where could I find this information?
- Is a solution within my control?
- Possible steps to a solution might include:

Closing Questions and Suggestions for Each Teacher Role

In our eighth professional learning opportunity, Identify Barriers to Academic English Language Acquisition, we learned about the different rates of language acquisition for various multilingual learners of English. This involved understanding the varying rates of language acquisition among different students and learning how to use proficiency level descriptors to assess individual progress in speaking, listening, reading, and writing. You also considered potential barriers that may prevent individual students from acquiring academic English and generated some solutions you can try in your instruction and classroom. As we conclude this professional learning opportunity, consider the following questions to reflect on your learning and plan actionable steps to support your students' academic language development.

Closing Questions and Suggestions for Each Teacher Role

Directions: Take a moment to write and reflect on your learning from Professional Learning Opportunity #8, Identify Barriers to Academic English Language Acquisition. We have included a few role-specific questions and suggestions to prompt your thinking.

Professional Learning Providers

Closing Questions
- Which activities did you choose to facilitate?
- What went well?
- What might you want to improve?
- In what ways do you feel teachers can now access and use proficiency level descriptors in their work with multilingual learners of English as a result of the learning you facilitated?
- Do your teachers have the information they need to identify and address potential barriers to language acquisition with every multilingual learner of English?

Suggestions for This Role
Before conducting professional learning sessions with teachers, it's important to feel confident in explaining the variations among levels of English language proficiency and knowing where to access related resources within your state. Your ELD teacher(s) can offer valuable knowledge and perspective on this topic. We recommend arranging meetings with your ELD teacher(s) to enhance your grasp of language acquisition for multilingual learners of English.

English Language Development Teachers

Closing Questions
- What were your key takeaways from these lessons?
- What impact did these lessons have on your work with your students?
- What points from this learning opportunity might you want to discuss with general education teachers in your school?

CONTINUED

Suggestions for This Role

Even veteran ELD teachers may overlook barriers that prevent students from progressing in English. To identify potential barriers for the students you support, you might consider reviewing each student's academic and language learning history to see if there is information you may have overlooked. You might also review Figure 3.6 to consider what intrinsic and extrinsic factors you may be able to address in your role as the ELD teacher in your school.

General Education Teachers

Closing Questions

- How did this go?
- What went well?
- What were your key takeaways?
- How did this learning inform how you design classroom instruction and make content accessible to multilingual learners of English?

Suggestions for This Role

Culture plays an important role in language acquisition. If you are not familiar with the home culture of your multilingual learners of English, start by learning more about each student's home language and home culture. Your ELD teacher would be a great resource for this work. By doing this, you can consider whether there might be materials or practices in your classroom that may create barriers to the language acquisition process for some students.

Note. ELD = English language development.

Wrapping Things Up

Postassessment

Just as we monitor student progress in our classrooms, measuring our progress in professional learning is also useful. At the beginning of this chapter, we offered a preassessment on objectives related to learning about English language acquisition. You may choose to reflect on your understanding of the standards-based learning targets by completing the Postassessment for English Language Acquisition shown in Table 3.11.

We have provided a continuum that starts with *1-Emerging* (no current understanding), moves to *3-Developing* (somewhat familiar but still needs information to take action), and *5-Proficient* (able to understand and take action on this learning target). After you have rated your level of understanding and skill on each learning target, consider how your results might inform which professional learning opportunities you would like to review or explore further as you practice the application of learning in your classroom.

Next Steps

Consider the following questions to guide your thinking around the process of English language acquisition, how it evolves, and what supports are needed to best facilitate this process for multilingual learners of English in your classroom, school, and district.

1. What learning do I need to clarify more in my understanding?
2. What would I still like to know about this topic?
3. What are my next steps in supporting English language growth for multilingual learners of English in my classroom?
4. What do multilingual learners of English in our classrooms, school, and district need to develop academic English that we are not yet providing?

Chapter Highlights

In this chapter, we learned that each U.S. state has aligned language standards and annual language assessments that monitor students' language growth in speaking, listening, reading, and writing. Teachers in each country should also identify the required language standards and assessments for English language teaching in their region. We do not use these language standards and assessments out of a sense of compliance but rather to design content instruction that meets multilingual learners of English at their current English language proficiency level.

When students increase their English language skills, they increase their potential to access content-area knowledge. We hope you became more aware of the education rights of multilingual learners of English in all classrooms because of the readings and lessons in this chapter. Access to learning in all content classrooms is the very definition of fair and equitable education for each multilingual learner of English. Your continued efforts to monitor and support the language development of multilingual learners of English in your classroom contribute to their overall academic success in your classroom, school, and district.

In Chapter 4, you will apply your new understanding of academic English development to designing effective lesson plans and practice embedding language supports throughout your instruction. You will also develop a deeper understanding of how to scaffold learning opportunities so they make content comprehensible for multilingual learners of English.

Table 3.11 *Postassessment for English Language Acquisition*

English Language Acquisition Professional Learning Opportunities #6–8		1 Emerging
#6 Academic Language Acquisition for Multilingual Learners of English	1. I can identify each student's home language and compare home language(s) with English to better support my student's acquisition of English.	
	2. I can identify newcomers, students with limited or interrupted formal education, and progressing multilingual learners of English in my classes.	
	3. I can analyze instructional plans for academic terms and concepts that may need explicit instruction and language support.	
#7 Analyze Annual Academic English Language Growth	4. I can locate the language standards and accompanying supports used in our state or region for multilingual learners of English.	
	5. I can forecast (predict) ways my multilingual learners of English may use current language skills to demonstrate their content knowledge and skills.	
	6. I can analyze the language development of multilingual learners of English over time in four language domains.	
#8 Identify Barriers to Academic English Language Acquisition	7. I can utilize proficiency level descriptors to describe what multilingual learners of English can do with their current academic English skills.	
	8. I can identify potential barriers that may impact English language acquisition.	

2	**3** **Developing**	**4**	**5** **Proficient**

References

Arizona Department of Education. (2024). *AZELLA assessment.* https://www.azed.gov/assessment/azella

Benegas, M., & Stolpestad, A. (2020). *Teacher leadership for school-wide English learning.* TESOL Press.

Bloom, L., & Lahey, M. (1978). *Language development and language disorders.* John Wiley.

California Department of Education. (2022). *Proficiency level descriptors for California English language development standards.* https://www.scoe.org/files/Proficiency_Level_Descriptors....pdf

Cárdenas-Hagan. E. (2020). *Literacy foundations for English learners.* Paul H. Brookes.

Civil Rights Act of 1964, Pub. L. No. 88-352, 78 Stat. 241 (1964). https://www.govinfo.gov/content/pkg/STATUTE-78/pdf/STATUTE-78-Pg241.pdf

Collier, V. (1995). Acquiring a second language for school. *Directions in Language Education, 1*(4), 3–14. https://www.ncela.ed.gov/files/rcd/BE020668/Acquiring_a_Second_Language__.pdf

Cummins, J. (1979). Cognitive/academic language proficiency, linguistic interdependence, the optimum age question, and some other matters. *Working Papers on Bilingualism, 19*(1), 121–129.

Cummins, J. (1981). The role of primary language development in promoting educational success for language minority students. In California State Department of Education (Ed.), *Schooling and language minority students: A theoretical framework* (pp. 3–50). Evaluation, Dissemination, and Assessment Center.

Cummins, J. (2000). *Language, power, and pedagogy: Bilingual children in the crossfire.* Multilingual Matters.

DeCapua, A., Marshall, H. W., & Tang, F. (2020). *Meeting the needs of SLIFE: A guide for educators* (2nd ed.). University of Michigan Press ELT.

Dutro, S., & Moran, C. (2003). Rethinking English language instruction: An architectural approach. In G. Garcia (Ed.), *English learners: Reaching the highest level of English literacy* (pp. 227–258). International Reading Association.

Elementary and Secondary Education Act of 1965, Pub. L. No. 118-42, 79 Stat. 27. (1965).

ELPA21. (2024a). *The ELP standards.* https://www.elpa21.org/elp-standards/

ELPA21. (2024b). *The ELPA21 assessment system.* https://www.elpa21.org/

ELPA21. (2024c). *Your next generation assessment system.* https://www.elpa21.org/assessments/

ELPAC. (2024). *ELPAC.* https://www.elpac.org/

Equal Educational Opportunities Act of 1974, Pub. L. No. 93-380, 88 Stat. 514. (1974).

Every Student Succeeds Act, 20 U.S.C. § 6301. (2015). https://www.congress.gov/bill/114th-congress/senate-bill/1177

Gottlieb, M. (2021). *Classroom assessment in multiple languages: A handbook for educators.* Corwin.

Haynes, J. (2007). *Getting started with English language learners: How educators can meet the challenge.* Association for Supervision and Curriculum Development.

Hymes, D. H. (1972). On communicative competence. In J. B. Pride & J. Holmes (Eds.), *Sociolinguistics: Selected readings* (pp. 269–293). Penguin.

LAS Links. (2024). *LAS Links: Leading the way in authentic language proficiency assessments.* https://laslinks.com/

Lightbown, P. M., & Spada, N. (2021). *How languages are learned* (5th ed.). Oxford University Press.

Llama, R., Cardoso, W., & Collins, L. (2009). The influence of language distance and language status on the acquisition of L3 phonology. *International Journal of Multilingualism, 7*(1), 39–57. https://doi.org/10.1080/14790710902972255

Louisiana Department of Education. (2024). *Welcome to the Louisiana portal.* https://la.portal.cambiumast.com/

Louisiana Department of Education. (n.d.). *LA connectors for English learners (ELS) one pager.* https://louisianabelieves.com/docs/default-source/english-learners/la-connectors-for-els-one-pager.pdf

Mississippi Department of Education. (n.d.). *English learners.* https://www.mdek12.org/EL

New York State Education Department. (2015–2024a). *Bilingual education and English as a new language.* https://www.nysed.gov/bilingual-ed

New York State Education Department. (2015–2024b). *State assessment.* https://www.nysed.gov/state-assessment/nyseslat-general-information

Purba, N. (2018). The role of psycholinguistics in language learning and teaching. *Teaching of English Language and Literature Journal, 6*(1), 47–54. https://doi.org/10.30651/tell.v6i1.2077

Reed, B., & Railsback, J. (2003). *Strategies and resources for mainstream educators of English Language learners.* Northwest Regional Educational Laboratory. https://educationnorthwest.org/sites/default/files/ell.pdf

Sağlam, G., & Salı, P. (2013). The essentials of the foreign language learning environment: Through the eyes of the pre-service EFL teachers. *Procedia—Social and Behavioral Sciences, 93,* 1121–1125. https://doi.org/10.1016/j.sbspro.2013.09.342

SERC. (2012). *State of Connecticut English Language Proficiency (CELP) standards.* https://ctserc.org/component/k2/item/77-state-of-connecticut-english-language-proficiency-celp-standards

Straubhaar, R., & Portes, P. (2022). Fifty definitions of English learner: A proposed solution to inconsistent state-by-state systems in the United States for classifying students who speak English as a second language. *Educational Considerations, 48*(1). https://doi.org/10.4148/0146-9282.2328

Tagliamonte, S. A. (2012). *Variationist sociolinguistics: change, observation, interpretation.* Wiley-Blackwell.

Texas Education Agency. (2007–2023). *Texas ELPS academy: Linguistic instructional guidance guide.* https://www.txel.org/elps

Texas Education Agency. (2024). *TELPAS.* https://www.texasassessment.gov/telpas.html

TESOL International Association. (2019). *Standards for initial TESOL Pre-K–12 teacher preparation programs.* TESOL Press.

TESOL International Association. (2024). *The 6 principles for exemplary teaching of English learners: Grades K–12* (2nd ed.). TESOL Press.

Trudgill, P. (2001). *Sociolinguistics: An introduction to language and society* (4th ed.). Penguin.

Turuk, M. (2008). The relevance and implications of Vygotsky's sociocultural theory in the second language classroom. *Annual Review of Education, Communication & Language Sciences, 5,* 244–262.

U.S. Department of Education. (n.d.-a). *Ensuring English learner students can participate meaningfully and equally in educational programs.* https://www2.ed.gov/about/offices/list/ocr/docs/dcl-factsheet-el-students-201501.pdf

U.S. Department of Education. (n.d.-b). *Fact sheet on the major provisions of the conference report to H.R. 1, the No Child Left Behind Act.* https://usinfo.org/enus/education/overview/facts.html

U.S. Department of Education, Office of English Language Acquisition. (2017). *English learner tool kit* (2nd ed.). https://www2.ed.gov/about/offices/list/oela/english-learner-toolkit/index.html

WIDA. (2024a). *Access for ELLs.* https://wida.wisc.edu/assess/access

WIDA. (2024b). *ELD standards framework.* https://wida.wisc.edu/teach/standards/eld

WIDA. (2024c). *WIDA.* https://wida.wisc.edu/

Wong-Fillmore, L. (1979). Individual differences in second language acquisition. In C. J. Fillmore, D. Kempler, & W. S.-Y. Wang (Eds.), *Individual differences in language ability and language behavior* (pp.203–228). Academic Press.

Zacarian, D., Alvarez-Ortiz, L., & Haynes, J. (2017). *Teaching to strengths: Supporting students living with trauma, violence, and chronic stress.* Association for Supervision and Curriculum Development.

Zwiers, J. (2008). *Building academic language: Essential practices for content classrooms.* Jossey-Bass.

Zwiers, J. (2014). *Building academic language: Grades 5–12.* Jossey-Bass.

Chapter 4

High-Quality Lesson Design

Getting Ready to Learn

Planning high-quality lessons with multilingual learners of English in mind reminds us of the expression of being unable to see the forest for the trees. Sometimes, we focus so intently on thinking of language supports to use during instruction that we lose sight of our focus, which is to provide multilingual learners of English equitable access to grade-level content and standards. High-quality lesson design recognizes each student's strengths and allows every student to master grade-level content standards, regardless of whether they enter our classroom as a fluent English speaker or as a multilingual student developing their academic English language proficiency.

If we wish to design equitable lesson plans in our classroom, we need to reassess the mental image we have formed of the students who will participate in our designed instruction. Instruction is often designed to meet the needs of what we may consider to be the average student in our class (Chardin & Novak, 2020); however, there is no such thing as an average student. Students vary on several dimensions of learning, exhibiting strengths and weaknesses in different areas. If we design our instruction to meet what we perceive to be the average student's needs, we likely aren't effectively meeting the learning needs of any student in our classroom (Rose, 2016).

In previous chapters, we learned that academic English skills develop at different rates and in different ways for each multilingual learner of English. Many general education teachers feel overwhelmed when considering the complex linguistic challenges represented by multilingual learners of English in their classroom and fear they cannot meet each student's language learning needs. We must shift our perspective on multilingual learners of English in content classrooms and focus on designing lessons that leverage student strengths. Our goal as teachers is not to design a separate lesson plan for each student in our classroom but to design lessons that provide opportunities for students to demonstrate their grade-level content knowledge and skills. This involves leveraging their existing strengths and abilities and supporting them in utilizing these strengths to enhance their academic English proficiency.

Table 4.1 *Preassessment for High-Quality Lesson Design*

High-Quality Lesson Design Professional Learning Opportunities #9–11		1 Emerging
#9 The Equitable Content Lesson Plan for Multilingual Learners of English	1. I can select relevant content and language standards to support my instruction with multilingual learners of English.	
	2. I can construct language learning objectives that align with academic content standards.	
	3. I can design plans that gather student evidence of learning appropriate for each student's current language proficiency levels.	
#10 Scaffold to Make Core Content Accessible	4. I can scaffold appropriately to enhance receptive and productive language while providing access to core content.	
#11 Putting It All Together	5. I can construct an equitable lesson plan structure that meets my students' content and language learning needs.	

2	3 Developing	4	5 Proficient

This chapter on high-quality lesson design offers three professional learning opportunities that demonstrate how teachers design instruction to support equitable learning for all students. First, we will evaluate the elements of lesson plan design and identify content standards and learning objectives that provide access to grade-level learning for multilingual learners of English. Next, our learning will focus on scaffolding instruction to enhance receptive and productive language for students learning English while providing access to core content. In our final professional learning opportunity in this chapter, we will implement a backward lesson design to proactively plan how to gather evidence of our students' learning. You will finish the chapter by practicing equitable lesson plan design skills and creating a high-quality lesson plan from start to finish.

Preassessment

Before designing high-quality lessons, consider your current understanding of each standard-based learning target by completing the Preassessment for High-Quality Lesson Design shown in Table 4.1, which is also part of the resources on the companion site for this book. As you complete the preassessment, reflect on your knowledge of each learning target and consider where you would place your current ability to meet this target in the content classroom.

We have provided a continuum that starts with *1-Emerging* (no current understanding), moves to *3-Developing* (somewhat familiar but still needs information to take action), and ends with *5-Proficient* (able to understand and take action on this learning target). After you have rated your level of understanding and skill on each learning target, consider how your results might inform which professional learning opportunities you would like to explore first in this chapter.

Professional Learning Opportunities

As we delve into lesson plan design, you may reflect on how lesson plans fit into your teaching practice up to this point in your education career. You may have memories of lesson plan assignments from teacher training or different lesson plan templates required in each school or district you have taught in. There are many ways to write lesson plans, and each style of lesson plan is designed to fit the needs of students in specific instructional settings. In this chapter, we offer three new professional learning opportunities that address high-quality lesson design that incorporate considerations for multilingual learners of English. You might choose to integrate elements of the lesson design template to incorporate language acquisition strategies into lesson plans that have already proven effective in your particular teaching area. Before beginning your professional learning opportunities, we encourage you to reflect on your preassessment responses in Table 4.1 and pursue one or all options that best fit your current learning needs. The three professional learning opportunities are as follows:

- The Equitable Content Lesson Plan for Multilingual Learners of English
- Scaffold to Make Core Content Accessible
- Putting It All Together

Professional Learning Opportunity #9: The Equitable Content Lesson Plan for Multilingual Learners of English

Lesson plans that are equitable are created to ensure that all students have access to learning opportunities. When engaging with multilingual learners of English, teachers must factor in both cultural and linguistic influences when making instructional decisions. In this chapter, lessons will focus on strategies to design high-quality lessons that support language development, including lesson preparation that targets clear outcomes (TESOL Principle 3, Practice 3a). In addition, lessons will address considerations for planning and implementing instruction to support standards and curricular objectives for multilingual learners of English in the content areas (Standard 3: Component 3a of the *Standards for Initial TESOL Pre-K–12 Teacher Preparation Programs*). The Equitable Content Lesson Plan for Multilingual Learners of English box outlines the components of the ninth professional learning opportunity.

The Equitable Content Lesson Plan for Multilingual Learners of English

TESOL's 6 Principles (Grades K–12)	**Principle 3. Design High-Quality Lessons for Language Development** **Practice 3a.** Teachers prepare lessons with clear outcomes and convey them to their students.
Standards for Initial TESOL Pre-K–12 Teacher Preparation Programs	**Standard 3: Planning and Implementing Instruction** **Component 3a.** Teachers plan for culturally and linguistically relevant, supportive environments that promote the learning of multilingual learners of English. Teachers design scaffolded instruction of language and literacies to support standards and curricular objectives for multilingual learners of English in the content areas.
Key Learning Targets	I can select relevant content and language standards to support my instruction with multilingual learners of English. I can construct language learning objectives that align with academic content standards. I can design plans to gather student evidence of learning appropriate for each student's current language proficiency levels.
Lessons and Activities	**Lesson 1: Explore the Equitable Content Lesson Plan** **Activity** 1. Explore the Equitable Content Lesson Plan for Multilingual Learners of English Template **Lesson 2: Lesson Preparation** **Activities** 1. Identify Standards for Your Lesson 2. Effective Language Objectives **Lesson 3: Prepare With the End in Mind** **Activity** 1. Backward Lesson Design for Multilingual Learners of English

CONTINUED

Notes for Each Teacher Role	**Professional Learning Providers:** The goals of professional learning in this professional learning opportunity highlight considerations to support multilingual learners of English during classroom instruction. Some teachers may not use lesson plans or are unsure about the essential elements to include in their daily instruction. Encourage teachers to incorporate new elements into their planning style gradually, rather than imposing an entirely new lesson plan template all at once. Consistent planning skills can be developed as teachers experiment with and gradually integrate new ideas into their current teaching approach.

Both Lessons 1 and 2 should require approximately 45 minutes of professional learning time with large or small groups of teachers. You may choose to add additional activities to the information provided here and should add time to your professional learning plans accordingly. You can access many online resources in this chapter on the companion site for this book and may choose to print or create electronic versions for your professional learning sessions with teachers.

English Language Development Teachers: General education teachers may not have prior experience in differentiating between instructional support with all students and language support for multilingual learners of English. You may hear some colleagues say that "good teaching benefits all students." You can support your colleagues by sharing methods to integrate language supports into their existing lesson plans. We can all learn from the expertise of each other, so this professional learning opportunity may create discussions that benefit all classrooms.

General Education Teachers: Lesson planning may feel daunting if you are new to teaching multilingual learners of English or have students from different countries or language levels in your classroom. Developing lesson plans that include language supports can build your confidence in delivering instruction with multilingual learners of English. Lesson planning with multilingual learners of English in mind may take additional time in the beginning, but with practice, you will begin to develop automatic planning skills and recognize which instructional strategies best support your students in their English language development and academic skills.

Lesson 1: Explore the Equitable Content Lesson Plan

When receiving multilingual learners of English in their classrooms for the first time, general education teachers might feel overwhelmed and have questions about the most effective ways to provide support for these students. Many teachers have expressed concerns that they do not have the time to create separate lesson plans to meet diverse learning needs in the classroom, and even if they did have extra time, they would have no way to implement those plans in the limited instruction time they have with their whole class each day. You might be happy to hear that planning instruction for multilingual learners of English in your classroom does not require a separate lesson plan or completely different learning objectives than those used in your regular daily lessons. Instead, simple, targeted adjustments can differentiate your lesson planning and instructional delivery for multilingual learners of English in our classrooms.

We must first consider the purpose of our lesson plans. Do we complete lesson plans out of compliance or because they help us better organize and prepare for instruction? If you have not used structured lesson plans before, you may discover that an intentional template will help you embed resources and learning scaffolds that you might otherwise overlook or forget to access during instruction. With practice, you will find that intentionally writing lesson plans may result in more streamlined instruction over time.

Lesson plans should be dynamic and adaptive to the purpose of student learning experiences. Learning will look different in each classroom and content area, and no single lesson plan design will meet the needs of all educational contexts. However, all educational settings can implement effective lesson plans that make content comprehensible for students learning English. In this chapter, we offer an equitable lesson plan template for multilingual learners of English that represents the most relevant areas of planning we have encountered in our professional practice. The proposed lesson plan template integrates components of the SIOP Model (Sheltered Instruction Observation Protocol) developed by Echevarria et al. (2023) with additional elements we have used or observed in English language development (ELD) teaching and learning.

The term *equitable* in our lesson plan template title signifies our intention to make grade-level content accessible for multilingual learners of English, ensuring they receive support and strategies to navigate instruction in English and address their language learning needs. Public schools are legally obligated to ensure that all students can participate meaningfully and equally in educational programs and access their grade-level curricula to meet promotion and graduation requirements (U.S. Department of Justice & U.S. Department of Education, 2015). Lesson plans that include intentional instructional strategies that make content comprehensible are the first step to creating access for multilingual learners of English to grade-level content. Table 4.2 illustrates our equitable lesson plan template for multilingual learners of English, available in the resources on the companion site for this book.

Table 4.2 *Sample Equitable Content Lesson Plan for Multilingual Learners of English Template*

Lesson Topic _____
Grade Level/Content Area _____

Student Accessibility Considerations Chapters 2 & 3	**English Language Proficiency Levels:** (What does current language development look like for the multilingual learners of English in this class? Beginning, intermediate, advanced, and which language domains?) **Other Student Background Information:** (What additional background information should you remember for instruction and assessment, e.g., home languages, educational background, interests, and other factors?)

CONTINUED

Lesson Preparation Professional Learning Opportunity #9	**Content and Language Standards** Common Core/Content Standard(s): English Language Proficiency Standard(s):
	Objectives: (What should students know and be able to do as a result of today's learning?) Content Objective: Language Objective:
	Materials Needed: (What will you need to deliver all elements of the lesson? Are there alternative language supports such as technology or translation needed to create access for multilingual learners of English?)
Academic Language Chapter 3	**Key Academic Vocabulary:** (What terms are crucial to understand in order to participate and connect to content knowledge/skills? What academic language challenges may students encounter at the word, sentence, discourse, and conceptual levels?)
Building Background Chapter 2	**Building Background:** (Connections to culture, funds of knowledge, student background knowledge on this topic, and/or previous lessons.)
Lesson Delivery Professional Learning Opportunity #10	**Scaffolding Receptive Language:** (How will you make the content comprehensible/accessible to your students? How will you enhance or scaffold receptive language when students are listening and reading to make it more comprehensible?
	Scaffolding Productive Language: (How will you plan for ways to encourage students to interact and use spoken and written language during class? How will you scaffold instruction to enhance oral language production? How will you encourage students to use written language?)
	Student Application: (Meaningful activities, interaction, strategies, practice and application, feedback, modeling, and gradual release.)
Review and Assessment Professional Learning Opportunity #9 and Chapter 5	**Review and Assessment:** (Review content and language objectives to assess learning. Did your student demonstrate their ability to meet the objectives for this lesson?) Student Evidence Produced: Method of Feedback and Student Self-Assessment:

| Activity | Explore the Equitable Content Lesson Plan for Multilingual Learners of English Template |

Key Learning Target: I can design plans to gather student evidence of learning appropriate for each student's current language proficiency levels.

Activity Goal: Examine and consider sections of the equitable content lesson plan.

Step 1: Identify Key Lesson Plan Elements

Refer to the sample lesson plan template provided in Table 4.2. This template includes the most common and effective elements we have identified for high-quality lesson plans used with multilingual learners of English.

You may download the lesson plan template we provided in this chapter from this book's online companion site or save it as an electronic copy for your work on this activity.

Arrange a time for general education teachers and English language development teachers to meet and explore the components included in this lesson plan. In that meeting, discuss how you could incorporate lesson plan elements into your instruction.

How do sections of the lesson plan support instruction in your grade-level or content classroom? What areas might need to be adapted to address unique requirements of content topics and standards?

Step 2: Review Student Accessibility Considerations

| Student Accessibility Considerations Chapters 2 & 3 | **English Language Proficiency Levels:** (What does current language development look like for the multilingual learners of English in this class? Beginning, intermediate, advanced, and which language domains?) |
| | **Other Background Information** (What additional background information should I remember for instruction and assessment, e.g., home languages, educational background, interests, and other factors)? |

In Chapter 2, we learned about the sociocultural identities that multilingual learners of English bring to their school. This learning was extended to consider the stages of language acquisition our students work through in each language domain of speaking, listening, reading, and writing.

When we consider how accessible our lessons are for each multilingual learner of English, we can review information in Chapters 2 and 3 to identify ways to support individual students' language development best.

CONTINUED

Step 3: Review Lesson Preparation

Lesson Preparation Professional Learning Opportunity #9	**Content and Language Standards** Common Core/Content Standard(s): English Language Proficiency Standard(s):
	Objectives: (What should students know and be able to do as a result of this learning?) Content Objective: Language Objective:
	Materials Needed: (What will you need to deliver all elements of the lesson? Are there alternative language supports such as technology or translation needed to create access for multilingual learners of English?)

Lesson 2 in Professional Learning Opportunity #9 addresses selecting appropriate content and language standards and content and language objectives for your lessons. Standards and objectives help teachers and students identify the day's learning goal and focus their teaching and learning in the direction of that goal. This section of the lesson plan also allows you to reflect on any specific materials you may need to carry out your plans during instruction with multilingual learners of English.

Step 4: Review Academic Language

Academic Language Chapter 3	**Key Academic Vocabulary:** (What terms are crucial to understand to participate and connect to content knowledge/skills? What academic language challenges may students encounter at the word, sentence, discourse, and conceptual levels?)

In Chapter 3, we explored ways to build academic language. In this section of the lesson plan template, teachers identify key vocabulary that may be crucial for student comprehension of the lesson. Key vocabulary may also include academic terms found in the standards and objectives we use to support student learning.

Step 5: Review Building Background

Building Background Chapter 2	**Building Background:** (Connections to culture, funds of knowledge, student background knowledge on this topic, and/or previous lessons.)

Culture plays an important role in learning for students learning the English language. We often focus on language development through attention to English language structures, but also must consider ways we may hinder student comprehension by neglecting to build background knowledge and establish connections between students' experiences and the context of classroom instruction (O'Reilly et al., 2019).
Building background may mean making connections to previous learning in the home culture, previous school, or recent lessons leading up to the current lesson you are teaching. Funds of knowledge refer to student abilities, prior accumulated knowledge, student strengths, and cultural ways of interacting with others that may serve as resources to enhance each student's academic progress (González et al., 2005).
For a review of how to identify and apply background knowledge and assets for each multilingual learner of English, review Chapter 2 in this book.

CONTINUED

Lesson Delivery Professional Learning Opportunity #10	**Scaffolding Receptive Language:** (How will you make the content comprehensible/accessible to your students? How will you enhance or scaffold language input when students are listening and reading to make it more comprehensible?)
	Scaffolding Productive Language: (How will you plan for ways to encourage students to interact and use spoken and written language during class? How will you scaffold instruction to enhance oral language output? How will you encourage students to use written language?)
	Student Application: (Meaningful activities, interaction, strategies, practice and application, feedback, modeling, and gradual release.)

In Professional Learning Opportunity #10, we guide you through instructional decisions that address scaffolding decisions that allow students to engage in content classroom learning.

Lesson delivery for multilingual learners of English considers both how we make academic content comprehensible as well as how we create opportunities for each student to use academic English to interact with instruction, texts, and classmates.

It is important to be intentional in our plans to scaffold students' productive and receptive language skills as they engage with new information. These scaffolds are not limited to direct instruction alone but should be integrated throughout the class period utilized during student interactions and applied during the practice and application of new learning.

Step 6: Review and Assessment

| Review and
Assessment
Professional Learn-
ing Opportunity #9
and Chapter 5 | **Review and Assessment:** (Review content and language objectives to assess learning. Did your student demonstrate their ability to meet the objectives for this lesson?)
Student Evidence Produced:
Method of Feedback and Student Self-Assessment: |

The Review and Assessment section of the lesson plan creates an intentional plan to gather student evidence and reinforce learning by providing feedback for students and creating opportunities for student self-assessment.

Within a lesson plan, the term *assessment* refers to the degree to which students have met their learning goals for that particular lesson. Methods to measure learning range from quick tools such as an exit ticket to more structured approaches such as an oral review with individual students.

When we plan each day's lesson with the end goal in mind, we consider the knowledge and skills we intend our students to acquire by the conclusion of class and examine how both students and we will use feedback and reflection to prepare for subsequent learning the next day or weeks in the classroom.

Step 7: Complete This Activity

Now that you have discussed the components of the suggested lesson plan template with colleagues, identify the initial actions you will take to introduce equitable lesson plans for multilingual learners of English in your lesson preparations.

Identify specific components you will apply during planning and instruction. We suggest that you plan to implement your ideas and follow up with colleagues to discuss how using this template enhances teaching and learning opportunities for multilingual learners of English in your classroom.

Lesson 2: Lesson Preparation

Interaction Between Content and Language Standards

As you grow in your knowledge of English language acquisition in the academic setting, you may wonder which standards you should use when working with multilingual learners of English: content standards or English language development standards. The answer is both! Content standards communicate *what* we want students to know, and English language development standards communicate *how* students will use their current academic English skills to meet the requirements of learning objectives and academic content standards. When we remind ourselves that academic English develops gradually across several language development levels, we recognize that the degree to which our students can access and apply knowledge of content standards depends on each student's current proficiency level in each language domain. Instruction with multilingual learners of English cannot be designed with a one-size-fits-all approach. In the following section, we will explore the diverse learning needs of these students and consider ways we can scaffold understanding to leverage student strengths and current abilities in academic English.

We can use four questions to identify a language standard that supports each content standard. These four questions are illustrated in the Identify Standards for Your Lesson activity box:

- What are the content standards I will use in my lesson?
- What are the academic demands of the standard?
- How will students use language to provide evidence of their learning?
- Which language standard best supports student learning goals?

In our next activity, we use a Next Generation Science Standard and demonstrate how to select relevant content and language standards to support instruction with multilingual learners of English. The next activity is not the only work that must be done in selecting language standards, but it walks you through the first step in selecting language standards that align to content standards.

Activity | Identify Standards for Your Lesson

Key Learning Target: I can select relevant content and language standards to support my instruction with multilingual learners of English.

Activity Goal: Connect language standards with content standards.

Step 1: Work individually or collaborate with a colleague or team to analyze connections between content and language standards in this activity. You may use the example provided here to discuss each question or access the example and a blank template on the companion site for this book.
As you work through the four questions listed in this activity, consider how your state language and content standards align. How do the language standards identify how students will use language to demonstrate mastery of the content standards?

Question 1. What are the content standards I will use in my lesson?

Example	HS-PS1-1: Use the periodic table to predict the relative properties of elements based on the patterns of electrons in the outermost energy level of atoms.

CONTINUED

Resource	HS-PS1-1 Matter and its Interactions (www.nextgenscience.org/pe/hs-ps1-1-matter-and-its-interactions)

There may be several academic tasks embedded in one content standard. There may also be conditions attached to provide success criteria for how students will provide evidence of their learning. To determine the academic task demand of a standard, we first identify the verb used in the standard. This tells us the main action that students must complete.

Question 2. What are the academic demands of the standard?

Identify the Task and Conditions	Task • predict the relative properties of elements Conditions • use the periodic table • based on the pattern of electrons in the outermost energy level of atoms

Identifying the main verb(s) listed in the content standard provides a clear picture of what we need all students to do in order to demonstrate mastery of that standard. For multilingual learners of English, we must then determine how these students will use one or more language domains to provide evidence of their learning.

Question 3. How will students use language to provide evidence of their learning?

What are the different ways students might use one or more of the language domains to receive information and then produce evidence of learning?

Example	Use the periodic table	Reading
	Predict the relative properties of elements	Speaking or writing
	Based on the patterns of electrons in the outermost energy level of atoms	Reading

Question 4. Which language standard best supports student learning goals?

Example	This task may require interactive language skills in accessing the information through listening or reading and sharing comprehension through speaking or writing. An appropriate language standard in a U.S. WIDA state would be Standard 4. Language for Science. (Other regional locations would identify interactive language standards from their state or country.)
Resource	**WIDA Standard 4. Language for Science:** English learners communicate information, ideas, and concepts necessary for academic success in the content area of science. EXPLAIN: Develop reasoning to illustrate and/or predict the relationships between variables in a system or between components of a system.

Step 2: After you have worked through the four questions in this activity example, you may choose to proceed by applying the same process to one of your classroom lessons with content and language standards.

Effective Language Objectives

As teachers, we have many goals for multilingual learners of English. We strive to foster a sense of self-confidence for every student in every classroom. We want to make sure all students receive the chance to learn what they need so they're ready for college or career choices after graduating from high school. Mastering content standards is one of the ways we monitor student progress through each grade level so they are ready for the next grade level of learning that eventually leads to graduation. Mastering content standards, however, is especially challenging for newcomers and students with limited or interrupted formal education (SLIfE) entering secondary grade levels (7–12). Not only are these students acquiring academic English language, they are also taking in cultural information necessary to understand the context of instruction and texts. Multilingual learners of English engage with progressively complex academic concepts as they advance through each grade level. When teachers ask us why students in the secondary grade levels take longer to reach English language proficiency than elementary students, we explain that grade-level academic language and content are increasingly difficult. This results in more demanding scaffolding challenges for students who have only been introduced to the English language in secondary grades.

As we prepare to design language objectives for our classroom, we must familiarize ourselves with each student's current proficiency in each English language domain and consider the student's current content and language knowledge in that subject area. Learning objectives designed to support the needs of multilingual learners of English are the first step in attaining mastery of content standards. For this reason, we introduce a simple approach to writing your language objectives. Table 4.3 outlines four steps to construct an effective language objective for multilingual learners of English in your classroom.

Table 4.3 *Writing Language Objectives*

	1. Connect to content objective(s) used with all students.
	2. Choose an academic verb connected to a language domain (speaking, listening, reading, writing) that will allow multilingual learners of English to use current language skills to meet the content objective.
	3. Add how students will use actions, supports, and resources to show their knowledge and skills.
	4. Indicate if student work will be done independently or in collaboration with classmates.

Next, we elaborate on these four steps, offering examples that demonstrate their application in writing language objectives for multilingual learners of English.

1. **Connect to content objective(s) used with all students.** Language standards are intended to provide equitable access to learning for multilingual learners of English by holding high learning standards consistent with those set for all students in the classroom. Although SLIFE may require additional support and time to address grade-level content standards, we should design language objectives that align with content objectives and provide options for students to use their current language skills to

show what they know. This approach avoids assumptions about students' abilities and encourages them to engage with the same learning objectives as their classmates.

Content Standard
Next Generation Science Standard 5—ESS1 Earth's Systems: Develop a model using an example to describe ways the geosphere, biosphere, hydrosphere, and/or atmosphere interact.

Content Objective
Students will create a group model showing the interactions between Earth's geosphere, hydrosphere, atmosphere, and biosphere.

Language Objectives for Listening and Speaking
Students will discuss and present their group model in a small group using domain-specific vocabulary, such as *geosphere, hydrosphere, atmosphere,* and *biosphere.*

2. **Choose an academic verb connected to a language domain.** Verbs anchor learning objectives by communicating what students need to know and/or be able to do by the end of the lesson. Content objectives describe *what* students will know or be able to do, while language objectives describe *how* multilingual learners of English will use their current language skills to demonstrate knowledge and skills of the content objective. Looking at the following example provided for Common Core State Standards (CCSS) Math Standard 8.EE.C.7, the main verb used in the content standard is *solve.* The content objective also uses *solve* as its primary verb and includes the verb *interpret* in the second part of the standard. The language objective focuses on reading skills and uses the verbs *read, comprehend, identify,* and *determine.* The teacher decided these four verbs best aligned with the verbs *solve* and *interpret* in the content standard. As the teacher supports multilingual learners of English with instruction aligned to these standards, they will lead their students through activities to demonstrate their proficiency in meeting the Common Core Math Standards. These activities will specifically focus on utilizing academic English skills in reading.

   Content Standard
   CCSS.MATH.CONTENT.8.EE.C.7 Solve linear equations in one variable: Solve linear equations with rational number coefficients, including equations whose solutions require expanding expressions using the distributive property and collecting like terms.

   Content Objective
   I can **solve** linear equations with one variable and **interpret** the solutions in the context of the problem.

   Language Objective for Reading
   I can **read and comprehend** word problems involving linear equations, **identify** key information, and **determine** the appropriate mathematical operations.

3. **Add how students will use actions, supports, and resources to show their knowledge and skills.** Language objectives clarify the demands of the content objective and provide a description of the resources and actions students will use to meet the goals of the learning objective. These added details help students visualize what they will do, helping them become self-directed and understand what they are asked to do in the classroom.

Content Standard

CCSS.ELA-LITERACY.RL.4.3: Describe in-depth a character, setting, or event in a story or drama, drawing on specific details in the text (e.g., a character's thoughts, words, or actions).

Content Objective

I can use tools like graphic organizers and charts to sort out my ideas and show the main messages of different stories.

Language Objective for Speaking

I can explain my thoughts about the main messages in stories using words on a graphic organizer or chart and share ideas with my classmates during discussions.

4. **Indicate if student work will be done independently or in collaboration with classmates.** As teachers, we guide students in producing independent evidence that demonstrates their ability to meet grade-level content standards. Content and language objectives can scaffold skill development through collaborative group work before students are required to show their individual ability to meet those standards. Additional information included in the language objective will be communicated to multilingual learners of English, indicating whether they are required to produce evidence of learning individually or in collaboration with their classmates.

Content Standard

CCSS.ELA-LITERACY.RH.9-10.8: Assess the extent to which the reasoning and evidence in a text support the author's claim.

Content Objective

I can assess how well the reasoning and evidence in a text support the author's claim and provide constructive feedback through active participation in peer reviews.

Language Objective for Speaking and Reading

I can provide constructive (helpful) feedback to a classmate when I peer review my classmates' analyses (study) of the author's claims (what the author says).

Many wonderful authors have addressed writing language objectives for multilingual learners of English in the content classroom. Our goal in this chapter is to introduce language objectives to teachers who may be new to working with students learning the English language or teachers who have not previously used language objectives to guide their instruction.

We recommend first trying predictable sentence starters or frames to introduce language objectives to your students. By using predictable sentence frames, your students can focus on the learning tasks and identify what they must do to provide evidence of learning for that lesson. This is one simple language frame that serves as an example.

A Simple Language Objective Sentence Frame

I can _____ by _____.

(action of the content standard)   (description of student actions)

While the structure of the simple language objective sentence frame may not apply to every standard in every content area, it offers a starting point as you design your first language objectives for multilingual learners of English. As we write these language objectives, we must reduce linguistic complexity without removing academic language terms or actions required in the standard. This may require you to use scaffolded language to represent terms used in the content standards until your students have learned the meaning of academic verbs.

For example, you may ask students to compare (same) and contrast (different) between two or more things in the language objective. Using synonyms in conjunction with the language of the standards provides accessibility to students who may be more familiar with the simpler terms and helps them connect their current knowledge to more complex academic vocabulary. See the following example of how to use a language objective sentence frame for multilingual learners of English.

Content Standard

CCSS RL.6.9: Compare and contrast texts in different forms or genres (e.g., stories and poems, historical novels and fantasy stories) regarding their approaches to similar themes and topics.

Content Objective

I can compare and contrast stories and poems, as well as historical novels and fantasy stories, by identifying and explaining how each genre approaches similar themes and topics.

Language Objective

I can compare (same) and contrast (different) kinds of text (writing), like stories or poems, by discussing (talking) with a classmate or small group about how these texts share similar themes and topics.

Add visuals to help students remember what actions are associated with academic terms. The following sample shows how inserting simple icon images can help students connect to academic terms in their initial exposure to such terms.

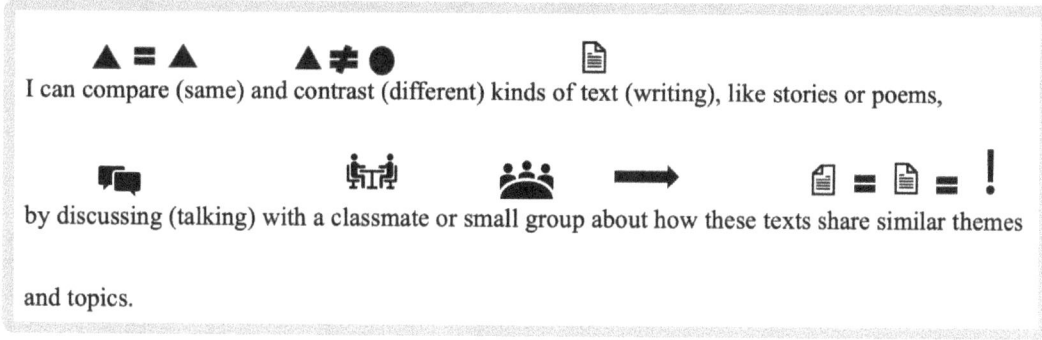

Over time, as you use the same icons with academic terms and clarify meaning for multilingual learners of English, you can remove the scaffolded terms and visuals and use the original language of the content standard. Table 4.4 shows two examples of how teachers might create language objectives aligned with content learning objectives. These language objectives could also be strengthened by adding visuals.

Table 4.4 *Examples of Language Objectives*

3rd-Grade Science, States of Matter

Content Area Standard	Content Area Objective	Language Objective
Students know that matter has three forms: solid, liquid, and gas.	I can distinguish between liquids, solids, and gases, and provide an example of each.	<u>Newcomer:</u> I can tell the difference between liquids, solids, and gases by matching labels with the right pictures showing each type of matter. <u>Progressing Student:</u> I can identify liquids, solids, and gases by describing each one with my classmate and giving an example of each.

7th-Grade Social Studies, Colonial Communities

Content Area Standard	Content Area Objective	Language Objective
Students will use various intellectual skills to demonstrate their understanding of the geography of the interdependent world in which we live.	I can show how geographic features affected colonial life by creating a map of colonial settlements and the nearby mountains and rivers in a small group.	<u>Newcomer:</u> I can show how geographic features (mountains, lakes, rivers, and valleys) caused people to build new settlements (towns) by writing and adding labels on a map and graphic organizer with our small group. <u>Progressing Student:</u> I can show how geographic features (mountains, lakes, rivers, and valleys) affected life for colonists (people) by creating a map of colonial settlements and the nearby mountains and rivers in a small group.

Our activity for this professional learning opportunity allows you to build your own language objectives that align with the content objectives used in your classroom. You may want to collaborate with your school's ELD teacher to practice identifying language objectives appropriate to each student's proficiency in each language domain. Even with the addition of sentence frames and visuals, it may be necessary to provide additional support to newcomer and beginner-level multilingual learners of English so they understand what each language objective asks them to do and comprehend by the end of the lesson.

Activity Effective Language Objectives

Key Learning Target: I can construct language learning objectives that align with academic content objectives.

Activity Goal: Design simple but effective objectives using a sentence frame.

Step 1: Create your language objective with the suggested simple language objective sentence frame.

I can _____ by _____ .

      (action of the content standard)   (description of student actions)

Step 2: Consult your notes on each student's current English proficiency level to determine what they know and are able to do with their academic language. If you are a general education teacher, you may want to collaborate with your English language development teacher to clarify what students can do with their English language skills at each level of proficiency.

Step 3: Consider ways you could make this language objective accessible to students at different language levels without changing the learning goal. Could you add synonyms for academic terms? Would embedded visuals presented with the learning objective make it more accessible to students with beginning language skills?

Step 4: Evaluate the effectiveness of your finished language objective by asking yourself these four questions:
1. Does this language objective connect to content standards used with all students?
2. Can I identify what I want students to know and/or be able to do by the end of this lesson using this language objective?
3. Will this language objective help students become self-directed in their personal content and language learning?
4. Is this language objective written so that student evidence is **specific, observable, and measurable?**
   - *Specific*: clearly states the desired outcomes
   - *Observable*: written so the teacher can see if learning has occurred
   - *Measurable*: defines how student evidence will be measured

A Final Note on Language Objectives

Writing learning objectives for your lessons is a skill that may be challenging for new teachers. Writing language objectives for multilingual learners of English is an additional challenge that takes time and practice. After you first implement language objectives with your students, reflect on how well your students were able to provide evidence of learning and if you need to adjust your objectives to be more specific, observable, or measurable in order to determine if students have clearly understood and met the learning objectives. Finally, consider if your objectives match each student's current language proficiency levels or if adjustments need to be made in future lessons.

While the main focus of this chapter has been on writing language objectives for use in the content classroom, we should remember that ELD teachers also utilize language objectives in their instruction and assessment of learning. Table 4.5 provides reflection questions to help both general education and ELD teachers consider how language objectives function within their classroom or targeted instruction time and how language objectives support students in meeting content classroom objectives and standards.

Table 4.5 *Language Objectives Considerations for Content and ELD Classrooms*

Content Objectives

- What knowledge and skill development do you want to target?
- How do these objectives align with the content area standard(s)?
- Is the objective(s) worded in a way that student evidence of learning is specific, observable, and measurable?

Language Objectives in the Content Classroom

- How will multilingual learners of English use language to demonstrate knowledge and skills of the content objective?
- How do language objectives connect to your state or regional language standards?
- Is the language objective designed to reflect the English language proficiency levels of students in the content classroom?

Language Objectives in the ELD Classroom

- How will multilingual learners of English target language skills that align with academic language requirements in the content classroom?
- How are learning objectives aligned to current student language proficiency levels and areas of language that need explicit language instruction?
- Do language objectives include work toward knowledge of English language structures?

Note. ELD = English language development.

Lesson 3: Prepare With the End in Mind

Now that we know what multilingual learners of English need to learn and how they will use language during instruction and classroom activities, we need to determine how our students will use language to provide evidence of their learning. In our next activity, we utilize a backward lesson design framework to demonstrate how to assess student learning before planning the instructional sequence and activities for your academic instruction (Wiggins & McTighe, 2005).

Activity   Backward Lesson Design for Multilingual Learners of English

Key Learning Target: I can design plans to gather student evidence of learning appropriate for each student's current language proficiency levels.

Activity Goal: Identify evidence of learning for multilingual learners of English by using a backward lesson design approach.

CONTINUED

Step 1: This activity suggests ways to identify appropriate student evidence according to student language proficiency levels in your classroom. To begin this activity, review the three steps of using a backward lesson design depicted in this step. You may find it beneficial to collaborate with a colleague during this activity and access insight from different teachers.

Identify Desired Results	Based on	Content Standards

Our desired result is having students meet the content standard in our lesson. Language objectives help make learning objectives accessible to multilingual learners of English; however, the goal for all students is mastery of each content standard highlighted during instruction.

Determine Acceptable Evidence	Based on	Plan for Student Evidence Tailored to Language Level

What will be accepted as evidence for meeting the content standard? While backward lesson requires teachers to identify learning evidence for all students, teachers of multilingual learners of English must also assess how students will display mastery of content standards. This involves considering the evidence of content knowledge and skills appropriate to their current English language proficiency levels in each language domain.

Plan Instruction	Based on	Scaffolded Learning Experiences

We can only plan effective instruction and activities after identifying acceptable evidence of learning. For example, consider our seventh-grade language objective example in Table 4.4 earlier in this chapter. The content objective asked students to create a map identifying geographical features. The language objective was adapted for newcomer and progressing multilingual learners of English:

Newcomer: I can show how geographic features (mountains, lakes, rivers, and valleys) caused people to build new settlements (towns) by writing and adding labels on a map and graphic organizer with our small group.

Progressing Student: I can show how geographic features (mountains, lakes, rivers, and valleys) affected life for colonists (people) by creating a map of colonial settlements and the nearby mountains and rivers in a small group.

To prepare our students to provide evidence of their learning, we must first provide instruction and resources that scaffold student knowledge and skills around using maps and identifying geographical features.

If we require multilingual learners of English to speak, listen, read, or write as a part of providing evidence of learning, we must build in activities and language scaffolds that offer multiple opportunities to learn and practice these skills.

Step 2: Read Table 4.6 to see an example of how a teacher applied the three steps of backward lesson design to their instructional plan for multilingual learners of English. When you are finished, you may choose to access a blank template of Table 4.6, found on this book's companion site, to practice working through the three steps of backward lesson design for multilingual learners of English.

Table 4.6 *Determining Acceptable Evidence of Learning With Multilingual Learners of English: Family Interviews Project Example*

Family Interviews Project (Unit)

1. What is the desired result?
(The desired result is the task demand in the content standard)

Content Standard (New York State) **SS.E.1 History of the United States and New York:** The student of New York and the United States requires an analysis of the development of American culture, its diversity and multicultural context, and the ways people are unified by many values, practices, and traditions.	Objectives for this lesson will first focus on family interviews and the remainder of the task demands in the content standard will be addressed in subsequent lessons in this learning project. **Content Learning Objective** I can demonstrate my understanding of American culture, diversity, and its multicultural context by conducting family interviews to gather information about our family's values, practices, and traditions and recording my notes for analysis. **Language Learning Objective** Language objectives vary according to each student's targeted language domain and proficiency level. **Sample Language Objective: Level 3, Writing** I can demonstrate my understanding of American culture, diversity, and its multicultural context by planning 10 questions to use in a family interview about our family's values, practices, and traditions, and writing responses into a graphic organizer.

2. What could be acceptable evidence?

- Evidence for each student will be determined by the language proficiency level and observed academic skills in the classroom.
- Evidence of family information will preferably be through face-to-face or video interviews.
- Students can gather information from their own family or any family available to them.
- Note: Some students may need to have a connection and family interviews arranged for them.
- Written evidence would consist of the following:
  - Graphic organizer using labels and phrases and verbal explanation of the graphic organizer
  - Summary of written notes applied to visual representation with labels put into categories

CONTINUED

Student Evidence by Language Level

Newcomer & Entering (1)	Emerging (2)	Transitions (3)	Expanding (4)	Commanding (5)
• Notes using graphic organizers with labels and short sentences to represent data for values, practices, and traditions. • Graphic organizers using labels in home language and English to represent data for values, practices, and traditions. • Summary of interviews may include graphic organizer that may include drawings and verbal explanations.	• Notes using graphic organizers with labels and short sentences to represent data for values, practices, and traditions. • Summary of interviews may include graphic organizers, visuals, and verbal explanations with notes.	• Notes using sentences or short paragraphs (3–4 sentences) to represent data for values, practices, and traditions. • Summary of interviews may include visuals and verbal explanation with notes.	• Notes using complete sentences arranged into short paragraphs (3–4 sentences) to represent data for values, practices, and traditions. • Summary of interviews may include visuals along with written paragraphs.	• Notes using complete sentences arranged into paragraphs (5–8 sentences) to represent data for values, practices, and traditions. • Summary of interviews may include visuals along with full paragraphs.

3. How will I plan for instruction and learning experiences to support my students in providing evidence of their learning?

- Plan lessons that define and describe culture, including values, practices, and traditions.
- Create activities in class to share and compare student values, practices, and traditions.
- Utilize graphic organizer options that students will use to organize the information from their interviews with families.
- Allow group work to collaboratively identify interview questions.
- Support students in adjusting interview questions for their chosen family and culture as needed.
- Provide word banks during instruction so students can identify familiar words to add to graphic organizers.

The Scaffolding Gap

Before we move on to learning about language scaffolds in the content classroom, we want to address how linguistic diversity among multilingual learners of English may impact your strategies for scaffolding learning for each student. If you have welcomed multilingual learners of English into your classroom before, you are most likely aware that student backgrounds can vary significantly from student to student. The optimal academic background possible for a new student includes a history of continual school attendance without interruptions. There are no gaps in their school education in their home country or the country where they resided before moving to their current country of residence. In many cases, new students may have received an education aligned with their new country's grade-level content and standards; however, schools may also need to examine transcripts and consider what academic content and standards must be augmented to help students work at the grade level in each content area. We do not have to wait to introduce content standards to new students who have had consistent, high-quality education experiences before their enrollment in a new school. Students with strong academic backgrounds and some previous exposure to the English language can usually understand academic concepts and participate in class when appropriate language scaffolds are integrated into instruction and assessment. Effective language scaffolds support students' comprehension of academic concepts, active class participation, and demonstration of their increased knowledge and skills in each content area.

As students increase their academic English proficiency, teachers can emphasize content learning objectives and use language objectives to monitor students' abilities to engage in content standards and grade-level tasks. Figure 4.1 illustrates the varying degrees of language scaffolding needed in the content classroom for multilingual learners of English with a history of continual school attendance without interruptions. The degree of language scaffolds implemented by teachers depends on their students' overall academic English proficiency level.

Figure 4.1 *Language scaffolds for new multilingual learners of English.*

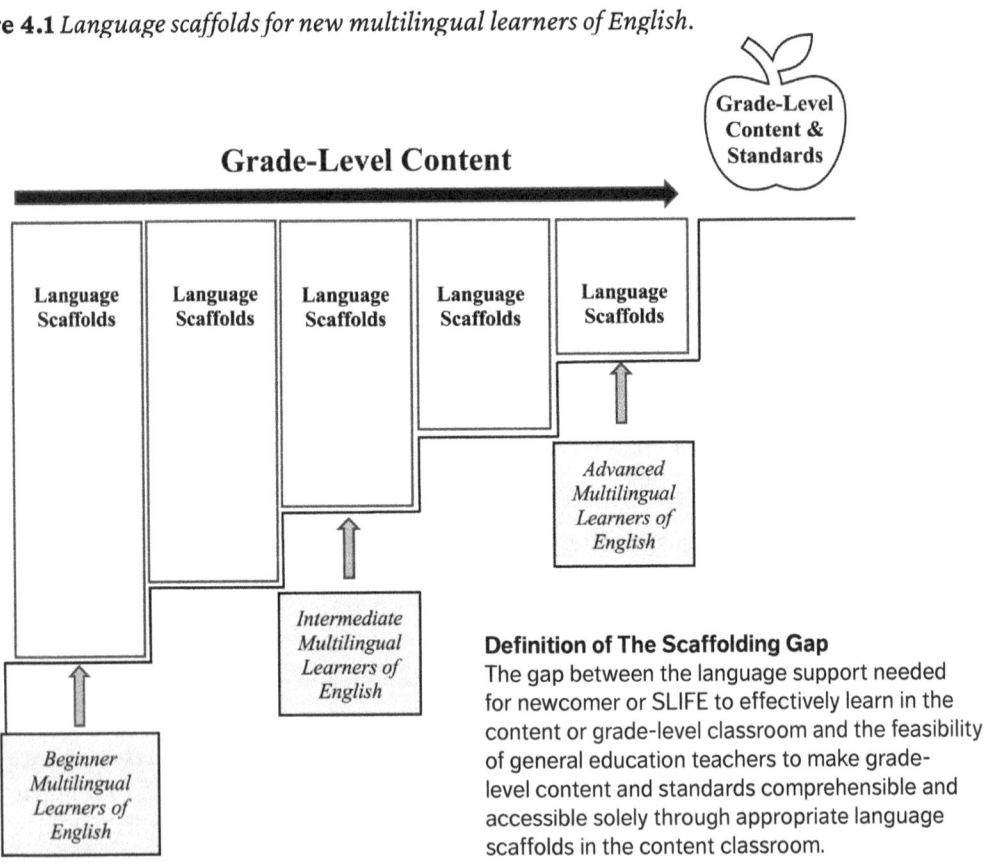

Definition of The Scaffolding Gap
The gap between the language support needed for newcomer or SLIFE to effectively learn in the content or grade-level classroom and the feasibility of general education teachers to make grade-level content and standards comprehensible and accessible solely through appropriate language scaffolds in the content classroom.

Students With Limited and/or Interrupted Formal Education

Language scaffolding may look different for students who have not experienced equitable education experiences or exposure to academic English language instruction in their previous country of residence. Each student's personal history can be impacted by factors related to the immigrant or refugee experience, including conditions in their home country that may have prohibited them from experiencing a continuous or adequate education. It is also important to remember that some new students in your classroom may not have had opportunities to become literate in their home language and may be below grade level in most academic skills (Freeman & Freeman, 2002).

Students with limited or interrupted academic backgrounds may have experienced traumatic experiences before arriving in their new country of residence. Addressing emotional, psychological, and physiological needs is often necessary before SLIFE can engage fully in the educational setting (WIDA, 2013). In addition to having these particular needs, our SLIFE may need to focus on developing essential literacy skills before fully engaging in all grade-level content standards. This does not mean students new to learning English cannot meet grade-level content standards, but rather the extent of scaffolding needed to support these students may initially depend on each student's history, grade level, and the task demands of learning objectives that guide daily instruction.

Consider the case of a student, referred to as Noa, who enrolled in an 11th-grade class in a rural midwestern U.S. school district at the age of 17. Noa enrolled as a new student, and his initial screener showed that he was a multilingual learner of English at the beginning level of English language proficiency. The ELD teacher visited with Noa and his family and learned that Noa had not attended school since he was 7. He was not literate in his home language and had no prior exposure to the English language before arriving at his new school.

The school had no newcomer program, and because of the low enrollment numbers of multilingual learners of English, their ELD teacher was only on a part-time contract. Teachers recognized these challenges immediately and committed to providing the support necessary to help Noa develop the English and foundational academic skills that were missing because of his limited educational background. The school counselor crafted a schedule mostly comprising elective courses for Noa's first semester in high school. They also arranged for the maximum time with the ELD teacher to concentrate on building foundational literacy and math skills. Noa had shared that he had an interest in welding as a career after high school. The school registered him for the welding class in his first semester, and the ELD teacher collaborated with the welding teacher to clarify safety procedures and signage in the classroom for Noa.

As we can see from Noa's example, having content teachers use appropriate language scaffolds alone in the content classroom would not have been enough to provide Noa with access to 11th-grade content standards. He needed a targeted plan to address the gap his limited education background created. We have often heard or read statements that claim every multilingual learner of English can demonstrate mastery of content standards when provided with adequate language support in the content classroom. We recognize the essence of advocacy behind such statements and believe this is often true for multilingual learners of English who are literate or mostly literate in their home language and have a consistent education history without significant gaps. However, planning language support exclusively through content classroom language scaffolds alone for SLIFE might result in schools encountering a scaffolding gap.

The Scaffolding Gap for SLIFE and Newcomer Students

All grade-level buildings, particularly secondary schools, should address the scaffolding gap for SLIFE by designing a plan to support the complex academic demands of grade-level information and tasks. General education teachers may struggle to meet the needs of SLIFE within their standard curriculum alone. Closing the scaffolding gap may involve introducing new classes or reconfiguring existing ones, such as offering newcomer ELD classes, sheltered instruction courses, and ELD elective courses that meet the specific learning needs of SLIFE, so that multilingual learners of English with limited or interrupted or formal education have the opportunity to receive explicit instruction that addresses the language structures of the English language. English language development classes at this level are crucial for SLIFE and for some newcomer students at the secondary grade levels so that they have sufficient language instruction to support them in generalizing new language skills in their content classrooms. Figure 4.2 illustrates possible solutions that schools might implement to address the scaffolding gap for SLIFE upon their arrival at their new school.

Figure 4.2 *Addressing the scaffolding gap.*

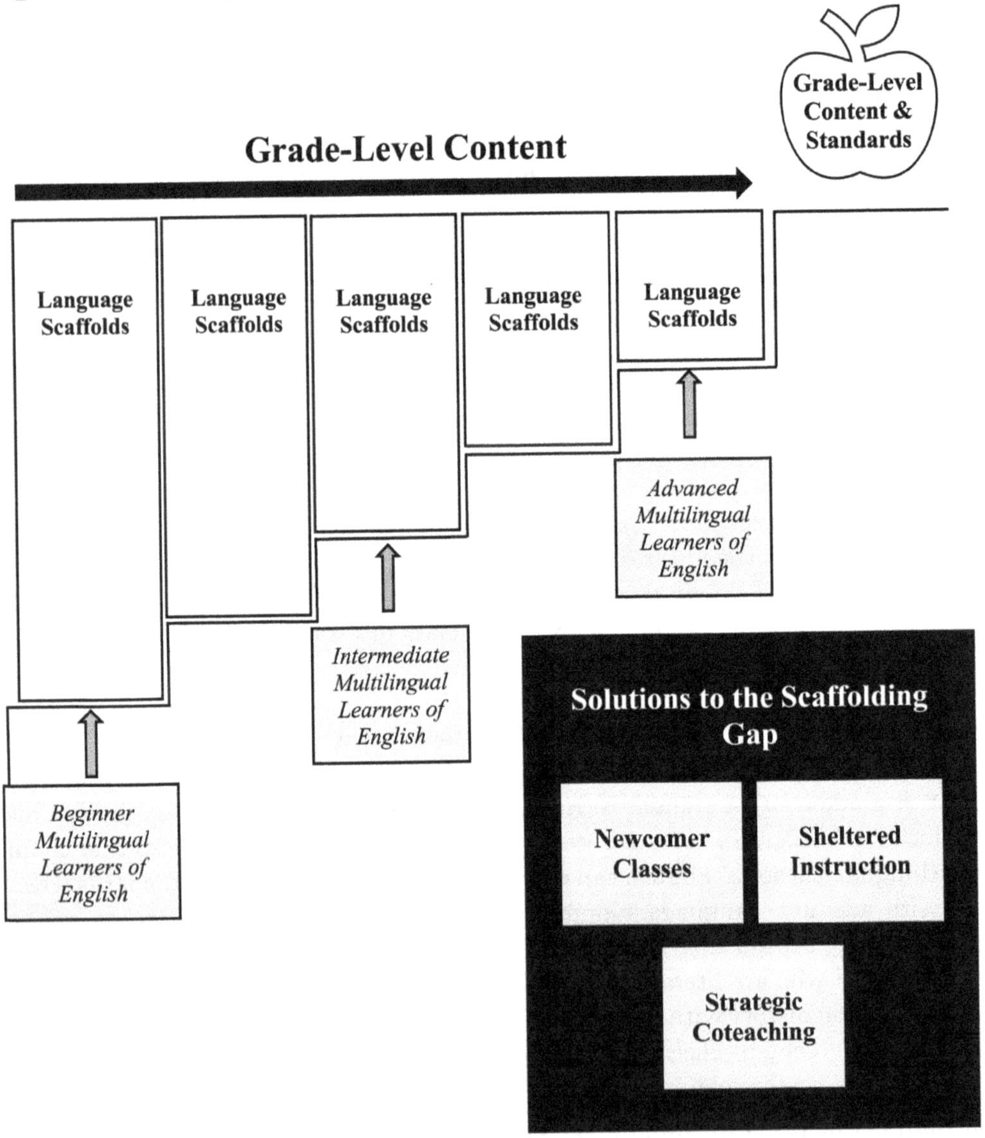

Closing Questions and Suggestions for Each Teacher Role

In Professional Learning Opportunity #9, you examined the significance of appropriately scaffolded instruction to develop language skills for multilingual learners of English while ensuring access to core content. Additionally, you explored strategies for crafting high-quality lessons tailored for these learners. As we wrap up this section, evaluate whether the language scaffolds currently utilized in your classroom adequately address your students' needs or if there might be scaffolding gaps in your school's language support system for all multilingual learners of English. As we conclude this section of the chapter, consider the following questions to reflect on your learning and plan actionable steps to support your students' academic language development.

Closing Questions and Suggestions for Each Teacher Role

Directions: Take a moment to write and reflect on your learning from Professional Learning Opportunity #9, The Equitable Content Lesson Plan for Multilingual Learners of English. We have included a few role-specific questions and suggestions to prompt your thinking.

Professional Learning Providers

Closing Questions
- Which activities did you choose to facilitate?
- What went well?
- What might you want to improve?
- In what ways do you feel teachers are now able to identify standards, design language objectives, and implement a backward lesson design for instruction with multilingual learners of English?
- What follow-up opportunities may you want to plan to further support teachers in your school or district?

Suggestions for This Role
Developing language objectives that complement content objectives could pose a challenge for teachers during professional development sessions at your school. To address this, consider starting by assisting teachers in designing the key components of effective learning objectives. Then, guide them in identifying language objectives that correspond with the learning objectives in their specific content area.

English Language Development Teachers

Closing Questions
- What were your key takeaways from these lessons?
- How did these lessons impact your work with your students?
- Which aspects of these lessons would you like to address and collaborate on with general education teachers in your school or district?

CONTINUED

Suggestions for This Role

General education teachers will likely depend on you to clarify the language skills progression for each student across different levels of English proficiency. If you're new to writing learning objectives, we suggest starting with writing language objectives for your English language development lessons. This will help you gain confidence in writing objectives and prepare you to provide examples of language objectives to your colleagues when they seek your assistance.

General Education Teachers

Closing Questions

- How did this go?
- What went well?
- What were your key takeaways?
- How did this learning inform how you will identify standards, design language objectives, and implement a backward lesson design for instruction with multilingual learners of English?

Suggestions for This Role

If you're new to teaching multilingual learners of English, you may choose to learn more about using a backward lesson design approach. Understanding the appropriate expectations for student evidence in your classroom is crucial. This allows you to integrate support during instruction, aiding students in effectively demonstrating their knowledge and abilities at their current language proficiency level.

Professional Learning Opportunity #10: Scaffold to Make Core Content Accessible

The key outcome of the 10th professional learning opportunity is to scaffold appropriately to enhance receptive and productive language for multilingual learners of English while providing access to core content. Lessons will focus on making lessons more comprehensible through varied approaches, techniques, and modalities (TESOL Principle 3, Practice 3b) and supporting language expression when speaking and writing (TESOL Principal 3, Practice 3c). In addition, lessons will build background for designing scaffolded instruction to support standards and curricular objectives for multilingual learners of English in the content areas (Standard 3: Component 3a of the *Standards for Initial TESOL Pre-K–12 Teacher Preparation Programs*). The Scaffold to Make Core Content Accessible box outlines the components of the 10th professional learning opportunity.

Scaffold to Make Core Content Accessible

TESOL's 6 Principles (Grades K–12)	**Principle 3. Design High-Quality Lessons for Language Development** **Practice 3b.** Teachers provide and enhance input through varied approaches, techniques, and modalities. **Practice 3c.** Teachers engage learners in the use and practice of authentic language.
Standards for Initial TESOL Pre-K–12 Teacher Preparation Programs	**Standard 3: Planning and Implementing Instruction** **Component 3a (partial).** Teachers design scaffolded instruction of language and literacies to support standards and curricular objectives for multilingual learners of English in the content areas.
Key Learning Target	I can scaffold appropriately to enhance receptive and productive language while providing access to core content.
Lessons and Activities	**Lesson 1: Introduction to Scaffolding** **Activity** 1. What is Scaffolding for Multilingual Learners of English? **Lesson 2: Scaffolding to Enhance Receptive and Productive Language** **Activities** 1. A Lesson Taught in Two Ways 2. Scaffolding Receptive and Productive Language While Providing Access to Core Content 3. Sample Equitable Content Lesson Plan for Multilingual Learners of English
Notes for Each Teacher Role	**Professional Learning Providers:** You can divide Lessons 1 and 2 into two brief sessions. For Lesson 1, you could introduce scaffolding in a brief session of approximately 30 minutes. In a subsequent professional learning session, you could then facilitate the Lesson 2 activities. These sessions could be back-to-back or on different days. You can access many online resources in this chapter on the companion site for this book and may choose to print or create electronic versions for your professional learning sessions with teachers. **English Language Development Teachers:** This professional learning opportunity aims to refine your practice related to scaffolding and adds ideas to your toolbox to support your collaboration with other teachers serving multilingual learners of English. **General Education Teachers**: This professional learning opportunity first aims to help you incorporate scaffolds to make content more accessible when multilingual learners of English are listening and reading. In addition, this opportunity helps you scaffold students' productive language when they are speaking and writing.

Lesson 1: Introduction to Scaffolding

Lesson 1 begins by defining scaffolding for multilingual learners of English, considering what it is and what it is like, and identifying some examples and nonexamples. You will also become familiar with different types of scaffolds recommended for instruction and assessment with multilingual learners of English.

Activity	What Is Scaffolding for Multilingual Learners of English?

Key Learning Target: I can scaffold appropriately to enhance receptive and productive language while providing access to core content.

Activity Goal: I can articulate a definition of scaffolding for multilingual learners of English based on reflecting, viewing a video, reading, and sharing with colleagues.

Step 1: Think, Write, Share

1. **Reflect** upon how you currently define scaffolding when serving multilingual learners of English.
2. Then, **write** your responses in each cell of the chart below. As an option, you can use the sentence starter provided in each cell to support your responses.
3. **Share** your responses with a partner or small group if working together.

What is it?	What is it like?
Scaffolding for multilingual learners of English is…	It is like…

What are some examples?	What are some nonexamples?
Some examples are…	Some nonexamples are…

Step 2: Video

1. **Watch** Dr. Cynthia Lundgren of Hamline University explain what scaffolding is and provide examples of how teachers can help newcomers with limited language proficiency access content (Colorín Colorado, 2012; www.youtube.com/watch?v=SWEtW70wzX0).
2. Then, **continue adding to or refining** the chart from Step 1.

CONTINUED

Step 3: Read, Write, Share

1. **Read** and reflect on the following questions from Step 1:
   a. What is scaffolding for multilingual learners of English?
   b. What is it like?
   c. What are some examples?
   d. What are some nonexamples?
2. **Continue adding to or refining** the chart from Step 1.
3. **Share** your growing definition with colleagues.

Step 4: Check Your Responses

1. **Compare** your responses to the sample responses provided on page 3 of the companion site version of this activity.

Scaffolding image by Daniel Larsen on Unsplash.

TESOL International Association (2018) defines scaffolding as "*temporary* structures that teachers use to support learning" (p. 56). Like a construction scaffold, "scaffolding...is a temporary structure that is often put up in the process of constructing a building. As each bit of the new building is finished, the scaffolding is taken down" (Gibbons, 2002, p. 10). To extend the construction analogy further, teachers could represent people on a scaffold who provide temporary instructional scaffolds to students so they can access grade-level expectations and then gradually remove those scaffolds when no longer needed (UnboundEd, 2020). In the first activity of Lesson 1, What Is Scaffolding for Multilingual Learners of English, the visual of construction workers sitting on a scaffold depicts this analogy.

In addition, WIDA (2014) shares that scaffolding for multilingual learners of English involves "careful shaping of the supports (e.g., processes, environment, and materials) used to build on students' already acquired skills and knowledge to support their progress from level to level of language proficiency" (p. 113). In addition to supporting language growth, these "supports facilitate students' access to grade-level material and enhance their opportunities to achieve academically" (Gottlieb, 2013, p. 49). Staehr Fenner and Snyder (2017) stress the importance of choosing scaffolds for multilingual learners of English based on their specific learning needs, such as their English proficiency levels, literacy levels in their home languages, and other factors, with the ultimate goal of removing scaffolds when they are no longer needed.

Wood et al. (1976) originally referred to scaffolding as a "process that enables a child or novice to solve a problem, carry out a task or achieve a goal which would be beyond his unassisted efforts" (p. 90). This process is similar to Vygotsky's zone of proximal development (ZPD) theory (Colorín Colorado, 2023c; Vygotsky, 1978), visualized in Figure 4.3, which has three circles:

- The inner circle represents *what I can do now* without any scaffolds.
- The middle circle represents *what I can do with assistance*. This area represents the ZPD. Multilingual learners of English will need scaffolding to get to the ZPD.
- The outer circle is *what I cannot do yet*. The key word in the outer circle is *yet* because it has more of a can-do, assets-based, and growth mindset connotation, and scaffolding will make it possible to reach the outer circle.

Figure 4.3 *Zone of Proximal Development (ZPD).*

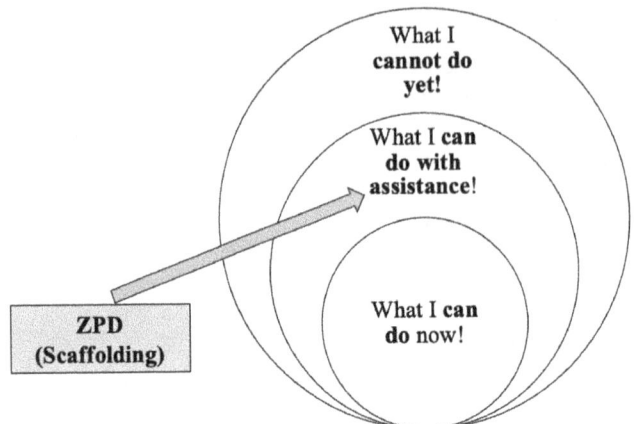

Inspired by Vdovina & Hengerer (2017), Vygotsky (1978), and WIDA (2020).

In addition, scaffolding in language development is similar to Krashen's (1982) input + 1 (or I + 1) hypothesis. In this hypothesis, Krashen described how language learners could reach language levels slightly above their current level when supported with linguistic, contextual, and background information. In addition, scaffolding is similar to Krashen's (1985) concept of comprehensible input. For this concept, Krashen stresses the importance of increasing comprehensibility when knowledge of the language of instruction is limited to ensure students are not just hearing incomprehensible noise that has no meaning (Krashen, 1985).

Finally, many of you are also familiar with accommodations. Accommodations are a type of scaffold; however, accommodations are supports that multilingual learners of English are legally entitled to with standardized assessments. Some examples include accommodations for setting, response, presentation, scheduling, and language translation (Colorín Colorado, 2023a, 2023c; Connecticut State Department of Education & RESC Alliance Initiative, n.d; Heartland Area Education Agency, n.d.). See Table 4.7 for more information about accommodations.

Table 4.7 *Accommodations for Multilingual Learners of English*

- Often recommended for multilingual learners of English to support success in testing or assessment situations.
- Students should use accommodations regularly during regular classwork before using them in assessments.
- "Assessment accommodations should not violate the construct being measured" (WIDA, 2024).
- Examples include adaptation to the following:
  - Setting (e.g., individual or small-group administration)
  - Response (e.g., word-to-word dictionary, oral reading of test content, repetition of directions)
  - Presentation (e.g., a person familiar to the student administers the test)
  - Scheduling (e.g., frequent monitored breaks, extended time)
  - Language translation (e.g., taking a test in the preferred language, explaining or paraphrasing test directions in the preferred language)

Source. Colorín Colorado (2023a, 2023c), Connecticut State Department of Education & RESC Alliance Initiative (n.d), Heartland Area Education Agency (n.d.), WIDA (2024).

Providing supports to enhance a learning experience is a form of scaffolding (UnboundEd, 2020). Relying on experts in English language teaching, we generated a list of their recommendations for ways to scaffold instruction and assessment for multilingual learners of English. See Table 4.8 for more details.

Table 4.8 *Recommendations for Scaffolding Instruction and Assessment With Multilingual Learners of English*

Experts in the Field of English Language Teaching	Recommendations for Scaffolding

Staehr Fenner & Snyder (2017), Staehr Fenner et al. (2024)	**Consider three categories of scaffolds**
	• **Instructional Materials:** Resources that teachers can create or select to support content and language acquisition
	  ◦ Examples include visuals and manipulatives, audio versions of texts, graphic organizers, word banks, word walls, bilingual and English dictionaries and glossaries, home language materials, sentence and paragraph frames, sentence stems and anchor charts, and amplified texts with embedded scaffolds such as visuals.
	• **Instructional Practices:** Ways teachers can support understanding of content
	  ◦ Examples include embedding academic language into instruction, activating and connecting to students' prior knowledge, reducing the linguistic load, using multimodal approaches, and clarifying, paraphrasing, and modeling.
	• **Student Grouping:** Ways teachers can group students to provide peer and teacher support and differentiated resources
	  ◦ Examples include structured whole-group, pair, and small-group work and home language group work.

Echeverria et al. (2023)	**Consider three scaffolding techniques** • **Verbal** (e.g., prompting, paraphrasing, questioning, repetition, using think-alouds or teachers verbalizing their thinking [Reading Rockets, 2024]) • **Procedural** (e.g., gradually increasing independence by first teaching and modeling, and then having students engage in guided and collaborative practice, and independent application) • **Instructional** (e.g., graphic organizers, models, sentence frames or starters, home language texts, and other visuals)

CONTINUED

Huynh (2017), WIDA (2014)	**Include supports for language learning** • **Sensory** (e.g., real-life objects, manipulatives, pictures, diagrams, physical activities, videos, models and figures, gestures and physical activities, and music and songs) • **Graphic** (e.g., charts, graphic organizers, tables, graphs, timelines, and number lines) • **Interactive Supports** (e.g., in pairs, triads, small groups, and whole groups; cooperative group structure; with mentors and with technology support; and home language group work)
Huynh (2017), Huynh & Skelton (2023)	**Consider five categories of scaffolds to increase comprehensible language input (as well as academic language output)** • **Background:** Connects students' experiential and cultural background to content; connects the known to the unknown; taps into knowledge of self, country, community, and world (e.g., student experiences, field trips, and world events) • **Sensory:** Incorporates senses (e.g., manipulatives, visuals, demonstrations, videos, models, role-playing, and artifacts) • **Graphic:** Visualizes numerical data in a graphic format (e.g., graphs, tables, charts, and timelines) • **Linguistic:** Increases comprehensibility of academic language and concepts (e.g., include annotating visuals, chunking content, and text engineering). *Text engineering* is making complex text more accessible without simplifying the text, which may include adding images, synonyms for challenging vocabulary, links to videos and teacher audio, headings, and labeled drawings in the margin. • **Interactive:** Requires collaboration (e.g., sentence starters for discussions, collaborative groups supported with word banks, sentence stems, protocols with clear step-by-step directions, and assigned roles).
Billings & Walqui (n.d.), Ferlazzo & Sypnieski (2021), Huynh (2018), Jmourko (2011/2016)	**Include verbal and textual supports** • Labeling • Word banks • Word walls • English and bilingual glossaries • Sentence starters and frames • Discussion frames • Repetition, paraphrasing, summarizing • Guiding questions, clarifying questions, probing questions, leveled questions, question prompts, and cues • Home language materials • Translation tools • Supplementary reading materials (e.g., read-alouds; age-appropriate, instructional-level texts aligned with content) • Engineered text ("amplify" text versus "simplify" text with white space, images, synonyms for definitions of words, graphics, word banks, annotations, etc.; Billings & Walqui, n.d.; Ferlazzo & Sypnieski, 2021, p. 20)

CONTINUED

Ottow (2019), Staehr Fenner & Snyder (2017), Staehr Fenner et al. (2024), TESOL International Association (2024)	**Make adjustments to instructional language** • Speak clearly • Adjust the rate of speech for beginners and more advanced language learners • Use word stress, intonation, and pauses • Avoid idioms, jargon, and slang • Reduce linguistic load

In Table 4.9, we share a few nonexamples of scaffolding.

Table 4.9 *Nonexamples of Scaffolding*

Modifications	Other Nonexamples
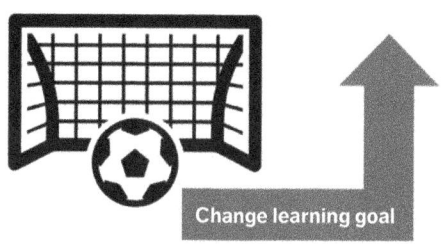 Change learning goal	
UnboundEd (2020) notes three considerations for modifications: • Modifications are "adaptations that change the learning goal and **lower the level of challenge** for students." • They "should be rare and are agreed upon in advance **within an IEP or 504.**" ○ An Individualized Educational Plan (IEP) comes from the educational law Individuals with Disabilities Education Act (IDEA). An IEP is a required plan or program to ensure a child attending an elementary or secondary school with a disability receives special education instruction to be successful in school. A Section 504 Plan comes from a civil rights law that says a child with a disability may receive accommodations and modifications without an IEP. For more details, see Bernal et al. (2024). • "Instructional modifications **change the grade-level goals.**"	Some additional nonexamples of scaffolding for multilingual learners of English include the following: • Providing supports or scaffolds when they are no longer needed • Providing no supports or scaffolds • Doing the work for a student • Lecturing without any visuals or context

As a reminder, continue to add to or refine your growing definition of scaffolding for multilingual learners of English in Step 1 of the What Is Scaffolding for Multilingual Learners of English? activity and share your growing definition with colleagues.

Lesson 2: Scaffolding to Enhance Receptive and Productive Language

In Chapter 3, we discussed the differences between receptive and productive language (see Figure 3.5, The New Language Reservoir). *Receptive language* refers to taking in information and learning through listening and reading, and *productive language* refers to expressing knowledge and skills through speaking and writing. When scaffolding instruction and assessment for multilingual learners of English, teachers should ensure that receptive English is comprehensible when students are listening and reading. They also should scaffold to support productive English when students speak and write.

In Table 4.10, we recategorize the different types of scaffolds into examples of scaffolding that enhance receptive and productive language while providing access to core content. Please note that the lists are not exhaustive, and there could be some crossover between the two lists.

Table 4.10 *Examples of Scaffolding to Enhance Receptive and Productive Language for Multilingual Learners of English While Providing Access to Core Content*

Enhance Receptive Language	Enhance Productive Language
Listening — Receptive Skills — Reading	Speaking — Productive Skills — Writing
Teachers can make language input more comprehensible when students are listening and reading with the following:	**Teachers can enhance oral and written output by students with the following:**

Sensory Supports
• Real-life objects (realia)
  ○ Physical models
  ○ Manipulatives
  ○ Visuals (e.g., photos, pictures, illustrations, drawings, diagrams, figures, color coding)
  ○ Gestures/physical activities
  ○ Technology (e.g., slides, videos, broadcasts, podcasts, software)
  ○ Music and songs or other auditory-musical supports
(Huynh, 2017; WIDA, 2014)
	Sensory Supports
	• Manipulatives
	• Visuals
	• Gestures
	• Technology
	(Huynh, 2017; Huynh & Skelton, 2023)

Graphic Supports • Charts • Graphic organizers • Tables • Graphs • Timelines • Number lines (Huynh, 2017, 2018; Huynh & Skelton, 2023; WIDA, 2014)	**Graphic Supports** • Charts • Graphic organizers • Tables • Graphs • Timelines • Number lines (Huynh, 2017; Huynh & Skelton, 2023)

CONTINUED

Textual Supports
- Labeling
- Word banks
- Word walls
- English and/or bilingual glossaries
- Home language materials
- Translation tools
- Supplementary reading materials (e.g., read-alouds; age-appropriate, instructional level texts aligned with content)
- Engineered text (e.g. "amplify" text versus "simplify" text with white space, images, synonyms for definitions of words, graphics, word banks, annotations, etc.; Ferlazzo & Sypnieski, 2021, p. 20)

(Billings & Walqui, n.d.; Ferlazzo & Sypnieski, 2021; Huynh, 2018; Huynh & Skelton, 2023; Jmourko, 2011/2016; Staehr Fenner et al., 2024)

Textual Supports
- Sentence stems
- Sentence frames
- Paragraph and essay frames

(Huynh, 2017; Huynh & Skelton, 2023)

Instructional Practices
- **Enhance vocabulary development** by preidentifying and preteaching prior to instruction, restating or defining while teaching, and reinforcing during and after instruction
- **Activate existing prior knowledge** or build background knowledge; connect what is familiar to students to new learning
- **Chunk content** (e.g., into key parts) or complex text (e.g., one paragraph or text excerpt at a time)
- **Simplify directions** or provide multistep directions one step at a time

(Huynh & Skelton, 2023; Staehr Fenner & Snyder, 2017; Staehr Fenner et al., 2024)

Instructional Practices
- **Intentionally sequence lesson** (e.g., spoken ➜ written language; concrete ➜ abstract)
- **Gradually** increase independence to support language output (e.g., teach, model, guided and collaborative practice, independent application)
- **Verbally scaffold output** by using "prompting, questioning, and elaboration to facilitate students' movement to higher levels of language proficiency, comprehension, and thinking" (Echeverria et al., 2023, p. 136; e.g., prompting, paraphrasing, summarizing, questioning, using repetition, and think-alouds or verbalizing thinking)

(Echeverria et al., 2023; Staehr Fenner & Snyder, 2017)

CONTINUED

Adjustments to Instructional Language
- Prompt, paraphrase question, use think-alouds and repetition
- Speak clearly
- Adjust rate of speech for beginners and more advanced language learners
- Use word stress, intonation, and/or pauses
- Avoid idioms, jargon, and slang
- Reduce linguistic load

(Ottow, 2019; Staehr Fenner & Snyder, 2017; Staehr Fenner et al., 2024; TESOL International Association, 2024)

Verbal Supports
- Discussion and discourse frames and stems for academic discussions

(Huynh, 2017; Huynh & Skelton, 2023)

Interactive or Social Supports
- Structured whole group led by teacher
- Structured small-group work (partners, triads, groups of four)
- Cooperative group structures
- Stations
- Home language group work

(Huynh, 2017; Huynh & Skelton, 2023; Staehr Fenner & Snyder, 2017; Staehr Fenner et al., 2024; WIDA, 2014)

Activity   A Lesson Taught in Two Ways

Key Learning Target: I can scaffold appropriately to enhance receptive and productive language while providing access to core content.

Activity Goal: Observe a lesson taught in two ways to experience the benefits of scaffolding from a beginning language learner's perspective when listening to a lesson in an unfamiliar language.

Step 1: Video 🎥 + ✏️

1. **Watch** the following lesson taught in Serbian from **0:00 to 0:30**: *Comprehensible Input Demonstration* (V. Gonzalez, 2017; www.youtube.com/watch?v=x7c429g-cu8).
2. **Then, in the Version 1 column,** list what made the lesson challenging for a beginning Serbian language learner to understand.
3. **Next, watch** the same video from **1:22 to 3:14** to see the same lesson taught in a different way.
4. **In the Version 2 column,** list what types of scaffolds supported your understanding of the lesson or how the instructor scaffolded your receptive language when you were listening to a lesson in an unfamiliar language.
5. **You may** refer to Table 4.8 or the first column of Table 4.10 for some ideas.

Version 1	Version 2
What made the lesson challenging as a beginning language learner?	What supported your understanding of the lesson? What did the instructor do to scaffold your receptive language or make it more understandable as you were listening to the lesson?

CONTINUED

Step 2: Reflection

Respond to the following questions **in writing** and then **orally** with colleagues:

a. How might this experience affect your future teaching of multilingual learners of English?

b. What scaffolds might you use to enhance receptive language, or how can you make your lessons more comprehensible for language learners when their knowledge of the target language is limited?

Based on Hiatt and Jones-Vo (2017-2018).

Activity Scaffolding Receptive and Productive Language While Providing Access to Core Content

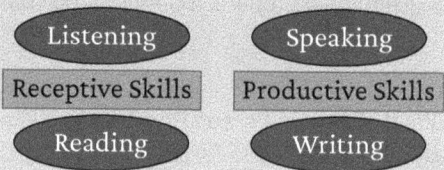

Key Learning Target: I can scaffold appropriately to enhance receptive and productive language while providing access to core content.

Activity Goal: Watch a middle school lesson with multilingual learners of English and identify how the instructor scaffolds receptive and productive language.

Directions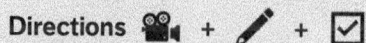

1. **Watch** the Answering Guiding Questions With Middle School ELLs (English language learners) video (Colorín Colorado, 2014; www.youtube.com/watch?v=Sda-_Nhocyg) in which Katie Soto incorporates scaffolding into her instruction with intermediate to high-intermediate multilingual learners of English at Poughkeepsie Middle School.
2. Next, **complete** the lesson delivery section of an equitable lesson plan for multilingual learners of English by identifying scaffolds the teacher used to scaffold receptive and productive language for her students. For some ideas, see Tables 4.8 and 4.10.
3. Finally, **compare** your responses to those provided with this activity on the companion site for this book.

You can find additional background information about this lesson at *Answering Guiding Questions With Middle School ELLs* (Colorín Colorado, 2023b; www.colorincolorado.org/classroom-video/answering-guiding-questions-middle-school-ells).

Lesson Delivery	**Scaffolding Receptive Language:** How did the teacher make the content comprehensible/accessible to her students? How did she enhance or scaffold receptive language when students were listening and reading to make it more comprehensible?
	Scaffolding Productive Language: How did the teacher plan for ways to encourage students to interact and use spoken and written language during class? How did she scaffold instruction to enhance oral language production? How did she encourage students to use written language?

To help prepare you for writing your own equitable content lesson plan for multilingual learners of English in the next professional learning opportunity (#11, Putting It All Together), you will first preview a completed lesson plan. This lesson plan includes the lesson delivery section you just completed in the second activity of Lesson 2. The lesson is also based on the video you watched in the previous lesson, *Answering Guiding Questions With Middle School ELLs*. Please note that the sample lesson is for one day; however, the planning template could also support planning for a larger unit of study.

Activity Sample Equitable Content Lesson Plan for Multilingual Learners of English

Lesson Target: I can scaffold appropriately to enhance receptive and productive language while providing access to core content.

Activity Goal: Review the completed Sample Equitable Content Lesson Plan for Multilingual Learners of English to help prepare you for writing your lesson plan.

Directions

1. **Review** the Sample Equitable Content Lesson Plan for Multilingual Learners of English based on the lesson presented in the video *Answering Guiding Questions With Middle School ELLs* (Colorín Colorado, 2014; www.youtube.com/watch?v=Sda-_Nhocyg). The lesson plan follows these directions.
2. As you review the lesson plan, **consider** how you might write your lesson using the Equitable Content Lesson Plan for Multilingual Learners of English template.

You can find additional background information about this lesson at *Answering Guiding Questions With Middle School ELLs* (Colorín Colorado, 2023b; www.colorincolorado.org/classroom-video/answering-guiding-questions-middle-school-ells).

CONTINUED

Sample Plan

Lesson Topic: Answering Guiding Questions for Multilingual Learners of English
Grade Level/Content Area: Grades 7–8 English language development with a language arts focus

Student Accessibility Considerations	**English Language Proficiency Levels:** What does current language development look like for the multilingual learners of English in this class? Beginning, intermediate, or advanced, and which language domains? Many of the multilingual learners of English are very likely "experienced multilinguals" or students who have not reached English language proficiency within 5 years as being identified as a multilingual learner of English (Every Student Succeeds Act, 2015; Huynh & Skelton, 2023). They are at the intermediate to high-intermediate levels of English language proficiency. **Other Background Information:** What additional background information should you remember for instruction and assessment (e.g., home languages, educational background, interests, and other factors)? Many of the students' home language is Spanish. Other languages and cultures could also exist, but the video does not identify those backgrounds.

Lesson Preparaation	**Content and Language Standards**
	• **Common Core/Content Standard(s)**
	  ◦ **Reading (Literature):** Determine a theme or central idea of a text and analyze its development over the course of the text; provide an objective summary of the text. (RL.7.2)
	  ◦ **Speaking and Listening:** Engage effectively in a range of collaborative discussions (one-on-one, in groups, and teacher-led) with diverse partners on grade 7 topics, texts, and issues, building on others' ideas and expressing their own clearly. (SL.7.1)
	  ◦ **Language**: Acquire and use accurately grade-appropriate general academic and domain-specific words and phrases. (Language 7.6)
	• **English Language Proficiency Standard(s)**
	  ◦ **English**: language learners communicate information, ideas, and concepts necessary for academic success in the content area of Language Arts (WIDA English Language Development Standard 2; WIDA, 2020).
	Objectives: What should students know and be able to do as a result of learning?
	• **Content Objectives**
	  ◦ **Reading (Literature)**: I can determine (find out) the central idea of the text. I will find details (pieces of information) in the text that support the central idea.
	  ◦ **Speaking and Listening**: I can discuss the text with a partner and with the whole class. I can express my ideas clearly, listen to what others say, and build on their ideas.
	  ◦ **Language**: I can acquire (learn) and use new words from the text.

Lesson Preparaation	**Language Objectives**
	○ I can discuss details that support the central ideas of the text using new words and complete sentences, first with a partner and then with the whole class.
	○ I can write complete-sentence responses to supplemental questions that describe details and the text's central idea with the support of a glossary, word bank, and partner.
	○ I can write a multiple-sentence response to the guiding question to describe details and the central ideas of the text with the support of sentence frames and small and whole groups.
	Materials Needed: What will you need to deliver all elements of the lesson? Are there alternative language supports such as technology or translation needed to create access for multilingual learners of English?
	• Text excerpt from *Travels With Charley* by John Steinbeck
	• Technology to teach vocabulary (display individual words with visual, student definition, and related sentence)
	• Glossary
	• Word bank
	• Supplementary and guiding questions
	• Sentence frames for answering a guiding question
Academic Language	**Key Academic Vocabulary:** What terms are crucial to understand in order to participate and connect to content knowledge and skills?
	Academic Language Levels: What academic language challenges may students encounter at the word, sentence, discourse, and conceptual levels?
	• **Word Level**: Eavesdrop, wayfaring, slip in, hold his peace, gather, inhabited, drawback, laconic, grunts, taciturnity, glorious, taciturn
	• **Sentence Level:** Complex sentences, question words
	• **Discourse Level:** Multiple sentence responses
	• The narrator prefers to eavesdrop in _____ and _____. When he enters new places, the narrator _____ and _____ so that he can learn more about the _____.
	• **Conceptual Level:** Find and discuss adequate details in the text to support the central idea of what happens to the narrator when being a stranger in a new place.
Background Knowledge	**Building Background:** Connections to culture, funds of knowledge, student background knowledge on this topic, and/or previous lessons.
	• Continued a story from the previous lesson.
	• Connected new vocabulary to student experiences.
	• It's possible that students were not familiar with a New England town; however, they might have been able to connect to being new or feeling like a stranger.

CONTINUED

Lesson Delivery	**Scaffolding Receptive Language:** How did the teacher make the content comprehensible/accessible to her students? How did she enhance or scaffold receptive language when students were listening and reading to make it more comprehensible?
	The teacher
	• Pretaught vocabulary with visuals, a student-friendly definition, a sentence, and by connecting to real-world examples
	• Embedded vocabulary introduction into instruction:
	  ◦ Substituted quick definitions for difficult vocabulary while reading the passage out loud to support comprehension
	  ◦ Provided a glossary
	• Chunked text by using a short text excerpt
	• Modeled a process of reading text and thinking through how to answer questions
	• Provided a word bank and glossary
	• Reviewed all questions before having students answer questions with a partner by going over key words (e.g., question words and other challenging words in the questions)
	• Intentionally sequenced questions, starting with supplementary questions (more specific) to guiding questions (more focused)
	
	Scaffolding Productive Language: How did the teacher plan for ways to encourage students to interact and use spoken and written language during class? How did she scaffold instruction to enhance oral language production? How did she encourage students to use written language?
	• Students worked in pairs to answer supplementary and guiding questions before sharing their responses with the whole group.
	• Students answered supplementary questions requiring more specific responses before answering guiding questions, which required responses with a larger focus. The supplementary questions scaffolded their understanding of the guiding questions.
	• The teacher provided sentence frames for the guided question responses.
	• The teacher continued to monitor work with verbal scaffolding, such as questioning and prompting.
	• The teacher gradually released responsibility to students (modeled and then released to pair work).
	
	Student Application: Meaningful activities, interaction, strategies, practice and application, feedback, modeling, and gradual release. Students engaged in the following meaningful applications:
	• Discussed the text excerpt with a partner
	• Listened to what others said and built on their ideas
	• Expressed ideas clearly with the whole group
	• Relied on a word bank and glossary to use grade-appropriate general academic and domain-specific words and phrases
	• Answered text-dependent questions

CONTINUED

Review and Assessment	**Review and Assessment:** Review objectives and vocabulary and assess learning. Did the students demonstrate their ability to meet the objectives for this lesson?
	• **Vocabulary Check for Understanding:** The teacher assessed students' ability to use grade-appropriate general academic and domain-specific words by having them connect words to real-world examples (e.g., Who is *taciturn* in this classroom?).
	• **Supplementary and Guiding Questions:** Students demonstrated the ability to discuss and write about the central idea with supporting details by answering questions in complete sentences with new vocabulary.
	• **Exit Slip:** The teacher closed the lesson with an exit slip. Students wrote what they learned on blue sticky notes and questions they had on green sticky notes.

In Lesson 2, you had the opportunity to observe scaffolded instruction and assessment in action to enhance receptive and productive language. You also had the chance to preview a sample lesson using the Equitable Content Lesson Plan for Multilingual Learners of English Template. These activities will help prepare you to apply scaffolding to your teaching context as you write a lesson plan in Professional Learning Opportunity #11, Putting It All Together.

Closing Questions and Suggestions for Each Teacher Role

In the 10th professional learning opportunity, Scaffold to Make Core Content Accessible, you defined scaffolding and became familiar with different types of scaffolds that could be incorporated into lessons to enhance receptive and productive language. In addition, you had the opportunity to observe scaffolded instruction and assessment in action and preview a sample lesson using the Equitable Content Lesson Plan for Multilingual Learners of English. The following box offers some role-specific questions and suggestions to help you reflect upon and extend your learning after engaging in this professional learning opportunity.

Closing Questions and Suggestions for Each Teacher Role

Directions: Take a moment to write and reflect on your learning from Professional Learning Opportunity #10: Scaffold to Make Core Content Accessible. We have included a few role-specific questions and suggestions to prompt your thinking.

Professional Learning Providers

Closing Questions
- What were your key takeaways from this professional learning opportunity?
- What types of scaffolding are your teachers currently using with multilingual learners of English?
- What types of scaffolding would your teachers like to incorporate more to enhance the receptive and productive language of their multilingual learners of English?

CONTINUED

Suggestions for This Role

We encourage you to use part of your team meetings to identify appropriate scaffolds for multilingual learners of English. In addition, it is important to have teachers refer to language and academic data to determine any shifting scaffolding needs. Finally, remember how essential it is to celebrate any wins your teachers are experiencing when embedding scaffolds into instruction and assessment.

English Language Development Teachers

Closing Questions

- Which scaffolds did you add to your toolbox to enhance receptive and productive language?
- How might you support your colleagues with scaffolding for multilingual learners of English to enhance receptive and productive language while providing access to core content?

Suggestions for This Role

We encourage you to support general education teachers to identify types of scaffolds they can incorporate into instruction and assessment based on the language, cultural, and academic needs of multilingual learners of English. You might attend planning meetings, or if your schedule does not allow for coplanning meetings, you might share ideas via an electronic shared document.

General Education Teachers

Closing Questions

- What surprised you in this professional learning opportunity?
- Which scaffolds would you like to implement to make your lessons more comprehensible for multilingual learners of English when they are listening and reading?
- Which scaffolds would you like to implement to enhance expressive language for your multilingual learners of English when they are speaking and writing?

Suggestions for This Role

We recommend working with your English language development teacher to further support you in identifying scaffolds you can embed into instruction and assessment for multilingual learners of English. This could happen during the school day in your professional learning communities or other team meetings, or through an electronic shared document.

Professional Learning Opportunity #11: Putting It All Together

Synthesize and Apply

As we begin Professional Learning Opportunity #11, Putting It All Together, our focus shifts to the work to synthesize and apply the insights you gained from the preceding sections of this chapter. After learning about the elements of designing an equitable lesson plan for multilingual learners of English, you can now apply that learning to designing an equitable lesson plan appropriate for your grade level and content area. As you work through this final section, remember the importance of identifying clear learning outcomes and how you can communicate lesson objectives to your multilingual learners of English (TESOL Principle 3, Practice 3a). In addition, the lesson addresses considerations for planning and implementing instruction to support standards and curricular objectives for multilingual learners of English in the content areas (Standard 3: Component 3a of the *Standards for Initial TESOL Pre-K–12 Teacher Preparation Programs*). The Putting It All Together box outlines the components of the 11th professional learning opportunity.

Putting It All Together

TESOL's 6 Principles (Grades K–12)	**Principle 3. Design High-Quality Lessons for Language Development** **Practice 3a.** Teachers prepare lessons with clear outcomes and convey them to their students.
Standards for Initial TESOL Pre-K–12 Teacher Preparation Programs	**Standard 3: Planning and Implementing Instruction** **Component 3a.** Teachers plan for culturally and linguistically relevant, supportive environments that promote the learning of multilingual learners of English. Teachers design scaffolded instruction of language and literacies to support standards and curricular objectives for multilingual learners of English in the content areas.
Key Learning Targets	I can plan for equitable instruction and assessment that meets my students' content and language learning needs.
Lessons and Activities	**Lesson 1: Plan for Student Evidence** **Activity** 1. Design Your Equitable Content Lesson Plan for Multilingual Learners of English
Notes for Each Teacher Role	**Professional Learning Providers:** The objective of this professional learning opportunity is to merge learning from previous lessons and apply that knowledge to the application of skills. The desired outcome is a complete lesson plan that makes learning accessible to multilingual learners of English. You may find that different areas from this or previous chapters need to be reviewed until your teachers feel confident working independently. Equitable lesson planning takes time and practice. You can support teachers in your school or district by providing consistent opportunities for reflection and continual support. This lesson will require approximately 45 minutes of professional learning time with large or small groups of teachers. You may choose to add time to review previous learning to cover all elements of the equitable lesson plan and should adjust your professional learning plans accordingly. You can access many online resources in this chapter on the companion site for this book and may choose to print or create electronic versions for your professional learning sessions with teachers. **English Language Development Teachers**: Building an equitable lesson plan may feel challenging for teachers who are new to this work. You may be called to provide background information about different cultures and languages. You may also need to look up information about the language and culture of students you have not previously worked with. As you work through your English language development lesson plans and support your colleagues in creating their classroom lesson plans, remember to always point instruction back to the appropriate standards. This will ground your work and help you and your colleagues keep the target in mind.

CONTINUED

> **General Education Teachers**: Lesson planning may feel daunting if you are new to teaching multilingual learners of English or you have students from different countries or language levels in your classroom this year. Lesson planning with multilingual learners of English in mind may take additional time in the beginning, but with practice, you will begin to develop automatic planning skills and recognize which instructional strategies best support your students in their English language development and academic skills.

Lesson 1: Plan for Student Evidence

Activity Design Your Equitable Content Lesson Plan for Multilingual Learners of English

Key Learning Target: I can plan for equitable instruction and assessment that meets my students' content and language learning needs.

Activity Goal: Integrate this chapter's learning on high-quality lesson design by designing an equitable lesson plan for multilingual learners of English.

Directions
In Professional Learning Opportunity #10, we practiced embedding language scaffolds to support our students' learning. Throughout this chapter, we have gradually designed the elements that create an effective and equitable lesson plan to use with multilingual learners of English in the content classroom.

In this final activity of Chapter 4, we ask you to design a lesson plan from start to finish, applying the knowledge you have developed in this and previous chapters. While we have not yet addressed assessment and student feedback issues, we encourage you to complete the lesson plan template shown in Table 4.11.

Use the guiding questions provided in each section of the lesson plan template to frame your thinking and note additional questions you may have as you work through your instruction with multilingual learners of English.

Table 4.11 *Designing Your Equitable Content Lesson Plan for Multilingual Learners of English Template*

Lesson Topic _____

Grade Level/Content Area _____

Student Accessibility Considerations Chapters 2 & 3	**English Language Proficiency Levels:** What does current language development look like for the multilingual learners of English in this class? Beginning, intermediate, or advanced, and which language domains? **Other Student Background Information:** What additional background information should you remember for instruction and assessment (e.g., home languages, educational background, interests, and other factors)?

CONTINUED

Lesson Preparation Professional Learning Opportunity #9	**Content and Language Standards** Common Core/Content Standard(s): English Language Proficiency Standard(s):
	Objectives: What should students know and be able to do as a result of today's learning? Content Objective: Language Objective:
	Materials Needed: What will you need to deliver all elements of the lesson? Are there alternative language supports such as technology or translation needed to create access for multilingual learners of English?
Academic Language Chapter 3	**Key Academic Vocabulary:** What terms are crucial to understand in order to participate and connect to content knowledge/skills? What academic language challenges may students encounter at the word, sentence, discourse, and conceptual levels?
Building Background Chapter 2	**Building Background:** Connections to culture, funds of knowledge, student background knowledge on this topic, and/or previous lessons.
Lesson Delivery Professional Learning Opportunity #10	**Scaffolding Receptive Language Skills:** How will you make the content comprehensible/accessible to your students? How will you enhance or scaffold language input when students are listening and reading to make it more comprehensible?
	Scaffolded Productive Language Skills: How will you plan for ways to encourage students to interact and use spoken and written language during class? How will you scaffold instruction to enhance oral language output? How will you encourage students to use written language?
	Student Application: Meaningful activities, interaction, strategies, practice and application, feedback, modeling, and gradual release.
Review and Assessment Professional Learning Opportunity #9 and Chapter 5	**Review and Assessment:** Review content and language objectives to assess learning. Did your students demonstrate their ability to meet the objectives for this lesson? Student Evidence Produced: Method of Feedback and Student Self-Assessment:

Closing Questions and Suggestions for Each Teacher Role

Directions: Take a moment to write and reflect on your learning from Professional Learning Opportunity #11, Putting It All Together. We have included a few role-specific questions and suggestions to prompt your thinking.

Professional Learning Providers

Closing Questions
- How did you choose to facilitate learning for this lesson?
- What went well?
- What might you want to improve?
- Do you feel you are now ready to independently create equitable lesson plans? If not, what follow-up opportunities may you want to plan to further support teachers in your school or district?

Suggestions for This Role
You may find that you need more than the usual 45-minute professional development session time to work through the entire equitable content lesson plan for multilingual learners of English. You may choose to target certain sections of the lesson plan with your school faculty and assign learning in other sections for grade-level/content meetings or group work.

English Language Development Teachers

Closing Questions
- How did this go?
- What went well?
- What were your key takeaways?
- How did this learning inform how you create equitable lesson plans that support your students learning English?

Suggestions for This Role
If you are supporting content teachers directly through coteaching or providing support in their classrooms, you may choose to first visit with the content teacher to discuss what areas of the equitable content lesson plan would be beneficial to explore together first.

General Education Teachers

Closing Questions
- How did this go?
- What went well?
- What were your key takeaways?
- How did this learning inform how you design classroom instruction and make content accessible to multilingual learners of English?

Suggestions for This Role
After you review the equitable content lesson plan template in this chapter, you might choose to further explore a section of the template that was new learning for you but learning that you think would be useful to support your instructional planning. Try different sections of the lesson plan template and reflect after each lesson on ways the intentional planning may support you or your students during instruction.

Wrapping Things Up

Postassessment

Lesson planning is a skill that develops with time and practice. Designing equitable content lesson plans that support multilingual learners of English is a skill that will develop over time as you apply new learning to your work and reflect on students' outcomes after each lesson. At the beginning of this chapter, we offered a preassessment of objectives related to designing high-quality lessons. You may choose to reflect on your understanding of each of the standards-based learning targets by completing the Postassessment for High-Quality Lesson Design shown in Table 4.12.

We have provided a continuum that starts with *1-Emerging* (no current understanding), moves to *3-Developing* (somewhat familiar but still needs information to take action), and ends with *5-Proficient* (able to understand and take action on this learning target).

Table 4.12 *Postassessment for High-Quality Lesson Design*

High-Quality Lesson Design Professional Learning Opportunities #9–11			1 Emerging
#9 The Equitable Content Lesson Plan for Multilingual Learners of English		1. I can select relevant content and language standards to support my instruction with multilingual learners of English.	
		2. I can construct language learning objectives that align with academic content standards.	
		3. I can design plans that gather student evidence of learning appropriate for each student's current language proficiency levels.	
#10 Scaffold to Make Core Content Accessible		4. I can scaffold appropriately to enhance receptive and productive language while providing access to core content.	
#11 Putting It All Together		5. I can construct an equitable lesson plan structure that meets my students' content and language learning needs.	

After you have rated your level of understanding and skill on each learning target, consider how your results might inform which professional learning opportunities you would like to review or explore further as you practice the application of learning in your classroom.

Next Steps

Consider the following questions to clarify your thinking around the process of English language acquisition, how it evolves, and what supports are needed to best facilitate this process for multilingual learners of English in your classroom, school, and district.

1. What areas of learning should I focus on to better understand lesson planning?
2. What would I still like to know about this topic?
3. What are my next steps in supporting English language growth for multilingual learners of English in my classroom?
4. What do I need to practice more to develop effective lesson plans to support my multilingual learners of English?

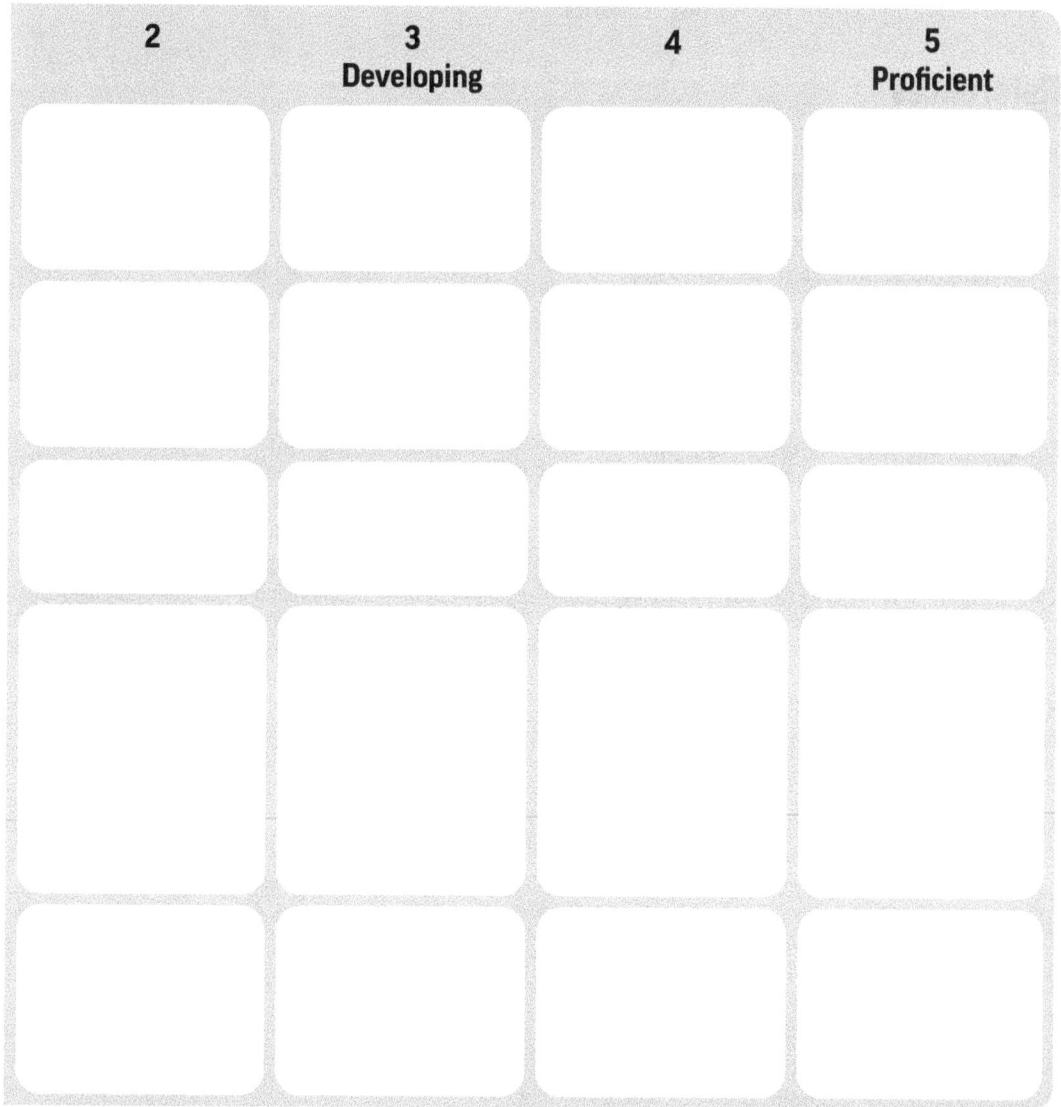

Chapter Highlights

Lesson plans are often underestimated as a teaching tool, yet they serve as one of the most valuable actions to use language support during instruction with multilingual learners of English. In this chapter, we learned the essential components to include in an equitable content lesson plan for multilingual learners of English. We practiced writing language objectives that align with content standards and objectives. We explored scaffolding instruction to build the receptive and productive language skills of our students. We finished the chapter by practicing creating our equitable content lesson plan with the learning needs of your students in mind.

In Chapter 5, you'll apply your newfound lesson planning knowledge and extend it to include designing effective assessment methods for multilingual learners of English. This includes gathering evidence of student learning in content knowledge, skills, and academic English language development. We'll learn to identify potential bias in current assessments and assess classroom evaluations for a more accurate measurement of content standards mastery. Reflecting on the connection between instruction and assessment will improve the overall learning experience for our students.

References

Bernal, E., Council, L., Emrich, J., & Pettus, C. (2024). *Special education essentials: 504 or IEP* [Webinar]. AFT: Share My Lesson Webinars. https://sharemylesson.com/webinars/special-education-essentials-iep-v-504

Billings, E., & Walqui, A. (n.d.). *Topic brief 3: De-mystifying complex texts: What are "complex" texts and how can we ensure ELLs/MLLs can access them?* New York State Education Department. https://www.nysed.gov/bilingual-ed/topic-brief-3-de-mystifying-complex-texts-what-are-complex-texts-and-how-can-we-ensure

Chardin, M., & Novak, K. (2020). *Equity by design: Delivering on the power and promise of UDL.* Corwin.

Colorín Colorado. (2012, December 5). *What is scaffolding* [Video]. YouTube. https://www.youtube.com/watch?v=SWEtW7OwzX0

Colorín Colorado. (2014, July 23). *Answering guiding questions with middle school ELLs* [Video]. YouTube. https://www.youtube.com/watch?v=Sda-_Nhocyg

Colorín Colorado. (2023a). *Accommodation (for English language learners).* WETA Public Broadcasting. https://www.colorincolorado.org/glossary/accommodation-english-language-learners

Colorín Colorado. (2023b). *Answering guiding questions with middle school ELLs.* WETA Public Broadcasting. https://www.colorincolorado.org/classroom-video/answering-guiding-questions-middle-school-ells

Colorín Colorado. (2023c). *What is "scaffolding" and how does it help ELLs?* WETA Public Broadcasting. https://www.colorincolorado.org/faq/what-scaffolding-and-how-does-it-help-ells

Connecticut State Department of Education & RESC Alliance Initiative. (n.d.). *Scaffolding to support English language development: Elementary.* https://drive.google.com/file/d/1qIuY6q5PoQ2iIGbaQkwEbZyHpQ7A77vd/view?usp=sharing

Echeverria, J., Vogt, M. E., Short, D. J., & Toppel, K. (2023). *Making content comprehensible for multilingual learners: The SIOP model* (6th ed.). Pearson.

Every Student Succeeds Act, 20 U.S.C. § 6301. (2015). https://www.congress.gov/bill/114th-congress/senate-bill/1177

Ferlazzo, L., & Sypnieski, K. H. (2021). Distance learning with English language learners. In *The ESL/ELL teacher's survival guide* (2nd ed.). Jossey-Bass. https://larryferlazzo.edublogs.org/files/2020/07/Chapter-22-Distance-Learning-With-ELLs-revrevised.pdf

Freeman, Y., & Freeman, D. (2002). *Closing the achievement gap: How to reach limited-formal-schooling and long-term English learners.* Heinemann.

Gibbons, P. (2002). *Scaffolding language scaffolding learning: Teaching second-language learners in the mainstream classroom.* Heinemann.

González, N., Moll, L.C., & Amanti, C. (2005). *Funds of knowledge: Theorizing practices in households, communities, and classrooms.* Lawrence Erlbaum.

Gonzalez, V. (2017, July 2). *Comprehensible input demonstration* [Video]. YouTube. https://www.youtube.com/watch?v=x7c429g-cu8

Gottlieb, M. (2013). *Essential actions: A handbook for implementing WIDA's framework for English language development standards.* Board of Regents of the University of Wisconsin System.

Heartland Area Education Agency. (n.d.). *Allowable accommodations for English learners on common academic assessments.* http://tinyurl.com/EL-Allow

Hiatt, J. E., & Jones-Vo, S. (2017-2018). *In-service educator of English learners' certificate program.* University of Iowa Baker Teacher Leader Center.

Huynh, T. (2017, April 14). #34. Three types of scaffolding: There's a scaffold for that. *Empowering ELLs.* https://www.empoweringells.com/scaffolding-instruction/

Huynh, T. (2018, May 25). #91. Language scaffolds: Lowering the barriers to comprehension. *Empowering ELLs.* https://www.empoweringells.com/language-scaffolds/

Huynh, T., & Skelton, B. (2023). *Long-term success for experienced multilinguals.* Corwin.

Jmourko, G. H. (2016). *Planning tool of math for ELLs* [Handout]. National Council of Teachers of Mathematics Conference, Session 40789.

Krashen, S. D. (1982). *Principles and practices in second language acquisition.* Pergamon Press.

Krashen, S. D. (1985). *The input hypothesis: Issues and implications.* Longman.

NGSS Lead States. (2013). *Next Generation Science Standards: For states, by states.* National Academies Press.

O'Reilly, T., Wang, Z., & Sabatini, J. (2019). How much knowledge is too little? When a lack of knowledge becomes a barrier to comprehension. *Psychological Science, 30*(9), 1344–1351. https://doi.org/10.1177/0956797619862276

Ottow, S. B. (2019). *The language lens for content teachers: A guide for K–12 teachers of English and academic language learners.* Learning Sciences International.

Reading Rockets. (2024). *Think-alouds.* WETA Public Broadcasting. https://www.readingrockets.org/classroom/classroom-strategies think-alouds

Rose, T. (2016). *The end of average: Unlocking our potential by embracing what makes us different.* HarperCollins.

Staehr Fenner, D., & Snyder, S. (2017). *Unlocking English learners' potential: Strategies for making content accessible.* Corwin.

Staehr Fenner, D., Snyder, S., & Gregoire-Smith, M. (2024). *Unlocking multilingual learners' potential: Strategies for making content accessible* (2nd ed.). Corwin.

TESOL International Association. (2018). *The 6 principles for exemplary teaching of English learners: Grades K–12.* TESOL Press.

TESOL International Association. (2019). *Standards for initial TESOL Pre-K–12 teacher preparation programs.* TESOL Press.

TESOL International Association. (2024). *The 6 principles for exemplary teaching of English learners: Grades K–12* (2nd ed.). TESOL Press.

UnboundEd. (2020). *Module 3: Accelerate student learning by scaffolding for equity.* Iowa Department of Education.

U.S. Department of Justice & U.S. Department of Education. (2015). *Ensuring English learner students can participate meaningfully and equally in educational programs.* https://www2.ed.gov/about/offices/list/ocr/docs/dcl-factsheet-el-students-201501.pdf

Vdovina, T., & Hengerer, A. (2017). *Using the sheltered instruction observation protocol (SIOP) to plan and implement effective instruction for English learners: SIOP institute trainer of trainers workshop: Foundations.* Center for Applied Linguistics.

Vygotsky, L. (1978). *Mind in society: The development of higher psychological processes* (M. Cole, V. John-Steiner, S. Scribner, & E. Souberman, Eds. & Trans.). Harvard University Press. (Original work published 1934).

WIDA. (2013). *RtI2: Developing a culturally and linguistically responsive approach to response to instruction and intervention for English language learners.* Board of Regents at the University of Wisconsin System. https://wida.wisc.edu/resources/response-instruction-and-intervention-english-language-learners

WIDA. (2014). *2012 amplification of the WIDA English language development standards: Kindergarten – Grade 12.* Board of Regents of the University of Wisconsin System. https://wida.wisc.edu/resources/2012-amplification-wida-english-language-development-standards

WIDA. (2020). *WIDA English language development standards framework, 2020 edition: Kindergarten–grade 12.* Board of Regents of the University of Wisconsin System. https://wida.wisc.edu/sites/default/files/resource/WIDA-ELD-Standards-Framework-2020.pdf

WIDA. (2024). *Advancing ALTELLA: Glossary.* Board of Regents of the University of Wisconsin System. https://advancingaltella.org/glossary

Wiggins, G., & McTighe, J. (2005). *Understanding by design* (2nd ed.). Association for Supervision and Curriculum Development.

Wood, D. J., Bruner, J., & Ross, G. (1976). The role of tutoring in problem-solving. *Journal of Child Psychology and Psychiatry, 17*(2), 89–100.

Chapter 5

Assessment and Evaluation

Getting Ready to Learn

Assessment is the bridge that connects teaching and learning (McTighe & Ferrara, 2021).

Only when we assess our students can we discover if our instructional practices resulted in their meeting learning goals. You may read those two sentences and think that we are advocating for intensive testing of our students; however, we present a conversation in this chapter that we hope will result in a more holistic view of assessment, one in which we become our students' academic coaches and greatest cheerleaders.

Teachers often associate assessment with testing and grading; however, grading and designing tests are not the primary purposes of assessment. The goal of assessment is to improve instructional methods and students' learning by gathering information on the progress of students' knowledge and skills in each content area. Before considering how to grade student work, we must evaluate our instructional methods, consider student work in the context of language acquisition, and provide actionable feedback that addresses content and language development knowledge. Only then can we approach equitable assessment with multilingual learners of English, confident that we have created opportunities for every student to learn.

Dual language programs are recognized as the most effective educational approach for multilingual students (Umansky et al., 2015); however, they may not always be available for the diverse range of languages found in urban areas or in rural areas where a lack of multilingual teachers make it challenging to maintain a dual language program. When evaluating content knowledge and skills, monolingual teachers can sometimes view multilingualism as something that prevents students from making academic progress. In reality, multilingual students often exhibit improved cognitive functions, such as better problem-solving skills, enhanced creativity, and a heightened ability to multitask. When teachers become more familiar with the benefits of multilingualism, they are better equipped to design assessments that support English language acquisition during assessments and provide actionable feedback.

This chapter discusses potential barriers to accurately assessing what multilingual learners of English know and can do in relation to content standards that drive classroom instruction. It also offers actions to increase accurate measures of learning and suggestions for ways to design assessments that will allow multilingual learners of English to use their current levels of English language proficiency to demonstrate content area knowledge and skills. Because this book focuses on professional learning, this chapter introduces key considerations in assessment and evaluation with multilingual learners of English in your classroom. As you read through these topics, we invite you to reflect on your current assessment practices and identify topics you may wish to delve deeper into after completing this chapter.

Preassessment

Before engaging with topics on assessment and evaluation, consider your current understanding of each standard-based learning target by completing the Preassessment for Assessment and Evaluation shown in Table 5.1. As you complete the preassessment, reflect on your knowledge of each learning target and consider where you would place your current ability to meet this target in the content classroom.

Table 5.1 *Preassessment for Assessment and Evaluation*

Assessment and Evaluation Professional Learning Opportunities #12–14		1 Emerging
#12 Assessment Bias	1. I can evaluate my classroom assessments for cultural and linguistic bias.	
	2. I can reduce the linguistic complexity of test questions so they are more accessible to students learning academic English as a new language.	
#13 Making Assessment Accessible	3. I can use technology to make a text accessible to students with different reading proficiency levels.	
	4. I can identify allowable accommodations for assessments used with multilingual learners of English in my classroom or school.	
#14 Formative Classroom Assessments	5. I can determine my process for gathering evidence of student learning toward both language development and grade-level content standards.	
	6. I can apply stages of the assessment cycle to my classroom to inform my instruction and my students' learning experiences.	

We have provided a continuum that starts with *1-Emerging* (no current understanding), moves to *3-Developing* (somewhat familiar but still needs information to take action), and ends with *5-Proficient* (able to understand and take action on this learning target). After you have rated your level of understanding and skill on each learning target, consider how your results might inform which professional learning opportunities you would like to explore first in this chapter.

Professional Learning Opportunities

Assessment and evaluation considerations with multilingual learners of English may feel intimidating if you are unfamiliar with the language acquisition process. Consider discussing the topics in this chapter with a colleague and English language development (ELD) teacher who works in your school or district for added insights. You will gain confidence as you practice new skills and determine what is appropriate for your grade level and content area. Your curiosity and openness to new ideas are crucial for creating an inclusive and supportive learning environment for all students.

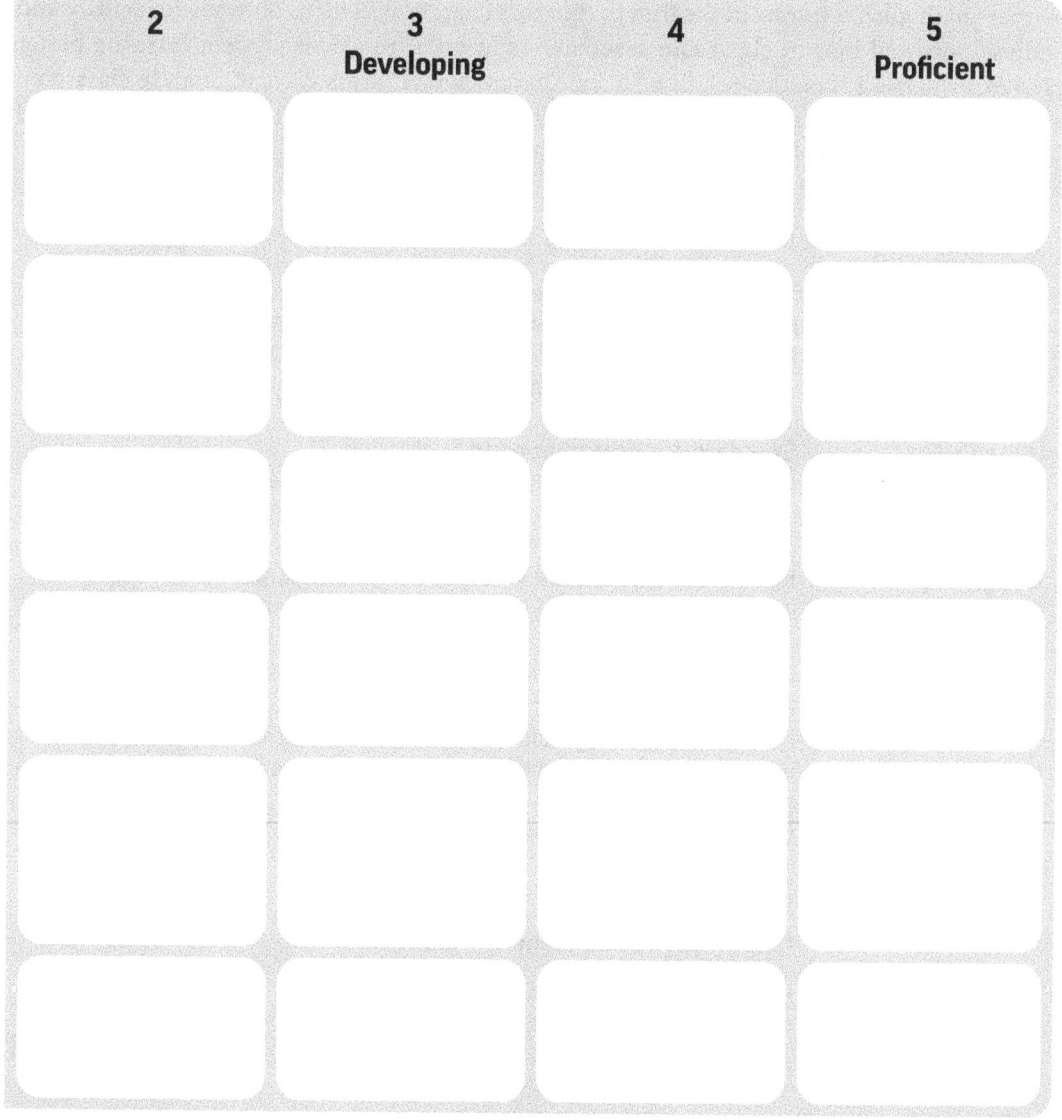

We encourage you to approach the subject of assessment and evaluation with curiosity as you explore best practices for collecting evidence of the knowledge and abilities of multilingual learners of English in using the English language in your classroom. You may engage in professional learning opportunities that best meet your learning needs or work through each lesson in the chapter. Before beginning your professional learning opportunities, we encourage you to reflect on your preassessment responses in Table 5.1 and pursue one or all options that best fit your current learning needs. The three professional learning opportunities are as follows:

- Assessment Bias
- Making Assessments Accessible
- Formative Classroom Assessments

Professional Learning Opportunity #12: Assessment Bias

All teachers should recognize that biases can exist in assessments and affect the accuracy of information we gather about the academic language skills and growth of our multilingual learners of English. Lessons in the first part of this chapter will focus on ways to identify and address potential bias in classroom assessments in order to assess student learning better (TESOL Principle 5, Practice 5c). In addition, lessons will address ways to analyze classroom assessment for bias and make corrections that allow teachers to interpret student data (Standard 4: Component 4a of the *Standards for Initial TESOL Pre-K–12 Teacher Preparation Programs*). The Assessment Bias box outlines the components of the 12th professional learning opportunity.

Assessment Bias

TESOL's 6 Principles (Grades K–12)	**Principle 5. Monitor and Assess Student Language Development** **Practice 5c**. Teachers design varied and valid assessments and supports to assess student learning.
Standards for Initial TESOL Pre-K–12 Teacher Preparation Programs	**Standard 4: Assessment and Evaluation** **Component 4a.** Teachers apply knowledge of validity, reliability, and assessment purposes to analyze and interpret student data from multiple sources, including norm-referenced and criterion-referenced tests. Teachers make informed instructional decisions that support language learning.
Key Learning Targets	I can evaluate my classroom assessments for cultural and linguistic bias. I can reduce the linguistic complexity of test questions so they are more accessible to multilingual learners of English.
Lessons and Activities	**Lesson 1: Bias in Assessments**
	Activity — 1. Five Potential Areas of Bias in Assessments
	Lesson 2: The Language of Assessments
	Activity — 1. Linguistic Bias in Text

CONTINUED

Notes for Each Teacher Role	**Professional Learning Providers:** The objectives of this professional learning opportunity focus on understanding how assessment bias can prevent multilingual learners of English from demonstrating their knowledge of content standards and objectives. Some teachers may need to be made aware of the unconscious ways bias can be embedded in the assessments we administer to students learning English.

We encourage you to support teachers by creating opportunities for them to learn how to identify bias in assessments and review their assessment materials for potentially biased assessment items. Learning to identify bias requires time, so it's helpful to revisit this topic and remind teachers of the various forms of bias and how to develop solutions in instruction and assessment. Teachers will enhance their skills in identifying assessment bias through examples and opportunities to review and practice creating assessments for multilingual learners of English.

Both Lessons 1 and 2 should require approximately 45 minutes of professional learning time with large or small groups of teachers. You may choose to add additional activities to the information provided here and add time to your professional learning plans accordingly. You can access many online resources in this chapter on the companion site for this book and may choose to print or create electronic versions for your professional learning sessions with teachers.

English Language Development Teachers: General education teachers may need to be more familiar with different kinds of bias and how it can create a barrier for multilingual learners of English during instruction and assessment. Some colleagues may say that all students should take the same tests. You can help your general education colleagues by demonstrating ways to reduce bias in their assessments without changing the content knowledge measured in the assessments. Then, observe how those changes impact how well multilingual learners of English can interact with the assessment. We can all learn from each other, so this professional learning opportunity may create discussions that benefit all classrooms.

General Education Teachers: Discovering that our assessments may sometimes be biased and challenging for multilingual learners of English can feel uncomfortable. It's natural to wonder how to address something we may not recognize. Remember, everyone has biases, which naturally stem from living and operating within our own familiar cultural contexts. The process of understanding potential assessment biases takes time. Approach this chapter with curiosity, noting new ideas to try in your classroom assessments. As you learn about various forms of assessment bias, you'll find it easier to recognize and make the needed adjustments to ensure your classroom assessments are accessible to multilingual learners of English.

Lesson 1: Bias in Assessments

Unintentional biases sometimes influence our instruction and assessment practices even without our knowledge. Assessment bias may appear in the form of unfair, skewed items on an assessment that potentially offend the student or make it more difficult to demonstrate their true level of knowledge related to test items. Assessment bias occurs when students of equal ability from different demographic groups are less likely to succeed on a task, test item, or another assignment because of elements within the assessment tool or the assessment process. This occurs when certain characteristics of the assessment tool systematically favor students from one demographic group over those from another group (Popham, 2012; Taylor, 2022). Assessment bias can lead to unfair or wrong evaluations of a student or demographic group's abilities, unintentionally causing students to suffer inequitable feedback or poor grades based on personal characteristics.

Bias can appear in different forms (Shallaita et al., 2021). By learning about different forms of bias, we can correct actions that promote inequalities in assessing our students. As teachers, these actions become evident in our choice of reading material for students, the selection of videos to support learning, or the graphics and illustrations we use during instruction. While there are many forms of bias in education, we want to bring three specific forms of bias to your attention because of their prevalence in education settings and materials. These areas are stereotyping, invisibility, and fragmentation/isolation. We define each type of bias and offer examples to aid in recognizing when these biases may appear in your instructional and assessment practices and in classroom resources.

Stereotyping: People from categories of difference are portrayed as having specific characteristics; holding specific occupations; having a certain living environment, specific possessions, or economic standing; or being from specific regions of the country or world.

Examples
1. Principals and teachers are shown as white people, while secretaries, custodians, and kitchen staff are depicted as people whose ethnicities are other than white.
2. Videos or scenarios in texts depict older adults as technologically challenged, contributing to age-based stereotypes.

Invisibility: People from different categories of difference are not represented, while members from other categories are consistently included.

Examples
1. Illustration exclusively features able-bodied individuals, contributing to the invisibility of people with disabilities.
2. High school websites show only male administrators, contributing to the invisibility of women in leadership roles.

Fragmentation/Isolation: In the text, a group is physically or visually isolated. This promotes the perspective that people from marginalized groups are peripheral members of society.

Examples
1. People from other countries who have emigrated to the United States are depicted as living in apartments or apartment complexes populated only by other immigrants.
2. Young people of color are depicted as hanging out in homogenous groups and in stereotypical locations such as the inner city, the basketball court, or the soccer field.

The presence of bias in texts and resources used in the classroom can be unconsciously revealed through stereotyping, invisibility, and fragmentation/isolation. These aspects demonstrate how authors may unintentionally incorporate bias into materials used with students. These forms often appear in examples or assessment questions linked to culture, gender, language, socioeconomic status, and prior knowledge. For example, a test creator might create a test question that stereotypes a particular culture or, in a health class assessment, exclusively uses examples portraying doctors as white men, thereby exhibiting both invisibility bias (excluding people of color) and gender-related stereotypes. We can identify and address these issues by explicitly stating that the assessment involves invisibility bias or gender stereotyping.

Various areas exist where different types of bias may be present, but for our purposes, we concentrate on five areas of bias to enhance our awareness of potential biases in assessments. Our next lesson provides an opportunity to practice recognizing five areas of bias that may be present in assessments.

Activity Five Potential Areas of Bias in Assessments

Key Learning Target: I can evaluate my classroom assessments for cultural and linguistic bias.

Activity Goal: Examine five areas of bias that may be present in educational settings and practice recognizing assessment items that promote bias.

Step 1: Review the Five Areas of Bias listed below. In Step 2 of this activity, you will take a short quiz addressing these areas of bias.

Five Areas of Bias

Bias	Examples
Culture	• Use of culturally specific references that may disadvantage students from different cultural backgrounds. • Examples or scenarios used in test questions that are familiar to certain cultural groups but not to others.
Gender	• Test questions that unintentionally favor one gender over others. • Stereotyped language or scenarios that may disadvantage certain genders.
Language	• Complex or ambiguous language that may be challenging for speakers with a home language(s) other than English. • Use of idiomatic expressions that are unfamiliar for students from a different geographical culture than the teacher.
Socioeconomic	• Examples or situations that are more relatable to students from certain socioeconomic backgrounds. • Assumptions about access to resources that may disadvantage students with different socioeconomic backgrounds.
Prior Knowledge	• Assuming certain prior knowledge that not all students possess. • Questions that unintentionally require external knowledge not covered during instruction.

CONTINUED

Step 2

- At the top of the following Five Areas of Bias Quiz, you will see five possible answers that may be used to fill in the blank with their matching sample quiz question. You will use some answers more than once.
- Identify which bias you think is represented by each quiz question and write the letter of the corresponding correct answer in the blank in front of each quiz question.

Five Areas of Bias Quiz

Directions

Use the five possible answers in this box (a, b, c, d, e) as answers to the questions in this quiz. You will use some answers more than once. You will use each possible answer at least once. Write the correct answer for each quiz question in the space to the left of each question number.

a. Gender   b. Language   c. Prior Knowledge   d. Socioeconomic   e. Culture

_____ **1. Multiple Choice**: Which of the following animals is most commonly associated with agricultural practices in North America?
A. Water Buffalo
B. Llama
C. Ox
D. Elephant

_____ **2. True/False**: Individuals from affluent families are more likely to succeed in academic pursuits because of better access to educational resources.

_____ **3. Multiple Choice**: Which career path is most suitable for a nurturing and empathetic woman?
A. Nursing
B. Engineering
C. Law
D. Computer Science

_____ **4. Essay Prompt**: In your opinion, should someone hit the nail on the head when addressing complex societal issues, or is it more effective to beat around the bush? Support your arguments with examples and consider how actions speak louder than words.

_____ **5. Reading Comprehension Question**: Examine the protagonist's internal conflict in the given passage. Elaborate on how the author utilizes intricate symbolism and nuanced language to convey the character's evolving emotional state. Provide specific examples from the text to support your analysis.

_____ **6. Word Problem**: In a baseball game, each team scored 5 runs. If the home team was the only team to score in the last inning, how many runs did they score?

CONTINUED

_____ **7. Word Problem**: If a family spends 20% of their monthly income on equestrian lessons and kayaking, and their monthly income is $5,000, how much money do they spend on extracurricular activities each month?

_____ **8. Essay Prompt**: Explain how student demonstrations advocating for changes in student loans might be seen as the contemporary equivalent of the Boston Tea Party for present-day students.

Step 3
- Now that you have practiced identifying areas of bias in the quiz questions, we encourage you to review questions used in your classroom assessments. Look for possible instances of bias related to culture, gender, language, prior knowledge, or socioeconomic factors in these assessments.
- Assess whether similar biases exist in your instructional materials and resources.
- If you identify such biases, consider strategies for eliminating them and explore alternative resources or test items that can be used instead.

Answers to the Quiz Questions
1. c. Prior Knowledge Bias or e. Culture Bias: Students need to have experience in North American culture or prior knowledge from living in North America or learning about North America to answer this question correctly.
2. d. Socioeconomic Bias: While students from wealthier families may have more opportunities to access educational opportunities, this does not necessarily mean they will be smarter or more academically successful than students from less wealthy families.
3. a. Gender Bias: This question assumes that only women are nurturing and empathetic.
4. b. Language Bias: The wording of this question includes idioms that would make the question unclear to students learning English or to students whose culture does not include these specific idioms.
5. b. Language Bias: As written, this question includes many technical terms that would make comprehending it difficult for multilingual learners of English or students in lower grade levels who have not yet learned these academic terms.
6. e. Culture Bias: This problem assumes familiarity with baseball, which may not be true for students from cultures where baseball isn't popular or well known.
7. e. Socioeconomic Bias: This question is biased because it assumes familiarity with equestrian lessons and kayaking as common extracurricular activities. However, not all families may have access to or participate in these specific activities because of factors such as location, cultural background, or socioeconomic status.
8. c. Prior Knowledge Bias: This question demonstrates prior knowledge bias because it assumes that students have prior knowledge of both the Boston Tea Party and contemporary student loan issues.

Lesson 2: The Language of Assessments

The complexity of language in assessments poses a considerable challenge for multilingual learners of English across all language proficiency levels. Students at lower language proficiency levels may struggle to comprehend what an assessment asks, or they may not be sure how to express their knowledge using English. Questions, tasks, and directions might include vocabulary or use syntactic structures not introduced during instruction, exposing multilingual learners of English to new terms for the first time on an assessment (Taylor, 2022).

We can gather better information about our students' academic knowledge and skills when we make assessments accessible to all groups of students. One way to make assessments more accessible for our multilingual learners of English is to reduce the linguistic complexity of assessments. Certain language structures in English may be unfamiliar to some multilingual learners of English, leading to difficulties in understanding the instructions of assessment questions or tasks. If students are uncertain about the type of response expected, teachers won't clearly understand their students' knowledge of academic standards. Some aspects of English that can be confusing include the following:

- *Multimeaning words*: Words that have more than one meaning. These meanings can be related or entirely different, depending on the context in which a word is used.
- *Idiomatic phrases*: A group of words with a meaning different from the literal interpretation of the individual words.
- *Dependent clauses*: A group of words that contains a subject and a verb but that does not express a complete thought. This type of clause relies on an independent clause to form a complete sentence.
- *Prepositional phrases*: A group of words in a sentence that begins with a preposition and typically includes a noun or pronoun as the object of the preposition. The preposition shows the sentence's relationship between the object and another element.

Activity Linguistic Bias in Text

Key Learning Target: I can evaluate my classroom assessments for cultural and linguistic bias.

Activity Goal: Identify ways linguistic complexity may create linguistic bias in assessments used with multilingual learners of English.

Directions
This activity provides practice in identifying linguistic features that may create barriers to student comprehension on academic assessments. While we address the ways language can create bias in assessments, we urge you to consider how linguistic complexity may appear in texts used for instruction and classroom resources.

Step 1
- Read and examine the examples of linguistic barriers and actions to simplify language for multilingual learners of English shown in Table 5.2.
- Examine one sample test question at a time and discuss with a colleague your understanding of what linguistic feature is creating a barrier and how that barrier was removed through actions to simplify the language.
- Note that the simplified language does not change the rigor of the academic task required by the revised language of the assessment question.

Table 5.2 *Linguistic Complexity in Assessment*

Linguistic Complexity in Assessment

Linguistic Barrier in Test Question	Initial Test Question	Action to Simplify Language	Accessible Test Question
Technical vocabulary unrelated to the targeted content concept	An *engineer* is *designing* a *suspension* bridge to *span* the distance between the *banks* of a river. The bridge must be *at least* 1,320 feet long. How long must the bridge be in miles?	Eliminate unnecessary technical language.	The city needs a new bridge over the river. The bridge must be 1,320 feet long. What will be the length of the new bridge in miles?
Multimeaning words unrelated to the subject area	Example 1 The *banks* of the river are 1,320 feet apart. How many miles are they apart?	Eliminate unrelated multimeaning words.	Example 1 The river is 1,320 feet wide. How wide is the river in miles?
	Example 2 Lisa put $100 in an *account*. After a year, her money had earned 10% in interest. How much money does she have now?		Example 2 Lisa had $100 in the bank. Her money earned 10% interest in one year. How much money does she have now?
Idiomatic phrases unfamiliar to multilingual learners of English	In the story, Mary is angry with her brother. Why is *her patience running out*?	Replace unfamiliar idiomatic phrases.	In the story, Mary is angry with her brother. Why is she angry?

Step 2
- Now that you're more acquainted with linguistic complexity issues in assessment items, review an assessment you use in your classroom. Identify and address any language in the questions and content that might confuse your multilingual learners of English.
- Table 5.3 provides questions to support your review of your classroom assessments for linguistic bias.

Sentence length	Jose wants to build a rectangular garden for his vegetables and he wants an area of 36 square feet. What dimensions will give him 36 square feet for his garden?	Break up sentences and decrease reading load.	Jose wants to build a rectangular garden. He wants an area of 36 square feet. What dimensions will give him 36 square feet for his garden?
Dependent clause	If Serge is going to build a garden with an area of 36 square feet, what dimensions can he use for his garden?	Separate clauses into sentences.	Serge is going to build a garden with an area of 36 square feet. What dimensions can he use for his garden?
Multiple prepositional phrases	Deng needs an area *of 36 square feet to build a garden in his backyard to grow vegetables.* What dimensions will give him 36 square feet of garden?	Break up sentences or eliminate unnecessary information.	Deng wants to build a vegetable garden in his back yard. He needs an area of 36 square feet. What dimensions will give him 36 square feet of garden?

Based on Taylor (2022).

Table 5.3 *Template to Evaluate Linguistic Complexity in My Classroom Assessment*

Linguistic Complexity in Assessment

Questions to Evaluate Linguistic Barrier in Test Questions	Initial Test Question	Action to Simplify Language	My New Accessible Test Question
Does my text include technical vocabulary that is unrelated to the targeted content concept?		Eliminate unnecessary technical language.	
Does my text include multimeaning words unrelated to the subject area?		Eliminate unrelated multimeaning words.	

CONTINUED

Does my text include idiomatic phrases unfamiliar to my students learning English?		Replace unfamiliar idiomatic phrases.	
Can sentences in my text be written more simply to clarify meaning?		Break up sentences and decrease reading load.	
Does my text use dependent clauses that could be rewritten as complete sentences?		Separate clauses into sentences.	
Does my text use multiple prepositional phrases that could make reading difficult?		Break up sentences or eliminate unnecessary information.	

Based on Taylor (2022).

In this professional learning opportunity, we focused on recognizing different forms of assessment bias in classroom assessments. It's important to note that biases in assessments are not always deliberate. By continually improving our understanding of how various biases affect our students, we can take steps to eliminate bias and ensure that academic content is accessible to students learning English.

The objective of assessing multilingual learners of English is to gauge their academic knowledge and skills accurately. Eliminating bias from assessments supports our students, enabling them to demonstrate their knowledge irrespective of their level of English language development in each language domain. We have highlighted only some potential areas of bias that can be found in classroom assessments. You may explore this topic further and consider ways to adjust your classroom's or school's current assessment resources to ensure they are accessible to all multilingual learners of English.

Closing Questions and Suggestions for Each Teacher Role

Closing Questions and Suggestions for Each Teacher Role

Directions: Take a moment to write and reflect on your learning from Professional Learning Opportunity #12, Assessment Bias. We have included a few role-specific questions and suggestions to prompt your thinking.

Professional Learning Providers

Closing Questions
- Which activities did you choose to facilitate with educators?
- What went well? What might you want to improve?
- If bias in assessments is a new topic for your group, what are some areas you may wish to reinforce around issues of unintentional bias in future sessions with educators?

Suggestions for This Role
As you prepare to plan for professional learning around assessment biases, you may want to locate more examples of each type of bias to use as examples in your learning sessions. If teachers in your school are unfamiliar with bias in assessments, they may require multiple examples of test items for each bias category to understand how to minimize bias in their own assessments.

English Language Development Teachers

Closing Questions
- What were your key takeaways from these lessons?
- What impact did these lessons have on your language development work with your students?
- Which aspects of these lessons would you like to address and collaborate on with general education teachers in your school or district?

Suggestions for This Role
Your colleagues might approach you for assistance in addressing linguistic bias in assessment items. If you're still unsure about grammar and wording in test items, consider delving into the examples provided in the activity in Lesson 2 to enhance your comprehension of how linguistic bias can affect understanding. For a reliable resource on explaining grammar to multilingual learners of English, we suggest books by Keith S. Folse, particularly *Keys to Teaching Grammar to English Language Learners: A Practical Handbook*.

General Education Teachers

Closing Questions
- How did this go?
- What went well?
- What were your key takeaways?
- What are some areas of unintentional bias you may want to explore in the assessments you use in your classroom?
- Are there aspects of English grammar you would like to review to better design questions used on classroom assessments?

CONTINUED

Professional Learning Opportunity #13: Making Assessments Accessible

Teachers need to ensure all assessments, whether gathered from instructional resources or self-created, are made accessible to students. It is important to gather an accurate measure of students' knowledge in relation to the assessment goals. While you may agree that making assessments accessible is important, knowing how to design appropriate accommodations for multilingual learners of English may be a skill you have not previously used. Our next professional learning opportunity will address ways to design assessments and supports to assess student learning (TESOL Principle 5, Practice 5c). We will also discuss how language accommodations are scaffolded for English language and content assessment (Standard 4: Component 4b of the *Standards for Initial TESOL Pre-K–12 Teacher Preparation Programs*). The Making Assessments Accessible box outlines the components of the next professional learning opportunity.

Making Assessments Accessible

TESOL's 6 Principles (Grades K–12)	**Principle 5. Monitor and Assess Student Language Development** **Practice 5c.** Teachers design varied and valid assessments and supports to assess student learning.
Standards for Initial TESOL Pre-K–12 Teacher Preparation Programs	**Standard 4: Assessment and Evaluation** **Component 4b (partial).** Teachers demonstrate an understanding of classroom-based formative, summative, and diagnostic assessments scaffolded for both English language and content assessment.
Key Learning Targets	I can use technology to make a text accessible to students with different reading proficiency levels. I can identify allowable accommodations for assessments used with multilingual learners of English in my classroom or school.
Lessons and Activities	**Lesson 1: AI Tools to Reduce Linguistic Complexity**
	Activities 1. Magic School Practice 2. ChatGPT Practice
	Lesson 2: Allowable Accommodations on Assessments
	Activity 1. Areas of Allowable Accommodations

CONTINUED

Notes for Each Teacher Role	**Professional Learning Providers:** The objectives of professional learning in this professional learning opportunity focus on creating assessments that are accessible to multilingual learners of English. Some teachers may be developing their knowledge of how language acquisition appears differently for students with different backgrounds. As you work through professional development opportunities with your teachers, consider ways you can make language acquisition conversations a part of your work. Teachers will enhance their skills in embedding language supports in classroom assessments or in administering standardized assessments through opportunities to discuss allowable options and practice creating assessment supports for multilingual learners of English. Both Lessons 1 and 2 should require approximately 45 minutes of professional learning time with large or small groups of teachers. You may choose to add additional activities to the information provided here and add time to your professional learning plans accordingly. You can access many online resources in this chapter on the companion site for this book and may choose to print or create electronic versions for your professional learning sessions with teachers.
	English Language Development Teachers: General education teachers may not be familiar with creating language supports for students with different levels of language proficiency. You can help your teacher colleagues by demonstrating ways to make assessments accessible to multilingual learners of English without changing the content knowledge being measured in the assessment itself, and then observe how those changes had an impact on how well multilingual learners of English are able to interact with the assessment. Your teacher colleagues may need to draw on your expertise in language acquisition to understand what language supports are most appropriate for multilingual learners of English with varying levels of academic English language development.
	General Education Teachers: We can increase the accessibility of assessments for our multilingual learners of English by improving how we present the assessments and administer them to our students. It is crucial to understand your students' language abilities and identify their ongoing language acquisition progress. With practice and reflection, you will become more familiar with making assessment accessible. This expertise will enable you to create assessment opportunities that allow multilingual learners of English to access and engage in classroom assessments successfully.

Lesson 1: AI Tools to Reduce Linguistic Complexity

Teachers have varied opinions about the wisdom of incorporating artificial intelligence (AI) into the classroom (Gordon, 2023). Some teachers are concerned that students will use AI to cheat on assignments or produce papers lacking genuine research or ideas, while others believe AI offers opportunities to enhance professional development and better prepare students for a future that regularly integrates the benefits of technology in their work (Ming & Mansor, 2023). Though the field of education has yet to agree on the value of students using AI, there are some promising benefits that teachers may find worth considering when it comes to incorporating AI in their lesson planning and accomplishing daily tasks.

In this next lesson, we discuss AI, defined as "a field of computer science that focuses on creating systems or machines that can perform tasks that typically require human intelligence" (OpenAI, 2023b). We purposefully utilized ChatGPT to generate a definition of AI and demonstrate how AI can be used and cited. We recognize the potential of AI in supporting teachers who work with multilingual learners of English. We believe teachers should broaden their understanding of AI to consider how it may or may not contribute to the teaching and learning of all students.

AI is rapidly evolving (Ming & Mansor, 2023), and teachers should not dismiss AI tools as a possible resource based on one initial observation or demonstration. While testing various AI tools, we found a need to edit AI responses through a lens of experience in the English language teaching field. In other words, some generated ideas were helpful, while others did not accurately reflect knowledge of academic English language structures or best teaching practices. AI responses did not always distinguish between the language proficiency levels of multilingual learners of English, and suggestions for academic support sometimes did not consider specific strategies that would benefit students at varying levels of English language development. As we explored AI tools, it became clear that teachers need to develop skills in using these tools before drawing conclusions about the advantages or disadvantages of their use.

Kulowiec (2023) suggests that teachers should consider AI as a personal assistant that is available to carry out routine tasks, allowing teachers more time to focus on the art and creativity of teaching. After hearing this suggestion, we approached AI differently, resulting in refocused interactions and goals. We began to discover ways AI tools could save teachers time in lesson preparation or daily routines. Some ways that AI can potentially benefit English language teachers include the following:

- Generate grammar writing samples to have students find errors in syntax, punctuation, pronoun use, and verb tenses.
  - Example Prompt: Create a writing sample at Lexile level 375 about recycling that is three sentences long. Include five syntax errors, three punctuation and capitalization errors, and two verb tense errors.
  - AI Output: Recyling are important. It help environment and save resources. Peopla should separates recyclables from trash for make positive impact. (OpenAI, 2023c).
- Generate word lists and sentences for using in lessons.
  - Example Prompt: Create a list of 10 words that use the eigh/sleigh pattern and rhyme.
  - AI Output: Eight, Weight, Sleigh, Neighbor, Reign, Feign, Vein, Deign, Eighty, Weighty (OpenAI, 2023d).
- Create example texts for pronunciation and conversation practice.
  - Example Prompt: Create a short conversation between two people about their spring break plans. The speakers should be a middle school student and a teacher. The text should be written at a Lexile level of 540.
  - AI Output:
  Student: Hey, Mr. Johnson! Have you made any plans for spring break?
  Teacher: Hi there! Not much, just looking forward to some relaxation. What about you?
  Student: Oh, cool! I'm thinking of spending time with my family. We might go on a short trip or just do some fun activities together.
  Teacher: That sounds wonderful! Quality time with family is always a good idea. Any specific place you're considering for the trip?

Student: Maybe a nearby beach or a national park. We haven't decided yet, but we want to enjoy the outdoors.

Teacher: Nice choice! Exploring nature can be so refreshing. Make sure to take lots of pictures and share your experiences when we get back to school.

Student: Definitely, Mr. Johnson! What about you? Any exciting plans?

Teacher: Well, I might catch up on some reading and visit a few local spots. Sometimes, a calm break is all you need.

Student: Sounds cool! Whatever you do, I hope you have a great time. See you after the break!

Teacher: Thank you! You too, enjoy your spring break! See you soon! (OpenAI, 2023a).

We recommend that you approach AI tools with cautious optimism. AI tools have demonstrated the potential to help teachers with busy tasks, but we should thoughtfully consider when and how to use each new AI tool after we have spent time practicing and vetting it before applying it to our work. AI can be a helpful assistant, but it should be overseen, edited, and reviewed before incorporating any final output into the classroom.

AI tools simplify intricate text while preserving the specified skills required by content standards. AI tools can also refine the wording of assessments to make test questions accessible for students in the early stages of English literacy comprehension. We were particularly interested in AI's ability to create assessment accommodations that reduce the linguistic complexity of test questions for multilingual learners of English. Our next activity demonstrates how we simplified the language of test questions using the AI tool Magic School.

Activity | Magic School Practice

Key Learning Target: I can use technology to make a text accessible to students with different reading proficiency levels.

Activity Goal: Identify ways an AI tool can reduce the linguistic complexity of test questions to accommodate multilingual learners of English.

Directions
The first step in this activity asks you to review an example of how we reduced the linguistic complexity of test questions using the AI tool Magic School. The second step of this activity gives you the opportunity to revise examples of assessment questions drawn from your own classroom assessment questions.

Step 1
Read through the steps we followed to generate test questions with Magic School.

1. We opened our browser and went to www.magicschool.ai.
2. We created a free account and logged in.
3. On the home page for the site, we chose to explore the Multiple Choice Assessment Generator.
4. The site asked us first to identify a grade level and the number of questions we wanted to generate. It also provided a box for us to enter the topic, standard, text, or description of the assessment. There was a prompt to make our request specific.
5. We entered a Common Core standard with the command to "Create questions for multilingual learners of English with beginning-level English language proficiency."

CONTINUED

Step 2

- Review the example of the test question we generated on Magic School.
- What do you notice in the different ways questions are posed to multilingual learners of English when comparing the original question with the simplified question generated from AI?

Magic School Multiple-Choice Assessment Generator Example

7th Grade Common Core Standard
CCSS.ELA-LITERACY.RL.7.6
Analyze how an author develops and contrasts the points of view of different characters or narrators in a text.

Magic School Command
Create questions for multilingual learners of English with beginning-level English language proficiency. Shorten original results.

Original Questions Generated on Magic School	Magic School Responses Simplified and Shortened
Question 1: In a story, the point of view refers to: a. The *setting* of the story b. The *time period* in which the story takes place c. The *perspective* from which the story is told d. The *genre* of the story	**Question 1: Point of view in a story refers to:** a. The story's *setting* b. The *time period* c. The narrative *perspective* d. The *genre*
Question 2: How does an author develop the point of view of a character? a. Through the use of *dialogue and actions* b. By describing the *physical appearance* of the *character* c. By including *flashbacks* in the story d. By changing the *setting* of the story	**Q2: How does an author develop a character's point of view?** a. Through *dialogue and actions* b. By describing *appearance* c. With *flashbacks* d. By changing the *setting*
Question 3: Which of the following is an example of contrasting points of view in a story? a. Two characters having a *friendly conversation* b. A character describing their *favorite place* c. Two characters arguing about a *decision* d. A character *reflecting* on a *past event*	**Question 3: Which is an example of contrasting points of view?** a. *Friendly conversation* b. Describing a *favorite place* c. Arguing about a *decision* d. *Reflecting* on a *past event*

Step 3

Reflect on our comments about creating these assessment questions with Magic School.

CONTINUED

1. We found that the initial multiple-choice questions provided were not accessible for most multilingual learners of English, especially those in the early stages of language acquisition. There was an option to shorten the questions that had been generated, so we chose that option and found the questions to be significantly improved.
2. We observed that the initial and shortened questions used the same key content vocabulary aligned with the Common Core standard. The shortened questions were straightforward and less linguistically complex yet retained the rigor of the original questions.
3. With adequate instruction by the teacher, including teaching key vocabulary and providing opportunities for multilingual learners of English to practice skills related to the standard, an advanced beginner could likely answer the questions when language supports were employed with the assessment method.
4. Note that our goal was to make assessment questions less complex in preparation for choosing an appropriate assessment method for multilingual learners of English at the beginning level of English language proficiency.
5. Note that we had to create the initial question. Magic School's role was to reduce the linguistic complexity, not write the original test questions.

We encourage you to take a moment to reflect individually or with a team on what you noticed about the AI-generated questions and how this may or may not be useful for creating assessment questions in your classroom or content area.

Step 4

- This section provides instructions for generating multiple-choice assessment questions with simplified language.
- After completing this activity, we recommend exploring the Magic School resource to discover tools that can enhance your instruction and assessment with multilingual learners of English.

1. Open your preferred browser and go to www.magicschool.ai.
2. Create a free account and log in.
3. On the home page for the site, choose the Multiple Choice Assessment Generator.
4. The site will ask you to identify a grade level and the number of questions you want to generate, and it also provides a box for you to enter the topic, standard, text, or description of the assessment. A more detailed description increases the likelihood of obtaining the desired result more quickly.
5. We recommend you start by entering a Common Core standard with the command to create questions for multilingual learners of English with the desired English language proficiency level of a student in your class.
6. If you are not satisfied with the initial set of multiple-choice questions generated, you can ask the site to shorten them or modify your initial request to generate responses more in line with your desired outcome.

ChatGPT was launched in November 2022 (Gordon, 2023) and has received mixed reviews from the education community. It is a language model developed by OpenAI designed to understand and generate human-like text based on the input it receives. The model is capable of performing various language-related tasks, such as answering questions, generating creative text, translating languages, and engaging in conversation.

ChatGPT is one tool that we again suggest teachers approach with cautious optimism. We can see definite opportunities to enhance and improve both teaching and learning experiences with this AI tool, and the key to identifying benefits will rely on teachers considering what work needs to be done and the best approach to meet that need.

We view AI not as a teacher replacement but as a tool that may amplify teachers' skills and provide opportunities to enhance instruction and assessment. Just as a hammer is a tool that achieves nothing when left on a workbench, AI requires knowledge and practice to use effectively. The person who picks up the hammer must have the ability to aim the face of the hammer and apply force, and also know how to turn the hammer around and use the claw to remove mistakes. Similarly, when utilizing AI tools, a teacher should be proficient at applying the tool, directing it skillfully toward the task, and engaging with the features it offers. This includes understanding how to redirect or correct mistakes if the initial task does not yield the desired outcome. The benefits of AI are just beginning to emerge. AI may offer the potential to assist teachers in teaching in previously unavailable ways (Najarro, 2023).

> Just as a hammer is a tool that achieves nothing when left on a workbench, AI requires knowledge and practice to use it effectively.

In our next activity, we suggest you interact with ChatGPT to observe how it may be able to support your work creating instructional supports or generating accessible assessment items.

Activity ChatGPT Practice

Key Learning Target: I can use technology to make a text accessible to students with different reading proficiency levels.

Activity Goal: Interact with a ChatGPT choice board to practice different commands you can use in ChatGPT to support your work.

Step 1
- Navigate to the ChatGPT site: chat.openai.com.
- Create a free basic account or log in if you already have an account.
- Once you are logged in, you will be taken to the home page. Here, you can view your options.
- Choose one of the sample commands on the ChatGPT Choice Board we have provided here, and type that command into the message box at the bottom of the ChatGPT home page that says Message ChatGPT.

ChatGPT Commands Choice Board

Generate a list of words that begin with specific blends or digraphs.	Create a list of 20 CVC words that rhyme using the vowel A.	Create a reading passage for Lexile level 450 that includes descriptive details.
What are examples of independent clauses?	Generate 10 sentences that use the past tense for Lexile level 250.	What are sentence starters for stating facts or an opinion?

CONTINUED

Create a math word problem about angles and planes at Lexile level 450.	List the major battles of the American Civil War.	What are ways that ChatGPT can assist teachers?

Step 2
After you have tried some of our suggested commands, create some of your own useful task commands for your content area.

Note. CVC = consonant-vowel-consonant

Lesson 2: Allowable Accommodations on Assessments

Teachers may access assessments from a variety of sources throughout the school year. These may include resources integrated into their textbooks or teaching materials, assessments supplied by the school district, standardized assessments, or assessments created by teachers specifically for their classrooms. When teachers create their own assessment tools, they are able to embed accommodations that respond to the specific needs of their students. Assessments supplied by education publishers or standardized tests do not offer this flexibility, but we can still utilize certain accommodations for multilingual learners of English on these types of assessments.

Standardized tests derive their name from the requirement to administer them using the same principles of consistency throughout administration; test takers in various settings are required to answer the same questions, and answers are scored in the same, predetermined way. Testing companies provide administration manuals to guide schools through the process of administering these tests. Some teachers may not be aware that companies also provide an accommodations manual that lists accommodations that are allowed for different groups of students, including multilingual learners of English.

The accommodations allowed on individual standardized tests are not always the same as accommodations/scaffolds typically used during instruction. However, teachers can create opportunities for the success of multilingual learners of English on standardized tests by acquainting themselves with the permitted accommodations for each test and developing a plan to apply these during test administration.

While classroom tests offer more leniency on how tests are administered, it may be helpful to consider how you might make your classroom tests accessible in five areas: setting, student response options, test presentation, scheduling, and translation. Table 5.4 introduces these five accommodation areas for teachers to explore methods of using language accommodations for multilingual learners of English in both standardized and classroom tests.

Table 5.4 *Allowable Accommodations on Tests for Multilingual Learners of English*

Setting Accommodations (the environment in which the test is taken)	
Allowed Accommodations	**Yes /No Or under what conditions**
Testing separately from non–multilingual learners of English	

CONTINUED

Flexible order of test administration	
Small-group administration	
Individual administration	
Optimal time of day administration for student	
Required to complete a test section in the same day	

Response Accommodations
(the ways students can provide answers to test prompts)

Allowed Accommodations	Yes /No Or under what conditions
Word-to-word dictionary	
Verbal response in English language to a scribe	
Small-group administration	
Verbal response in preferred language to a scribe	
Oral reading of test content	
Repetition of directions	

Presentation Accommodations
(the ways students interact with test content)

Allowed Accommodations	Yes /No Or under what conditions
Person familiar to the student administers the test	
Explain or paraphrase the test directions	
Read aloud and/or repeat directions for written and/or oral test	
Oral reading of test content	
Home language translation of test directions	

CONTINUED

Provide a written version of test directions	
Newcomer exempt	
Minimum attempts required	

Scheduling Accommodations
(the length of time spent on each section of a test)

Allowed Accommodations	Yes /No Or under what conditions
Frequent monitored breaks	
Extended time (This may not be an appropriate accommodation for all language proficiency levels. For example, newcomers who are not able to read in English may not benefit from extended time on required standardized tests.)	

Language Translation Accommodations
(test material presented in English or the student's dominant language)

Allowed Accommodations	Yes /No Or under what conditions
Take test in home language or dominant language other than English	
Explain or paraphrase the test directions in home language or dominant language other than English	

Activity Areas of Allowable Accommodations

Key Learning Target: I can identify allowable accommodations for assessments used with multilingual learners of English in my classroom or school.

Activity Goal: Consider the five basic areas of allowable accommodations and identify accommodations I can embed in my classroom assessments and utilize during standardized assessments.

Step 1
- Before you begin, reach out to a colleague, team, or English language development teacher to work through this activity with you. It may be beneficial to discuss considerations in similar content areas or consider how accommodations might look different for different academic areas.

CONTINUED

- Choose one area of accommodations from Table 5.4 to focus on first. You may choose from setting, response, presentation, scheduling, or language translation.
- Identify an assessment you would like to evaluate for allowable accommodations. We recommend you practice first on an assessment you have created for your classroom.
- Work through the left column of allowable accommodations in Table 5.4 and consider if the assessment you are evaluating is able to use the suggested accommodation (yes), is not able to use the suggested accommodation (no), or is possible under certain conditions. If the accommodation is possible under certain conditions, do you have the capacity to put that accommodation in place for your student(s)?

Step 2
- After you have worked through different accommodation areas, access a standardized test's accommodations manual provided by the testing company to determine if sections of Table 5.4 are allowed with that test.
- As you work through each area of allowable accommodation in Table 5.4, make a note of which accommodations are allowed, are not allowed, or are allowed under certain conditions with that assessment.
- What are some allowable accommodations you could use in the future that you were not previously aware of and were an option when testing multilingual learners of English in your classroom?
- To see how one education agency applied these sections to assessments used in its state, visit Allowable Accommodation for English Learners on Common Academic Assessments (Heartland Area Education Agency, n.d.; tinyurl.com/EL-Allow).

At the beginning of this chapter, we stated that assessment is the bridge that connects teaching and learning. During the assessment phase, teachers identify gaps in their students' understanding and refine their instruction to meet each student's learning needs. Assessment results should never come as a surprise to teachers but should rather be a confirmation of what they have already observed during instruction and interaction with their students. Multilingual learners of English should not encounter questions or tasks on an assessment they have not already worked through with support in the classroom. When our assessments consistently align with our instructional practices, we increase the likelihood of obtaining accurate information about our students' knowledge and skills in relation to content and language standards.

In the same way that we provide learning scaffolds for multilingual learners of English during instruction, language scaffolds must be used as accommodations in classroom assessments. Assessment accommodations clarify the questions posed to students so that they have the opportunity to demonstrate their understanding of the academic content. If assessment accommodations are not provided for multilingual learners of English, the assessment becomes an English language proficiency test rather than a test to measure content area knowledge and skills.

Some teachers have expressed concerns that adding language accommodations to classroom assessments unfairly advantages their students learning English. We would argue that the unfair advantage is given to fluent speakers of English when multilingual learners of English are asked to engage in the same assessments without language supports that clarify the questions to which language learners must respond. Well-designed language accommodations provide clarity, not answers.

Other teachers may learn about language accommodations and decide to use them with all their students because if it's helpful for multilingual learners of English, it must be helpful for all students. They share their perspective that language support for multilingual learners of English during instruction or administering assessment is just good teaching practice. These teachers don't see the need to differentiate between language accommodations and useful instructional strategies for all students because they view specific accommodations as just good teaching practices with all their students.

Consider the analogy of students using pool noodles during a swimming class to illustrate our point. Imagine taking your entire class to the swimming pool for a swimming lesson. Some students have a lot of experience with swimming and are even on the local swim team. Some students swim for fun and spend a good amount of time each summer at the local lake or swimming pool. Another group of students is learning to swim, and while they enjoy being in the water, some are mostly at the dog paddle stage, while others are learning how to stay afloat. Now, imagine equipping each student entering the water with a pool noodle.

The pool noodles may enhance the swimming experience for all your students. Some of the advanced swimmers might use their pool noodles to create innovative swimming strokes and techniques. However, since these proficient swimmers can swim effectively without the pool noodles, some students become distracted and engage in play instead of improving their swimming abilities. A good number of experienced swimmers are using the noodles to multitask as they experiment with ways to use the pool noodles to swim or float, chat with their friends, and compare techniques to invent new games. When you watch the novice swimmers, you see that they are using the pool noodles to stay afloat and practice kicking their legs to propel themselves forward. They are having fun but must also concentrate on using the pool noodles effectively to stay afloat. Without the pool noodles, these novice swimmers would need your attention to stay afloat and keep their heads above water.

Language accommodations for multilingual learners of English in our classrooms are like the pool noodles in the swimming pool analogy. Language accommodations during assessment and targeted language scaffolds delivered during instruction are crucial for the language development of multilingual learners of English. We agree that good teaching practices may enhance the learning experience of all students in the classroom; however, assessment accommodations tailored for specific student groups are not appropriate with all students. Even more importantly, if we regard scaffolding instruction for multilingual learners of English solely as good teaching practice, we risk overlooking their unique language learning needs and fail to provide adequate support.

Language accommodations don't have to be complex or demand a great amount of time to create. Many language accommodations involve making simple adjustments or additions to clarify the purpose of an assessment question for multilingual learners of English. Consider the following list of simple language accommodations you can add to improve student access to assessments used in your classroom.

1. *Clarifications and Definitions*: Provide clarifications or definitions for challenging vocabulary or concepts used in the test when vocabulary terms are not the focus of the assessment.
2. *Bilingual Glossaries and Word-to-Word Dictionaries*: Include a bilingual glossary or a word-to-word dictionary to assist students in understanding key terms in both their home language and English.
3. *Simplified Language*: Present questions and instructions using simplified language without compromising the integrity of the assessment.

4. *Visual Aids*: Incorporate visual aids, such as images, charts, or graphs, to help illustrate concepts and enhance understanding.
5. *Flexible Response Formats*: To accommodate different language proficiency levels, allow for varied response formats, such as multiple choice, short answer, or oral responses.
6. *Chunking Information*: Break down test content into manageable chunks with clear headings, aiding comprehension for multilingual learners of English.
7. *Preview and Preteach Vocabulary*: Preview and preteach essential vocabulary before the test to familiarize students with key terms.
8. *Language Support Tools*: Depending on the assessment guidelines and policies, provide language support tools, including but not limited to translation tools.
9. *Oral Instructions*: Provide oral instructions in addition to written ones to ensure clarity for multilingual learners of English.
10. *Flexible Scheduling*: Consider flexible scheduling options, such as allowing multilingual learners of English to take the test at a time of day when they are most alert.
11. *Culturally Relevant Content*: Ensure the test content is culturally relevant and inclusive, reducing potential cultural bias.
12. *Teacher Support:* Offer teacher support or clarification sessions before the test to address language-related concerns.

Closing Questions and Suggestions for Each Teacher Role

Closing Questions and Suggestions for Each Teacher Role

Directions: Take a moment to write and reflect on your learning from Professional Learning Opportunity #13, Making Assessments Accessible. We have included a few role-specific questions and suggestions to prompt your thinking.

Professional Learning Providers

Closing Questions
- Which activities did you choose to facilitate with teachers?
- What went well?
- What might you want to improve?
- What areas of information may you need to clarify before exploring AI tools in a school professional development session?
- How might your school and district consider ways to make more accommodations allowable for teachers to use with multilingual learners of English in test settings?

Suggestions for This Role
If you decide to organize professional development sessions about AI tools in your district, it's advisable to initially reach out to your district administration office to inquire about any existing district policies governing the use of AI.

English Language Development Teachers

Closing Questions
- What were your key takeaways from these lessons?
- How did these lessons impact your language development work with your students?

CONTINUED

- AI tools may offer even more advantages to you as teachers of English language structures. What potential AI tasks would enhance your work with multilingual learners of English?
- In what ways might you collaborate with general education teachers in your school to provide allowable accommodations on assessments?

Suggestions for This Role
Utilizing language accommodations in content area assessments can improve outcomes for multilingual learners of English. We suggest first reaching out to general education teachers and initiating a discussion about potential collaborative efforts to enhance student success on content classroom assessments.

General Education Teachers

Closing Questions
- How did this go?
- What went well?
- What were your key takeaways?
- How might you use AI tools to reduce linguistic complexity on assessments in your classroom?
- How familiar are you with providing language accommodations on assessments with your students?
- Is there an area of accommodations you would like to try using first?

Suggestions for This Role
To increase accessibility for multilingual learners of English in your classroom assessments, try implementing one language accommodation initially. Observe how students at different English proficiency levels engage with the assessment items. As you gain confidence, gradually adapt assessment items and incorporate additional accommodations.

Professional Learning Opportunity #14: Formative Classroom Assessments

Formative assessment enhances language learning for multilingual learners of English by offering prompt feedback on student work and language use in content classrooms. Formative assessment practices also help teachers by facilitating observations of student language interactions and creating opportunities for immediate adjustments to instruction, clarifying student learning, and providing focused language support. This professional learning opportunity addresses how teachers use the formative assessment process to strategically provide ongoing effective feedback (TESOL Principle 5, Practice 5b and 5c). We also discuss how teachers determine language and content learning goals, based on observations from the formative assessment process (Standard 4: Component 4b of the *Standards for Initial TESOL Pre-K–12 Teacher Preparation Programs*). The Formative Classroom Assessments box outlines the components of this professional learning opportunity.

Formative Classroom Assessments

TESOL's 6 Principles (Grades K–12)	**Principle 5. Monitor and Assess Student Language Development** **Practice 5b.** Teachers strategically provide ongoing, effective feedback. **Practice 5c.** Teachers design varied and valid assessments and support to assess student learning.
Standards for Initial TESOL Pre-K–12 Teacher Preparation Programs	**Standard 4: Assessment and Evaluation** **Component 4b.** Teachers demonstrate an understanding of classroom-based formative, summative, and diagnostic assessments scaffolded for both English language and content assessment. Teachers determine language and content learning goals based on assessment data.
Key Learning Targets	I can determine my process for gathering evidence of student learning toward both language development and grade-level content standards. I can apply stages of the assessment cycle to my classroom to inform my instruction and my students' learning experiences.
Lesson and Activities	**Lesson 1: The Process of Formative Assessment** **Activities** 1. The Assessment Cycle 2. The Teaching and Learning Assessment Cycle
Notes for Each Teacher Role	**Professional Learning Providers:** Professional learning goals in this professional learning opportunity focus on understanding the assessment cycle and its links to teaching and learning experiences during the instruction and assessment phases. Teachers might already be acquainted with the concept of backward lesson design, which aligns with the assessment cycle. Encouraging teachers to bring their lesson plans to professional development sessions can create opportunities to collaborate and reflect with their colleagues. Each activity in Lesson 1 should require approximately 45 minutes of professional learning time with large or small groups of teachers. You may choose to add additional activities to the information provided here and add time to your professional learning plans accordingly. You can access many online resources in this chapter on the companion site for this book and may choose to print or create electronic versions for your professional learning sessions with teachers. **English Language Development Teachers:** The assessment cycle applies to all learning settings, including the English language development classroom. If you have your own language classroom, we encourage you to include your students in assessing their learning and reflecting on which aspects of language development they need to clarify and practice to become more proficient in using English in academic settings. If you collaborate or coteach with general education teachers, you may wish to discuss how to use the assessment cycle with all students in the grade-level or content classroom.

CONTINUED

General Education Teachers: You might already be acquainted with the concept of backward lesson design, which aligns with the assessment cycle. This approach to identifying the ways we will assess our students' knowledge before planning instruction will help us stay focused on providing the instruction and supports each student needs to meet their learning goals. We encourage you to consider how both you and your students can reflect on instruction and assessment in your classroom as you work to meet learning objectives for each lesson.

Lesson 1: The Process of Formative Assessment

When we talk to teachers on the topic of assessment, the discussion often focuses on how to assign meaningful grades to students learning English equitably. This question is asked so frequently that we have formed the opinion that many teachers consider the terms *assessment* and *grading* interchangeable. It's important to clarify that this perspective doesn't imply that teachers only prioritize grading; rather, we believe that questions related to grading stem from a sincere desire to identify students' knowledge and abilities accurately.

Research indicates that teachers dedicate a significant portion of their daily activities, ranging from 33% to 50%, to assessment-related tasks (Stiggins & Conklin, 1992). This time is invested in gathering information about students' skills and demonstrates teachers' commitment to using assessment to gather more information about students' progress toward academic goals. Through discussions with both ELD and general education teachers, it is apparent that teachers genuinely want to ensure they are using fair grading practices with multilingual learners of English and want to provide constructive feedback that supports students' learning.

We can understand the pressure for teachers to find ways to assess their students and gather accurate insight into how students are or are not making progress toward their grade-level learning goals. Grading is a part of assessment, but there is so much more to assessment than determining a formative or summative grade for each student. Assessment is derived from the Latin word *assidere*, which means to sit beside, assist, or guide (McTighe & Ferrara, 2021). Ken O'Connor (2018) describes assessment as gathering and interpreting information about student performance to measure content knowledge and skills progress. According to these definitions, assessments are intended to serve as ongoing guidance leading to a final result but are not the final result itself. Classroom assessments gauge progress toward a goal, and progress reports offer feedback to students on their journey toward academic learning goals.

The Challenge of Classroom Assessment With Multilingual Learners of English

Classroom assessments can either empower multilingual learners and teachers through linguistic and culturally sustaining practices, fostering engagement and advancing student learning, or they can serve as a tool to reinforce academic deficits and highlight performance differences among student groups (Gottlieb, 2022). Understanding classroom test items and assignment directions is influenced by each student's language proficiency level and their teacher's ability to make content comprehensible for multilingual learners of English. Individual factors such as life experiences, prior knowledge, academic history, language proficiency, and cultural perspective shape how students comprehend and interpret texts across different content subjects. Because our multilingual learners of English have such complex backgrounds and skills, test and assignment scores may not fully capture the depth of students' true knowledge (Taylor, 2022), especially if teachers are not familiar with their students' backgrounds or current language proficiency skills in all four language domains.

If assessments are designed without language learners in mind, they may prevent multilingual learners of English from demonstrating their true knowledge through their current English language proficiency skills. A strengths-based approach to assessing multilingual learners of English first considers the assessment environment to ensure it provides opportunities for students to showcase their knowledge and skills in the relevant content area (Clark & Chrispeels, 2022). In this final section of this chapter, we concentrate on formative assessment and how it fits into a strengths-based approach that allows students to demonstrate what they have learned. Well-designed formative assessments are crucial in helping teachers and students acquire accurate information about these students and their learning progress.

Defining Formative Assessment

The definition of formative assessment within the education literature varies, with different interpretations linked to the specific intent and purpose assigned by those providing the definitions. Testing companies and publishers promote formative assessments as a set of measures that can be internal or external to instruction (Staehr Fenner & Snyder, 2017).

Formative assessments are sometimes defined as tools used to identify specific students' mistakes or misconceptions that occur while the material is being taught (Kahl, 2005). One example of this is common formative assessments, which are created collaboratively by a team of teachers at the grade or course level. These assessments evaluate students' comprehension of specific standards emphasized in a series of related lessons or a current curricular unit (Ainsworth & Viegut, 2014).

In contrast to viewing formative assessment solely as a tool, it is also recognized as an essential set of practices integrated into teaching and learning to improve instruction and gain insights into student learning. This perspective views formative assessment as a process to enhance instructional effectiveness (Gottlieb, 2021; Stiggins, 2005; Stiggins & Chappuis, 2011; Wiliam, 2018). Formative assessment as a process has led some in education to replace the term *formative assessment* with the descriptor *assessment for learning*, which they believe more accurately captures the essence of the process. Broadfoot et al. (1999) list seven components that capture the practices of assessment for learning:
1. It is embedded in a view of teaching and learning.
2. It involves sharing learning goals with students.
3. It aims to help students know and recognize the applied standards.
4. It involves students in self-assessment.
5. It provides actionable feedback that leads to students recognizing their next steps and how to take them.
6. It is underpinned by confidence that every student can improve.
7. It involves both teachers and students reviewing and reflecting on assessment data.

There are many ways to gather information about the language development and academic progress of multilingual learners of English. However, the information you gather is only useful when interpreted with a well-informed understanding of language acquisition. Teachers should avoid making assumptions about each student's progress that do not consider each student's current language proficiency development. Instead, teachers must engage in processes that involve giving feedback to students and incorporating multilingual learners of English in self-assessments of their individual progress. Through this communication process focused on teaching and learning, teachers gain a deeper understanding of required language supports while students develop a better understanding of the teacher's instructions and expectations in the classroom. The importance of including multilingual learners of English in the process of assessment leads us to adopt Wiliam's (2018) definition of formative assessment:

> An assessment functions formatively to the extent that evidence about student achievement is elicited, interpreted, and used by teachers, learners, or their peers to make decisions about the next steps in instruction that are likely to be better or better founded than the decisions they would have made in the absence of that evidence.

Though we acknowledge that *assessment for learning* best captures the teaching and learning process with multilingual learners of English, if not all students, we will continue to use the term *formative assessment* to promote clarity with teachers who are more familiar with that terminology.

As you proceed through this next activity, consider formative assessment as a constant, ongoing process of providing opportunities for students to showcase their content knowledge and skills and then observing the degree to which students have demonstrated knowledge and skills toward academic standards.

The Assessment Cycle

Assessment cycles involve planning, implementing, evaluating, and adjusting processes. The concept of the assessment cycle has evolved over time, and its development is attributed to the collective contributions of teachers, researchers, and professionals in various fields. In education, for instance, assessment cycles have roots in educational philosophy and research on effective teaching and learning. While the number of stages and descriptors of each stage in the cycle may vary, the process typically begins by identifying a desired outcome, gathering evidence, reviewing findings, and making necessary changes before beginning the process again.

Figure 5.1 *The assessment cycle.*

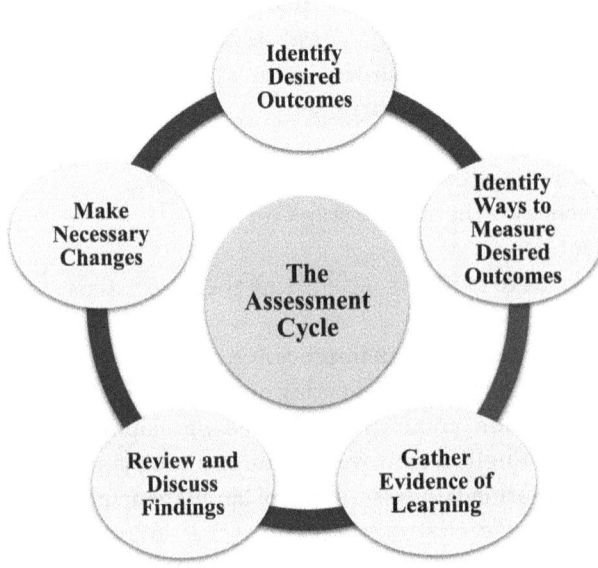

The assessment cycle shown in Figure 5.1 centers on collecting student evidence to assess how well instruction has aided multilingual learners of English in achieving their desired outcomes. In this case, the desired outcome is students' capacity to demonstrate knowledge and skills related to grade-level language and content standards by meeting the lesson's learning objectives.

Key Learning Target: I can apply stages of the assessment cycle to my classroom to inform my instruction and my students' learning experiences.

Activity Goal: Evaluate ways to apply the assessment cycle to monitoring student progress toward meeting learning objectives in your classroom.

Step 1

Engage in this reflection independently or collaborate with a colleague to exchange ideas on different ways to use the assessment cycle or incorporate its stages into your assessment approach.

Step 2

Consider the various stages of the assessment cycle by assessing the following corresponding questions.

Assessment Cycle Stage 1: Identify Desired Outcomes

- Which standards will you use to inform learning outcomes or goals for your assessments?
- How do you consider your multilingual learners of English when planning assessments?

Assessment Cycle Stage 2: Identify Ways to Measure Desired Outcomes

- What will successful student evidence of learning look like for multilingual learners of English?
- Do multilingual learners of English at different levels of English language development have options to demonstrate their knowledge and skills toward the standards represented in the assessment?

Assessment Cycle Stage 3: Gather Evidence of Learning

- How have you used language supports to make the assessment accessible to multilingual learners of English?
- Are there assessment accommodations that might support the ability of multilingual learners of English to demonstrate their knowledge of the standards?

Assessment Cycle Stage 4: Review Findings

- How do you analyze the assessment results to gauge student understanding?
- How do student data provided by multilingual learners of English compare to the data gathered for students who are not multilingual learners of English?
- Did the language supports provided in the assessment allow multilingual learners of English to show you what they know in relation to the content standards?

Assessment Cycle Stage 5: Make Necessary Changes

- In what ways do you use assessment data to inform your teaching practices?
- How do you address the needs of students who may be struggling based on assessment results?

Step 3

- Reflect on the assessment cycle. In what ways do you see the assessment cycle promoting student learning?
- If you have previously used the assessment cycle or a similar approach, what difficulties did you face in implementing this method, and how did you address those challenges?

The assessment cycle involves more than teachers independently providing instruction and assessment; it is a collaborative process that requires teachers' and students' input and reflection (Black & Wiliam, 2010). Figure 5.2 illustrates the connections between teaching and learning at each stage of the assessment cycle.

Figure 5.2 *Teaching and learning assessment cycle.*

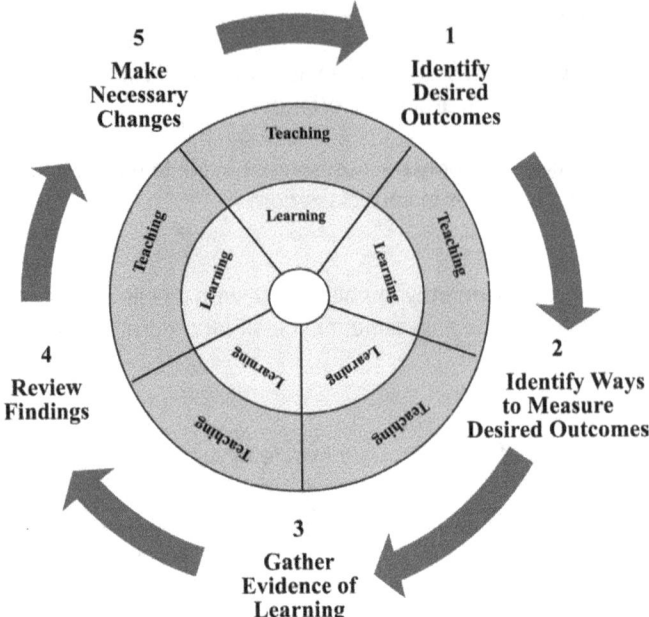

Advocates of formative assessment stress the importance of involving students in assessing their own learning. This is particularly important when working with students from bilingual or multilingual backgrounds who are learning academic English. Some multilingual learners of English in the early stages of developing English listening and reading skills may not fully comprehend their teachers' instructions or assignment directions. For this reason, it is even more important to provide clear expectations and allow students to reflect on their learning throughout classroom instruction and assessments.

Our second activity for Lesson 1 uses Figure 5.2 to think through implications for teaching and learning at each stage of the assessment cycle.

Activity The Teaching and Learning Assessment Cycle

Key Learning Target: I can apply stages of the assessment cycle to my classroom to inform my instruction and my students' learning experiences.

Activity Goal: Consider teacher and student actions at each stage of the assessment cycle to increase student engagement in self-reflection and monitoring their academic progress.

Step 1
- Use Figure 5.2 as a guide and consider working through this exercise with a colleague, a grade-level or content team, and an English language development teacher.
- On the next couple of pages, you will find the steps of the teaching and learning assessment cycle along with examples illustrating actions that both teachers and students can take at each stage of the assessment cycle.
- Individually or with a team, review the teaching and learning examples and consider how language support can be provided to make assessments accessible for multilingual learners of English at various language proficiency levels.

CONTINUED

Assessment Cycle Stage	Teaching and Learning Examples
1. Identify Desired Outcomes 	**Teachers** • Post the guiding standards for daily lessons and/or unit projects where students can see them. • Add language supports using synonyms for complex academic terms and visuals representing processes. **Students** • Highlight task demands in the standard with the support of the teacher. • Discuss with the teacher and/or peers to describe the learning objectives and what meeting the standard may look like by including success criteria.
2. Identify Ways to Measure Desired Outcomes 	**Teachers** • Provide success criteria and grading rubrics for assignments and projects. • List success criteria with visual supports in checklist format so students can keep track of work that aligns with the standards. • Ensure rubrics include visuals and actions that have been previously used during instruction or previous assignments. • Display models of finished assignments or projects in the classroom to show possible ways to demonstrate evidence of learning. **Students** • Use the success criteria checklist provided by the teacher to plan work assignments and projects. • Review the grading rubric with the teacher to clarify understanding of what needs to be turned in and how points will be assigned to work. • Access models of assignments or projects and make notes of ideas to clarify and apply to personal work.
3. Gather Evidence of Learning 	**Teachers** • As you work through the responses provided by multilingual learners of English on your classroom assessment, make note of where information gaps occur and evaluate ways you might have created additional support to make information accessible. • Do you notice differences in student evidence between students with different levels of language proficiency? • Are there additional ways you might adapt question responses for multilingual learners of English with beginning-level language skills? For example, could you conduct an oral interview in place of essay questions? **Students** • Provide evidence of learning using a checklist of success criteria and reviewing the grading rubric before turning in work.

CONTINUED

4. Review Findings 	**Teachers** • Give students feedback to make corrections and share ways to improve skills and fill any gaps in knowledge. • Initiate a discussion with students to find out what portions of the assessment were unclear or most difficult for them to complete. **Students** • Engage in self-reflection using feedback from the teacher and peers. • Make notes about areas of the assessment that were confusing and academic information that may need to be clarified.
5. Make Necessary Changes 	**Teachers** • Using student feedback and your own observations, make notes on ways to improve future classroom assessment. • Develop a plan to apply new ideas during instruction or in checks for understanding to gauge the effectiveness of the new approach with multilingual learners of English. **Students** • Develop a plan to use success criteria checklists on future assignments or assessments. • Plan to access grading rubrics for future assignments or assessments and discuss them with the teacher in preparation for studying or completing assignments.

Step 2
After reading through the example for each stage, brainstorm additional examples that you might use in your classroom that are most relevant to your grade level and classroom context.

Closing Questions and Suggestions for Each Teacher Role

Closing Questions and Suggestions for Each Teacher Role

Directions: Take a moment to write and reflect on your learning from Professional Learning Opportunity #14, Formative Classroom Assessments. We have included a few role-specific questions and suggestions to prompt your thinking.

Professional Learning Providers

Closing Questions
• Which activities did you choose to facilitate with teachers?
• What went well?
• What might you want to improve?
• In what ways do you feel teachers are now able to use the assessment cycle when working with multilingual learners of English?
• What follow-up opportunities may you want to plan to further support teachers in your school or district?

CONTINUED

Suggestions for This Role

As you start planning professional development on formative assessment, consider beginning with the teaching and learning assessment cycle. This will aid teachers in considering classroom actions. Break down the cycle step by step, encouraging teachers to apply their new skills in their classrooms and share observations in the next professional learning session.

English Language Development Teachers

Closing Questions

- What were your key takeaways from this lesson?
- What impact did this lesson have on your language development work with your students?
- Which aspects of this lesson would you like to address and collaborate on with general education teachers in your school or district?

Suggestions for This Role

English language development teachers can initially concentrate on clarifying learner actions appropriate for multilingual learners of English at different proficiency levels within the assessment cycle. You might plan ways to differentiate student actions based on language proficiency levels, to support your own work and to provide examples for general education colleagues.

General Education Teachers

Closing Questions

- How did this go?
- What went well?
- What were your key takeaways?
- How did this learning inform how you use the assessment cycle to evaluate how you use classroom assessments and create opportunities for your multilingual learners of English to reflect on their progress toward learning goals in your classroom?

Suggestions for This Role

If you're new to teaching multilingual learners of English, your initial step could be setting up a system to save ideas for supporting various language proficiency levels during instruction and assessments. As you become more skilled at distinguishing between language proficiency levels, you'll discover additional methods to integrate language support into your teaching and assessment practices.

Wrapping Things Up

Postassessment

Just as we monitor student progress in our classrooms, measuring our progress in professional learning is also useful. At the beginning of this chapter, we offered a preassessment of objectives related to assessment and evaluation with multilingual learners of English. You may choose to reflect on your understanding of each of the standards-based learning targets by completing the Postassessment for Assessment and Evaluation shown in Table 5.5.

We have provided a continuum that starts with *1-Emerging* (no current understanding), moves to *3-Developing* (somewhat familiar but still needs information to take action), and ends with *5-Proficient* (able to understand and take action on this learning target). After you have rated your level of understanding and skill on each learning target, consider how your results might inform which professional learning opportunities you would like to review or explore further as you practice the application of learning in your classroom.

Next Steps

Consider the following questions to guide your thinking about the assessment and evaluation process with multilingual learners of English in your classroom.

1. What learning do I need to clarify more in my understanding?
2. What would I still like to know about this topic?
3. What are my next steps in supporting English language growth for multilingual learners of English in my classroom?
4. What do multilingual learners of English in our classrooms, school, and district need to demonstrate their knowledge and skills related to academic knowledge and skills?

Table 5.5 *Postassessment for Assessment and Evaluation*

Assessment and Evaluation Professional Learning Opportunities #12–14		1 Emerging
#12 Assessment Bias	1. I can evaluate my classroom assessments for cultural and linguistic bias.	
	2. I can reduce the linguistic complexity of test questions so they are more accessible to students learning academic English as a new language.	
#13 Making Assessment Accessible	3. I can use technology to make a text accessible to students with different reading proficiency levels.	
	4. I can identify allowable accommodations for assessments used with multilingual learners of English in my classroom or school.	
#14 Formative Classroom Assessments	5. I can determine my process for gathering evidence of student learning toward both language development and grade-level content standards.	
	6. I can apply stages of the assessment cycle to my classroom to inform my instruction and my students' learning experiences.	

Chapter Highlights

As you reflect on Chapter 5, consider how unconscious bias might appear in materials or assessments you use in the classroom. Simplifying the language in texts is an effective method for tackling language bias, and modern AI tools can assist in this effort. The chapter concluded with a discussion on the assessment cycle, emphasizing the importance of teacher and learner actions in the formative assessment process within the classroom.

In Chapter 6, you will engage in opportunities to develop an understanding of the legal rights of multilingual learners of English and their families. This understanding will help you develop skills to advocate for multilingual learners of English based on student and family backgrounds. Another focus in Chapter 6 is the professionalism and leadership required in educating multilingual learners of English and providing essential learning opportunities. These opportunities include understanding the rights that provide access to equitable education and applying federal guidance in practical K–12 settings.

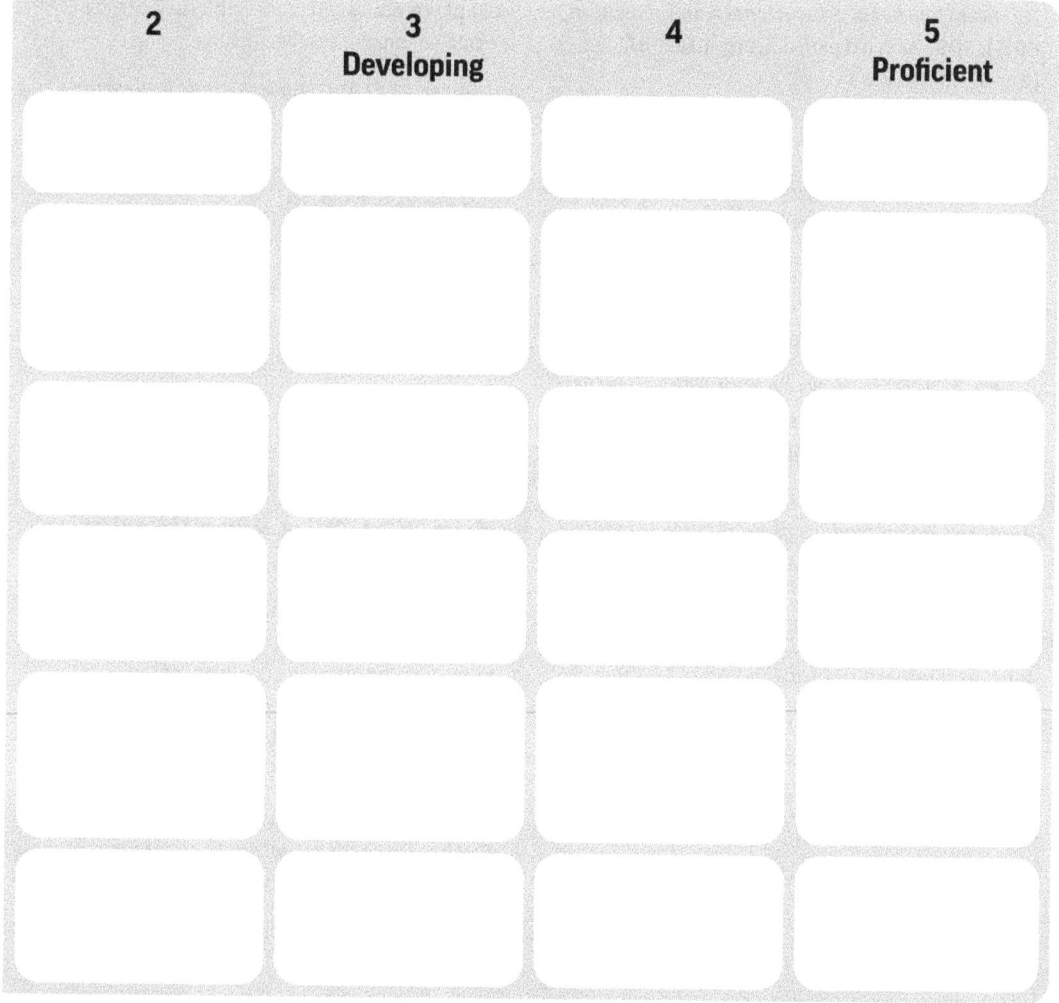

References

Ainsworth, L., & Viegut, D. (2014). *Common formative assessments 2.0: How teacher teams intentionally align standards, instruction, and assessment*. Corwin.

Black, P., & Wiliam, D. (2010). Inside the black box: Raising standards through classroom assessment. *Phi Delta Kappan, 92*(1), 81–90. https://doi.org/10.1177/003172171009200119

Broadfoot, P. M., Daugherty, R., Gardner, J., Gipps, C. V., Harlen, W., James, M., & Stobart, G. (1999). *Assessment for learning: Beyond the black box*. Nuffield Foundation and University of Cambridge.

Clark, J. T., & Chrispeels, J. H. (2022). Using multiple leadership frames to understand how two school principals are influencing teachers' practices and achievement of Hispanic English learners. *Journal of Educational Administration, 60*(3), 303–322. https://doi.org/10.1108/JEA-03-2021-0054

Gordon, C. (2023, April 30). How are educators reacting to Chat GPT? *Forbes.* https://www.forbes.com/sites/cindygordon/2023/04/30/how-are-educators-reacting-to-chat-gpt/?sh=6d9c93a12f1c

Gottlieb, M. (2021). *Classroom assessment in multiple languages*. Corwin.

Gottlieb, M. (2022). *How can multilingual learners and their teachers make a difference in classroom assessment?* Center for Applied Linguistics.

Heartland Area Education Agency. (n.d.). *Allowable accommodations for English learners on common academic assessments*. http://tinyurl.com/EL-Allow

Kahl, S. (2005, November 30). Coming to terms with assessment. *Education Week, 25*(13), p. 26.

Kulowiec, G. (2023, September 28). *AI in EDU Open Q+A with Greg Kulowiec* [Video]. YouTube. https://www.youtube.com/live/IRuRZgdKIgw?si=aRGTv7X0V6p0N_IO

Liu, X. (2008). *Measuring teachers' perceptions of grading practices: Does school level make a difference?* [Paper presentation]. Northeastern Educational Research Association Annual Meeting, Rocky Hill, CT, United States.

McTighe, J., & Ferrara, S. (2021). *Assessing student learning by design: Principles and practices for teachers and school leaders*. Teachers College Press.

Ming, G. K., & Mansor, M. (2023). Exploring the impact of Chat-GPT on teacher professional development: Opportunities, challenges, and implications. *Asian Journal of Research in Education and Social Sciences, 5*(4), 54–67.

Najarro, I. (2023, September 28). AI with English learners: What teachers need to know. *Education Week.* https://www.edweek.org/events/webinar/ai-and-english-learners-what-teachers-need-to-know

O'Connor, K. (2018). *How to grade for learning: Linking grades to standards* (2nd ed.). Corwin.

OpenAI. (2023a). *Conversation for pronunciation and practice*. ChatGPT. https://www.openai.com/chatgpt

OpenAI. (2023b). *Definition of AI*. ChatGPT. https://www.openai.com/chatgpt

OpenAI. (2023c). *Grammar writing sample*. ChatGPT. https://www.openai.com/chatgpt

OpenAI. (2023d). *Word list*. ChatGPT. https://www.openai.com/chatgpt

Popham, W. J. (2012). *Assessment bias: How to banish it* (2nd ed.). Allyn & Bacon.

Shallaita, B. A., Nawawi, N., & Amin, M. (2021). Analysis of English language teaching materials on gender representation. *International Journal of Multicultural and Multireligious Understanding, 8*(2), 419–434. https://doi.org/10.18415/ijmmu.v8i2.2423

Staehr Fenner, D., & Snyder, S. (2017). *Unlocking English learner's potential: Strategies for making content accessible*. Corwin.

Stiggins, R. J. (2005). *Student-involved assessment FOR learning* (4th ed.). Pearson.

Stiggins, R. J., & Chappuis, J. (2011). *An introduction to student-involved assessment FOR learning* (6th ed.). Prentice Hall.

Stiggins, R. J., & Conklin, R. F. (1992). *In teachers' hands: Investigating the practice of classroom assessment*. State University of New York Press.

Taylor, C. S. (2022). *Culturally and socially responsible assessment: Theory, research, and practice*. Teachers College Press.

TESOL International Association. (2019). *Standards for initial TESOL Pre-K–12 teacher preparation programs*. TESOL Press.

TESOL International Association. (2024). *The 6 principles for exemplary teaching of English learners: Grades K–12* (2nd ed.). TESOL Press.

Umansky, I. M., Valentino, R. A., & Reardon, S. F. (2015). *The promise of bilingual and dual immersion education* [CEPA Working Paper No. 15-11]. Center for Education Policy Analysis. http://cepa.stanford.edu/wp15-11

Wiliam, D. (2018). *Embedded formative assessment*. Solution Tree Press.

Additional Resource

Folse, K. S. (2016). *Keys to teaching grammar to English language learners: A practical handbook*. University of Michigan Press.

Chapter 6

Professionalism and Leadership

Getting Ready to Learn

We would like to introduce you to Cecilia. Cecilia has been referred to a school team to determine if she would qualify for special education. The team reports the following information for Cecilia:

- **Grade:** 8th grade
- **English Reading Level**: Pre-emergent level
- **General Education Work**
  - Not proficient on grade-level exams
  - Easily distracted in general education core classes
- **Early Thoughts**: The team is strongly considering a special education evaluation.

As advocates of multilingual learners of English, we should pause and consider other factors before making a final determination about Cecilia. We should also consider who else should be involved. Upon further review and with the inclusion of an English language development (ELD) teacher at the team meeting, the team reports the following additional data for Cecilia:

- **English Language Development Levels**
- **Language Identification Screener:** All level 1 in listening, speaking, reading, and writing, or at the emerging/beginning stages of English language development
- **Most Recent Annual Language Assessment**
  - Listening: Level 2
  - Speaking: Level 2
  - Reading: Level 1
  - Writing: Level 1
- **Home Language:** Cecilia speaks Spanish in the home. Cecilia's mom reports she comprehends Spanish well; however, she is not able to read or write in Spanish.
- **Country of Origin/Immigrant/Refugee:** Cecilia and her family were born in El Salvador. Cecilia's mom reports that there was much gang activity in the home country.
- **Length of Time in the United States:** 2.5 years
- **Educational Background:** Cecilia has experienced interrupted schooling. She went to school for one year in El Salvador, where there was a 1:50 teacher-to-student ratio. Mom reports that Cecilia did not learn well in this environment.

CONTINUED

- **Physical:** Hearing and vision were tested, and they were normal.
- **Current Reading Instruction:** The school placed Cecilia in an 8th-grade general education language arts class.
- **Interests:** Cecilia enjoys music and art and has an interest in pursuing teaching in the future.

Table 6.1 *Preassessment for Professionalism and Leadership*

Professionalism and Leadership Professional Learning Opportunities #15–17		1 Emerging
#15 Know the Rights of Multilingual Learners of English and Their Families	1. I can identify key rights and policies that impact instruction and daily interaction with multilingual learners of English and their families.	
#16 Application of Federal Guidance	2. I can apply information from federal guidance to support immigrant and refugee families in our school.	
	3. I can evaluate my current knowledge of federal protections for multilingual learners of English and identify areas where I can improve my understanding.	
#17 Advocate on Behalf of Multilingual Learners of English and Their Families	4. I can build my capacity to advocate for multilingual learners of English and their families to ensure they are afforded an equitable education.	

To ensure special education is reserved "for students with documented disabilities" (Morando Rhim et al., 2023), a language specialist needs to be part of the determination team. It is also crucial to gather essential background information (referenced in Chapter 2), including English language proficiency levels, educational history, home language literacy level, country of origin, life experiences/interests, social-emotional information, and other factors to make this critical decision. As advocates, we want to ask how these additional data might impact special education placement or other service decisions. Ultimately, the referral team determined Cecilia needed additional scaffolded opportunities to access content, continued

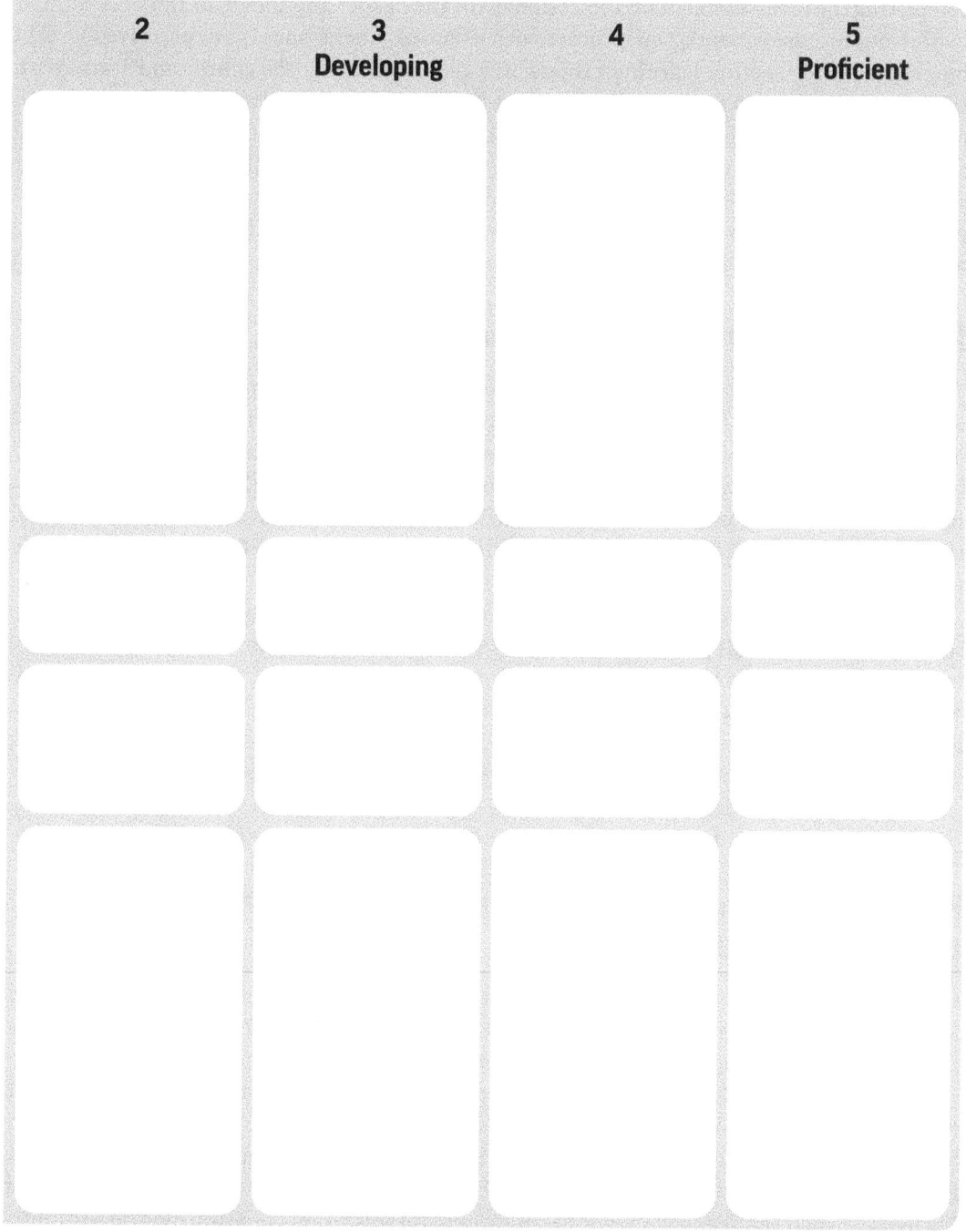

language development, and support with English literacy before they could confidently determine if she would benefit from being evaluated for special education services.

In this chapter, you will become familiar with the legal rights of multilingual learners of English and their families. You will also build your capacity to take appropriate action on behalf of multilingual learners of English to ensure they are afforded an equitable education.

Preassessment

Before participating in this chapter's professional learning opportunities, we recommend completing the Preassessment for Professionalism and Leadership shown in Table 6.1. Similar to previous preassessments, you indicate with a date or other symbol your perceived level of progress toward meeting learning targets on a 1–5 continuum. The continuum starts with *1-Emerging* (little to no understanding), moves to *3-Developing* (somewhat familiar but still need information to take action), and ends with *5-Proficient* (I feel confident that I understand and can take action on this learning target). The survey results will help determine your priorities for professional learning opportunities for the Professionalism and Leadership pathway. You may also compare your progress toward meeting the learning targets before and after participating in this chapter's learning opportunities.

Professional Learning Opportunities

This chapter addresses professionalism and leadership as teachers of multilingual learners of English. Key professional learning opportunities include learning about the rights of multilingual learners of English and their families that impact their access to education and becoming familiar with how to apply federal guidance to real-life K–12 educational contexts. In addition, there are opportunities to identify sample areas of advocacy for multilingual learners of English and their families and address one or more issues that impact equitable education.

This chapter has three professional learning opportunities. You may engage in those that meet your learning needs. However, before beginning your professional learning opportunities, we encourage you to reflect on your preassessment responses and pursue options that fit your current learning needs. The three professional learning opportunities are as follows:
- Know the Rights of Multilingual Learners of English and Their Families
- Application of Federal Guidance
- Advocate on Behalf of Multilingual Learners of English and Their Families

Professional Learning Opportunity #15: Know the Rights of Multilingual Learners of English and Their Families

One of the first steps in advocating for the rights of multilingual learners of English (Standard 5, Component 5b of the *Standards for Initial TESOL Pre-K–12 Teacher Preparation Programs*) is noticing and identifying issues that stem from rights and policies related to their education (Linville & Whiting, 2022). In Professional Learning Opportunity #15, you will become familiar with some key legislation, court cases, and policies that impact access to equitable education for language learners and their families (TESOL Principle 1. Know Your Learners and TESOL Principle 2. Create Conditions for Learning). The Know the Rights of Multilingual Learners of English and Their Families box shows the components of this professional learning opportunity.

Know the Rights of Multilingual Learners of English and Their Families

TESOL's 6 Principles (Grades K–12)	**Principle 1: Know Your Learners** **Principle 2: Create Conditions for Language Learning**
Standards for Initial TESOL Pre-K–12 Teacher Preparation Programs	**Standard 5: Professionalism and Leadership** **Component 5b.** Teachers apply knowledge of school, district, and governmental policies and legislations that impact the educational rights of students in order to advocate for multilingual learners of English.
Key Learning Target	I can identify key rights and policies that impact instruction and daily interaction with multilingual learners of English and their families.
Lesson and Activities	**Lesson 1: Know Key Legislation, Court Cases, and Policies Impacting the Educational Rights of Multilingual Learners of English and Their Families** **Activities** 1. Freedom to Talk Anticipation Guide and Video 2. Noticing and Wondering
Notes for Each Teacher Role	**Professional Learning Providers:** You can facilitate Lesson 1 in an approximate 30- to 45-minute whole-group staff meeting or small-group professional learning community. You can access many online resources in this chapter on the companion site for this book and may choose to print or create electronic versions for your professional learning sessions with teachers. **English Language Development Teachers:** This professional learning opportunity will serve as a reminder of key legislation, court cases, and policies that impact the educational rights of multilingual learners of English and their families. This reminder aims to strengthen your advocacy when issues arise that require speaking or acting on behalf of students learning English to ensure they receive an equitable education. **General Education Teachers**: Lesson 1 will allow you to gain background on the legal rights of multilingual learners of English and their families. Knowledge of educational rights helps build the capacity to advocate for multilingual students learning English and their families when issues arise.

Lesson 1: Know Key Legislation, Court Cases, and Policies Impacting the Educational Rights of Multilingual Learners of English and Their Families

In Lesson 1, you will first build background knowledge for key legislation, court cases, and policies that impact the educational rights of multilingual learners of English and their families. You will then consider the implications of these rights for the students and their families you serve in your school or district.

Key Learning Target: I can identify key rights and policies that impact instruction and daily interaction with multilingual learners of English.

Activity Goal: Build background for the educational rights of multilingual learners of English.

Directions
1. **Before viewing** the video *Freedom to Talk* (Stanford University, 2015), read each statement in the middle column below.
2. **Then**, in the Before Viewing column, mark if you agree or disagree with each statement.
3. **Next**, view and reflect on the video *Freedom to Talk* (Stanford University, 2015; vimeo. com/133969433).
4. **After that,** reread each statement in the middle column, and in the After Viewing column, mark if you agree or disagree with each statement.
5. **Finally**, discuss your before and after viewing responses with colleagues.

Before Viewing	Statements	After Viewing
Agree Disagree	There are very few landmark court rulings protecting the education rights of multilingual learners of English.	Agree Disagree
Agree Disagree	Martin Luther King Jr. played a role in advocating for the rights of multilingual learners of English to receive legal education.	Agree Disagree
Agree Disagree	Equality of treatment for multilingual learners of English is mainly about providing students with the same facilities, textbooks, teachers, and curriculum.	Agree Disagree
Agree Disagre	No Child Left Behind increased district accountability for multilingual learners of English.	Agree Disagree
Agree Disagree	The Common Core State Standards include language demands.	Agree Disagree

Activity Noticing and Wondering

Key Learning Target: I can identify key rights and policies that impact instruction and daily interaction with multilingual learners of English and their families.

Activity Goal: Consider what you notice and wonder about the rights of multilingual learners of English and their families.

Directions
1. **First**, review Table 6.2, which summarizes key legislation, court cases, and policies that impact the education of multilingual learners of English and their families in the United States.

CONTINUED

2. **Next**, **review Table 6.3,** which presents resources from the U.S. Department of Justice and U.S. Department of Education (2015a, 2015b, 2015c). These resources provide jointly issued guidance to education officials and fact sheets for students and parents regarding state and local-level civil rights obligations to multilingual learners of English and their families.
3. **Then**, **answer the following questions** about what you notice and wonder about in Tables 6.2 and 6.3 related to the educational rights of multilingual learners of English and their families.

Noticing	What do you notice about the legal rights of multilingual learners of English and their families in Tables 6.2 and 6.3?
Wondering	What are you wondering about the potential implications of these legal rights for the multilingual learners of English and the families you serve? Also, how might these rights impact instruction and daily interaction with multilingual learners of English and their families?

Table 6.2 *Key Legislation, Court Cases, and Policies Impacting the Educational Rights of Multilingual Learners of English*[1]

Legislation, Court Cases, and Policies	Implications
Title VI of the Civil Rights Act of 1964 	• Prohibits discrimination on the grounds of race, color, or national origin. • The Title VI regulatory requirements prohibit denial of equal access to education because of a language minority student's limited proficiency in English. Civil Rights Act (1964)

CONTINUED

---

1   Image Attributions
Martin Luther King to Represent His Impact on the Civil Rights Act (1964): Photo by David Erickson, I Have a Dream Speech (https://www.flickr.com/photos/e-strategycom/1054179588). Attribution 2.0 Generic (CC BY 2.0).
Signing Ceremony Elementary and Secondary Education Act (1965): White House Photographer Frank Wolfe, Public domain, via Wikimedia Commons, https://commons.wikimedia.org/wiki/File:ESEAJohnson.jpg
Lau v. Nichols (1974): U.S. Supreme Court, Public domain, via Wikimedia Commons, https://commons.wikimedia.org/wiki/File:-Supreme_Court.jpg
Castañeda v. Pickard (1981): Child, School, Classroom image. Free for use. https://pixabay.com/photos/child-school-class-room-717168/
Plyler v. Doe (1982): U.S. Supreme Court, Public domain, via Wikimedia Commons, https://commons.wikimedia.org/wiki/File:Supreme_Court.jpg
No Child Left Behind Act (2001): Public Domain. No Child Left Behind Act. (2024, March 15). In Wikipedia. https://en.wikipedia.org/wiki/No_Child_Left_Behind_Act
Every Student Succeeds Act (2015): File: President Barack Obama signs Every Student Succeeds Act (ESSA). Jpg. In Wikipedia. https://commons.wikimedia.org/wiki/File:President_Barack_Obama_signs_Every_Student_Succeeds_Act_(ESSA).jpg

Elementary and Secondary Education Act of 1965 	• Provides money for children in disadvantaged schools. • Ensures funding is for supplementing and not supplanting (e.g., federal funds cannot be used for something a district should already be paying for, such as bussing and textbooks for core instruction). Title III is an example of federal funding intended to improve the education of multilingual learners of English. Elementary and Secondary Education Act (1965)
May 25, 1970 Memorandum 	Addresses four areas of school compliance: • Instructional programming must not exclude multilingual learners of English from effective participation. • Multilingual learners of English may not be placed in special education based on language proficiency alone or be denied college preparation because of limited language. • Ability groups based on language skills must not be a permanent track for multilingual learners of English. • Schools must notify the parents of multilingual learners of English of any school activities shared with other parents, preferably in a language best understood by parents. U.S. Department of Health, Education, and Welfare (1970)
Equal Educational Opportunities Act of 1974 	• Prohibits discrimination due to race, gender, or national origin. • Schools are required to overcome language barriers that impede equal school participation. • Schools are required to provide information to the families of multilingual learners of English in a language most easily understood. Equal Education Opportunities Act (1974)
Lau v. Nichols (1974) 	• The Supreme Court ruled that "there is no equality of treatment merely by providing students with the same facilities, textbooks, teachers, and curriculum; for students who do not understand English are effectively foreclosed from any meaningful education." • Determines schools must address language barriers for multilingual learners of English. • Schools must take steps to overcome educational barriers faced by non-English-speaking students, including a specialized language instruction educational program. Lau v. Nichols (1974)

CONTINUED

Castañeda v. Pickard (1981) 	Schools are required to provide a language program that • Is theoretically sound or based on sound educational theory (e.g., English language development [ELD] or bilingual program). • Is implemented with appropriate resources and qualified personnel (e.g., ELD teacher, appropriate books and resources). • Achieves beneficial results over time; if not, the program needs to be evaluated and adjusted so it meets the linguistic and academic needs of multilingual learners of English. Castañeda v. Pickard (1981)
Plyler v. Doe (1982) 	• The Supreme Court ruled that schools must not deny admission of children and young adults because of immigration status (doing so violates the Equal Protection Clause of the Fourteenth Amendment). • Determined schools are not responsible for the enforcement of U.S. immigration laws (WIDA Consortium, 2015). • Also determined Social Security numbers were not required to enroll students or for families to be eligible for free and reduced-price meals (WIDA Consortium, 2015). Plyler v. Doe (1982)
No Child Left Behind Act of 2001 	• Increased accountability for the achievement of multilingual learners of English. • Required multilingual learners of English to participate in standardized testing. • Districts receiving Title III funding needed to set annual objectives and document progress in language acquisition and academic achievement. • The Every Student Succeeds Act (2015) subsequently replaced the No Child Left Behind Act of 2001. No Child Left Behind Act (2001)
Every Student Succeeds Act (2015) 	Requires states to have the following: • Standardized identification and exit procedures for multilingual learners of English with clear criteria for entering and exiting or reclassifying students from language programs • Language proficiency standards that align with state content standards and include the language domains of listening, speaking, reading, and writing • Annual language assessments • Reporting on the progress of multilingual learners of English • Monitoring the progress of exited students or students who were former multilingual learners of English Every Student Succeeds Act (2015); Linville & Whiting (2022)

Table 6.3 *Additional Resources: Schools' Civil Rights Obligations to Multilingual Learners of English and Their Families*

Resource Title	Audience	Description	References
Dear Colleague Letter: English Learner Students and Limited English Proficient Parents	Education Officials	• Reminders to state agencies and public schools of their civil rights obligations to ensure equitable educational opportunities for multilingual learners of English • Overview of common civil rights compliance issues when serving multilingual learners of English • Guidance on how to meet civil rights obligations	U.S. Department of Justice & U.S. Department of Education (2015a; www2.ed.gov/about/offices/list/ocr/letters/colleague-el-201501.pdf)
Ensuring English Learner Students Can Participate Meaningfully and Equally in Educational Programs (Fact Sheet)	Students and Parents/Guardians	• A brief overview of schools' and states' civil rights obligations that are outlined in the Dear Colleague Letter (described above)	U.S. Department of Justice & U.S. Department of Education (2015b; www2.ed.gov/about/offices/list/ocr/docs/dcl-factsheet-el-students-201501.pdf)
Information for Limited English Proficient Parents and for Schools and School Districts that Communicate With Them (Fact Sheet)	Students and Parents/Guardians	• Answers questions about the rights of parents and guardians who are not proficient in English • Includes information about when schools are required to communicate information to the parents/guardians of multilingual learners of English in a language they can understand	U.S. Department of Justice & U.S. Department of Education (2015c; www2.ed.gov/about/offices/list/ocr/docs/dcl-factsheet-lep-parents-201501.pdf)

Note. The term *limited English proficient* is included in this chapter when it refers to U.S. legislation. Please note that TESOL and the authors do not use this deficit-based term and caution the reader to use only asset-based terminology when talking about multilingual learners of English, their parents, and other family members. For additional information, see TESOL International Association's updated acronyms webpage, which includes a position statement on asset-based language (TESOL International Association, 2024b; www.tesol.org/careers/career-tools/beginning-your-career/common-acronyms-in-the-english-language-teaching-profession).

Closing Questions and Suggestions for Each Teacher Role

In Professional Learning Opportunity #15, Know the Rights of Multilingual Learners of English and Their Families, you began to notice issues that stem from the rights and policies of educational rights related to multilingual learners of English. You also became familiar with some key legislation, court cases, and policies that impact access to equitable education for language learners. The following box offers some role-specific questions and suggestions to help you reflect upon and extend your learning after engaging in this professional learning opportunity.

Closing Questions and Suggestions for Each Teacher Role

Directions: Take a moment to write and reflect on your learning from Professional Learning Opportunity #15, Know the Rights of Multilingual Learners of English and Their Families. We have included a few role-specific questions and suggestions to prompt your thinking.

Professional Learning Providers

Closing Questions
- What went well in this professional learning opportunity?
- What might you want to improve?
- Which legal rights stood out to you and your participants?

Suggestions for This Role
A suggestion to get started is to discuss the implications of legal rights for the multilingual learners and families you support in your school. As a professional learning provider, it is highly likely you have a larger sphere of influence and ability to advocate for schoolwide issues.

English Language Development Teachers

Closing Questions
- Were there any surprises or was there new learning regarding the legal rights of multilingual learners of English and their families?
- How might you use information about legal rights to advocate for equitable educational opportunities for the multilingual learners of English and the families you serve?

CONTINUED

Suggestions for This Role
To help you get started, consider some common issues for advocacy. For example, English language development teachers often advocate for communication in a family's home language or access to appropriate resources for English language development programs. In addition, you could advocate for your school to follow standardized exit and entrance procedures for multilingual learners of English or for general education teachers to receive professional learning specific to supporting multilingual learners of English.

General Education Teachers

Closing Questions
- What were your key takeaways about legal rights for multilingual learners of English and their families?
- Was there anything surprising to you?
- Were there legal rights that resonated with you to help ensure equitable opportunities for multilingual learners of English and their families?

Suggestions for This Role
A suggestion to get started is to first focus on one area to help build your capacity for advocacy. You can also start by advocating for the multilingual learners and families in your classroom and gradually expand your sphere of influence to colleagues in other classrooms.

Professional Learning Opportunity #16: Application of Federal Guidance

Teacher education programs in the United States do not always include comprehensive instruction on the civil rights of immigrant and refugee students and families in schools. Teachers should develop a practical understanding of these rights and be able to apply knowledge of relevant policies and legislations at school, district, and governmental levels. This knowledge is essential to advocate for equitable education and aligns with Standard 5, Component 5b of the *Standards for Initial TESOL Pre-K–12 Teacher Preparation Programs*. In this professional learning opportunity, we focus on the civil rights of multilingual learners of English and their families, offering resources to familiarize you with federal guidance. By engaging with case scenarios and the accompanying resources, you will discover solutions to common challenges faced by immigrant students and families in our communities. The Application of Federal Guidance box shows the components of the 16th professional learning opportunity.

Application of Federal Guidance

TESOL's 6 Principles (Grades K–12)	**Principle 1. Know Your Learners** **Principle 2: Create Conditions for Language Learning** **Principle 6: Engage and Collaborate Within a Community of Practice**
Standards for Initial TESOL Pre-K–12 Teacher Preparation Programs	**Standard 5: Professionalism and Leadership** **Component 5b.** Teachers apply knowledge of school, district, and governmental policies and legislations that impact the educational rights of multilingual learners of English in order to advocate for multilingual learners of English.

CONTINUED

Key Learning Targets	I can apply information from federal guidance to support immigrant and refugee families in our school. I can evaluate my current knowledge of federal protections for multilingual learners of English and identify areas where I can improve my understanding.
Lessons and Activities	**Lesson 1: Case Scenarios for Student and Family Rights** **Activities** 1. Enrollment Questions Case Scenario and Quiz 2. Access to Interpretation or Translation Case Scenarios and Quiz 3. SLIFE and High School Attendance Case Scenario and Quiz 4. Special Education and ELD Program Schedules Case Scenario and Quiz **Lesson 2: Federal Guidance Self-Assessment** **Activity** I Used to Think but Now I Know
Notes for Each Teacher Role	**Professional Learning Providers:** The objectives of professional learning in this professional learning opportunity provide opportunities for teachers to explore topics related to the civil rights of immigrant and refugee students in our schools. Some topics may interest some teachers more than others, or better relate to their work with students at different grade levels. It is recommended to direct teachers to federal guidance when they have questions about school responsibilities toward immigrant and refugee students and their families. Both Lessons 1 and 2 should require approximately 45 minutes of professional learning time with large or small groups of teachers. You may choose to add additional activities to the information provided here and add time to your professional learning plans accordingly. You can access many online resources in this chapter on the companion site for this book and may choose to print or create electronic versions for your professional learning sessions with teachers. **English Language Development Teachers:** General education teachers may not be familiar with some of the challenges faced by immigrant and refugee students in your school district. You can help your general education colleagues by sharing your personal experiences in supporting students and families and directing them to the resources that clearly define the responsibilities of all teachers toward immigrant students and families in our schools. **General Education Teachers**: You may not have the opportunity to know your immigrant or refugee students and their families as well as you would like. While federal guidance may at times feel limiting, learning about the backgrounds of the families we serve helps us understand the need to make education and information accessible.

CONTINUED

The case scenarios in this section will give you an opportunity to reflect on situations you may not previously have considered in advocacy for immigrants and refugees. We encourage you to access your school's English language development teacher to discuss issues for which you would like more information and to discuss questions that may arise from participating in the following activities.

Lesson 1: Case Scenarios for Student and Family Rights

At times during our school day, our immigrant or refugee students and families may ask questions that you may not have an answer to. You also might witness circumstances that seem to violate the civil rights of these students and families, but you are not sure of what federal guidance is provided to address these situations. You may feel uncertain about how to respond to requests for help or find yourself at a loss for where to look for answers to pressing questions. These incidents often occur during a busy day, and you may find yourself without the resources or opportunity to answer requests for help promptly. Lesson 1 introduces four case scenario activities designed to help you identify some of the rights of immigrant and refugee students in our schools, and some key resources that can help provide answers. We should emphasize that teachers or schools should never give immigration status advice or information to our students and their families, but you may choose to locate immigration lawyers or nonprofit agencies in your area that are able to give legal guidance. Our goal is that by interacting with these lessons and resources, you will build a toolbox of resources and answers to address simple questions confidentially.

Activity Enrollment Questions Case Scenario and Quiz

Key Learning Target: I can apply information from federal guidance to support immigrant and refugee families in our school.

Activity Goal: Identify resources that help us and others recognize the rights of immigrant and refugee students related to enrollment in our schools.

Step 1
Read through Case Scenario 1. Make a note of any questions you have or any additional information you think would be important to have when making a decision in this situation.

Case Scenario 1, Enrolling in School
Mr. and Mrs. Alfaro moved to a small town in the midwestern United States after Mr. Alfaro was hired as a new engineer at a local company. They enrolled their two children, Nelson and Cynara, at the local middle school 2 weeks before the start of the new school year. During enrollment, the office manager asked the Alfaro family to provide the Social Security number for each family member. They were also asked to provide proof of legal residency in the United States with a visa or green card.

CONTINUED

The family received all necessary school paperwork and forms in English without any offers of translated documents or an interpreter to guide them through the documents. The application for the free and reduced-price lunch program was included with the enrollment documents, but the office manager informed them that noncitizens are not eligible for the program. While Mr. and Mrs. Alfaro were somewhat proficient in English, they left the school district office feeling stressed. They were concerned about how their children would be received in their new school.

Step 2
- Read through the questions of the Enrollment Question Quiz.
- Choose whether each statement in the quiz is true or false. You can make an initial guess or review the resource provided for each statement before answering the true or false question based on your knowledge of the topic.

Enrollment Question Quiz

Statement	True	False	Resources
All children have a right to attend public school in the United States, regardless of their residency status.			Dear Colleague Letter, U.S. Department of Justice and U.S. Department of Education, 2015, www2.ed.gov/about/offices/list/ocr/letters/colleague-el-201501.pdf Fact Sheet: Information on the Rights of All Children to Enroll in School, U.S. Department of Education, 2011, www.ed.gov/media/document/dcl-factsheet-201405pdf
Schools have the right to require a Social Security number for every student who enrolls in their school district.			Fact Sheet: Information on the Rights of All Children to Enroll in School, U.S. Department of Education, 2011, www.ed.gov/media/document/dcl-factsheet-201405pdf
All families are required to provide proof of local residence in order to enroll in public school.			Fact Sheet: Public Education for Immigrant Students: Understanding Plyler v. Doe, American Immigration Council, 2016, www.americanimmigrationcouncil.org/research/plyler-v-doe-public-education-immigrant-students

CONTINUED

Free and reduced-price lunch is only available to families who are legally residing in the United States.			Applying for Free and Reduced-Price School Meals, U.S. Department of Agriculture, Food and Nutrition Services, n.d., www.fns.usda.gov/cn/applying-free-and-reduced-price-school-meals Non-Citizen Communities, U.S. Department of Agriculture, Food and Nutrition Services, n.d., www.fns.usda.gov/non-citizen-communities Translated Applications, U.S. Department of Agriculture, Food and Nutrition Services, n.d., www.fns.usda.gov/schoolmeals/model-application/translations

Step 3
- If you are working through this activity on your own, consider initiating a discussion with an English language development teacher in your building to discuss ways you can ensure the rights of students and families are protected in your school/district.
- If you are working through this activity in a team, consider initiating a discussion with an English language development teacher if that person is not already a part of your team. Consider ways you can advocate for practices that ensure the rights of students and families are protected in your school/district.

Step 4
You can check your answers for all quizzes in Lesson 1 Case Scenarios 1–4 Answer Key (Table 6.4) located at the end of Lesson 1.

Activity Access to Interpretation or Translation Case Scenario and Quiz

Key Learning Target: I can apply information from federal guidance to support immigrant and refugee families in our school.

Activity Goal: Identify resources for appropriate interpretation and translation that protects the rights of immigrant and refugee families to clear communication with schools.

Step 1
Read through Case Scenario 2. Make a note of any questions you have or any additional information you think would be important to have when making a decision in this situation.

Case Scenario 2, Access to Interpretation and Translation
Mrs. Choi arrived early with her son for their first third-grade parent-teacher conference in his new school. She and her family had just moved to the United States from South Korea 6 months ago, and she knew she needed extra time to park and find the gym where conferences were being held. Neither Mrs. Choi nor her son were able to read the welcome signs in English that guided parents to sign in and provided directions to the gym, but she followed other parents, and eventually, her son recognized his teacher, Ms. Manning, who was seated at the third-grade conference table.

CONTINUED

Ms. Manning smiled, motioned for Mrs. Choi and her son to sit opposite her, and pulled out her smartphone. Ms. Manning said something in English into the phone and then showed the phone to Mrs. Choi. Ms. Manning then began speaking into her phone, pausing every few moments to show the screen with Korean translations on the phone screen to Mrs. Choi. While some of the words on the screen were understandable, Mrs. Choi struggled to understand the questions or know how to respond completely. When she tried to respond to Ms. Manning's phone in Korean, incorrect words showed up on the screen. Mrs. Choi finally remained silent and nodded yes to everything Ms. Manning said. Mrs. Choi left the meeting unsure of her son's academic progress in school or what she could do at home to support her child.

Step 2
- Read through the Interpretation and Translation Rights Quiz questions.
- Choose whether each statement in the quiz is true or false. You can make an initial guess or review the resource provided before answering the true or false question based on your knowledge of the topic.

Interpretation and Translation Rights Quiz

Statement	True	False	Resource
Apps like Google Translate are appropriate methods of interpreting or translating for families.			Information for Limited English Proficient (LEP) Parents and Guardians and for Schools and School Districts that Communicate With Them, U.S. Department of Justice & U.S. Department of Education, 2015c, www.ed.gov/media/document/dcl-factsheet-el-students-201501pdf
It is not appropriate to use multilingual students or siblings as interpreters in family meetings.			

Step 3
- If you are working through this activity on your own, consider initiating a discussion with an English language development teacher in your building to discuss ways you can ensure the rights of students and families are protected in your school/district.
- If you are working through this activity in a team, consider initiating a discussion with an English language development teacher if that person is not already on your team. Consider ways you can advocate for practices that ensure the rights of students and families are protected in your school/district.

Step 4
You can check your answers for all quizzes in Lesson 1 Case Scenarios 1–4 Answer Key (Table 6.4) located at the end of Lesson 1.

Key Learning Target: I can apply information from federal guidance to support immigrant and refugee families in our school.

Activity Goal: Identify resources that provide information about the allowed age of enrollment for immigrant or refugee students in U.S. schools.

Step 1
Read through Case Scenario 3. Note any questions you have or any additional information you think would be important to have when making a decision in this situation.

Case Scenario 3, SLIFE and High School Attendance
Ghazal Shinwari, age 18, and her brother Aaban Shinwari, age 17, recently arrived in the United States as refugees from Afghanistan. Both siblings and their parents resided in a refugee camp for several months before relocating to the United States. When the Shinwari family left Afghanistan, Ghazal had 1 remaining year of secondary school, while Aaban had 2 years to fulfill his diploma.

Before the Shinwari family left Afghanistan, a new Afghan policy prohibited girls from attending secondary school. Because Ghazal had begun her final year of school when this policy went into effect, her school granted her a diploma even though she had not completed all the required classes for graduation. Ghazal was aware that she had not completed all the math and science courses necessary to prepare her to attend college. High school–level classes were unavailable in the refugee camp, but Ghazal and Aaban brought some of their school notebooks with them and tried to review as much as possible. Ghazal would like to pursue a career in medicine but is aware that she missed out on the math and science courses she should have had in her final year of secondary school in Afghanistan.

When the Shinwari family attempted to enroll their children in the local U.S. high school, they were informed that the traditional high school was not an option because of their children's ages of 17 and 18. The school suggested attending the district's alternative school, citing concerns about the students' lack of academic progress compared to U.S. standards and their older ages, which might prevent them from graduating by the end of their senior year. The school also said they were unsure they could enroll Ghazal even in the alternative school because her transcript indicated she had already graduated from a secondary school in Afghanistan.

Step 2
- Read through the SLIFE and High School Attendance Quiz questions.
- Choose whether each statement in the quiz is true or false. You can make an initial guess or review the resource provided for each statement before answering the true or false question based on your knowledge of the topic.

CONTINUED

SLIFE and High School Attendance Quiz

Statement	True	False	Resources
Students who arrive in the Unites States at the age of 18 are not allowed to enroll in school.			Equal Educational Opportunities Act of 1974, www.justice.gov/crt/types-educational-opportunities-discrimination
SLIFE who arrive after age 17 are better served in alternative schools to help them learn through modified instruction.			Fact Sheet: Information on the Rights of All Children to Enroll in School, U.S. Department of Education, 2011, www.ed.gov/media/document/dcl-factsheet-201405pdf
			Title VI of the Civil Rights Act of 1964, U.S. Department of Justice, n.d., www.justice.gov/crt/fcs/TitleVI

Step 3
- If you are working through this activity on your own, consider initiating a discussion with an English language development teacher in your building to discuss ways you can ensure the rights of students and families are protected in your school/district.
- If you are working through this activity in a team, consider initiating a discussion with an English language development teacher if that person is not already a part of your team. Consider ways you can advocate for practices that ensure the rights of students and families are protected in your school/district.

Step 4
You can check your answers for all quizzes in Lesson 1 Case Scenarios 1–4 Answer Key (Table 6.4) located at the end of Lesson 1.

Note. SLIFE = students with limited or interrupted formal education.

Activity   Special Education and ELD Program Schedules Case Scenario and Quiz

Key Learning Target: I can apply information from federal guidance to support immigrant and refugee families in our school.

Activity Goal: Identify resources that provide information about the access of multilingual learners of English to both special education instruction and English language development (ELD) instruction in our schools.

Step 1
Read through Case Scenario 4. Note any questions you have or any additional information you think would be important to have when making a decision in this situation.

CONTINUED

Case Scenario 4, Special Education and ELD Program Schedules

Cherish is a fifth-grade student who arrived in the United States 3 months ago. She had no previous exposure to the English language, and her transcript indicates that she had the equivalent of an Individualized Education Program (IEP) in her home country. Upon enrollment, the school team established a schedule for Cherish incorporating 45 minutes of daily special education instruction and 45 additional minutes of daily newcomer language instruction with the school ELD teacher.

After 1 month on this schedule, Mrs. Nairn, Cherish's classroom teacher, invited Ms. Parrish, the special education teacher, and Mr. Biswa, the ELD teacher, to a meeting to discuss Cherish's schedule. Mrs. Nairn shared that she was concerned Cherish was being pulled from her class for too much of the school day.

During the meeting, Mrs. Nairn expressed her opinion that Cherish's primary need was to support her IEP goals, and she did not need to be pulled for additional ELD instruction. She believed that focusing solely on her IEP goals would be sufficient to meet her academic requirements, and therefore, ELD newcomer group time was not necessary. Ms. Parrish agreed and said that if Mr. Biswa would like to give her some tips on working with multilingual learners of English, she would happily incorporate those strategies into her lessons with Cherish.

Mr. Biswa explained that learning a new language requires focused and specific instruction in language acquisition, which is essential for all newcomers to develop academic knowledge and skills. Mrs. Nairn and Ms. Parrish assured him that Cherish's primary need was instruction aligned with her IEP goals, and they would plan her schedule to maximize instructional time in special education.

Step 2

- Read through the Special Education and ELD Program Schedules Quiz questions.
- Choose whether each statement in the quiz is true or false. You can make an initial guess or review the resource provided before answering the true or false question based on your knowledge of the topic.

Special Education and ELD Program Schedules Quiz

Statement	True	False	Resource
School districts are not obligated to factor in the English language proficiency of multilingual learners of English when conducting evaluations to determine suitable assessments and other evaluation materials.			Dear Colleague Letter, U.S. Department of Justice and U.S. Department of Education, 2015a, www2.ed.gov/about/offices/list/ocr/letters/colleague-el-201501.pdf
Schools only need to inform parents of multilingual learners of English about the details of an IEP and do not have to include information on how the language instruction education program aligns with the child's IEP objectives.			
When a multilingual learner of English is identified with an IEP, the student should continue to receive both language instruction and specialized education support.			

CONTINUED

Step 3

- If you are working through this activity on your own, consider initiating a discussion with a special education teacher and an ELD teacher in your building to discuss ways you can ensure the rights of students and families are protected in your school/district.
- If you are working through this activity in a team, consider initiating a discussion with a special education teacher and an ELD teacher if those people are not already a part of your team. Consider ways you can advocate for practices that ensure the rights of students and families are protected in your school/district.

Step 4

You can check your answers for all quizzes in Lesson 1 Case Scenarios 1–4 Answer Key (Table 6.4) located at the end of Lesson 1.

Table 6.4 *Lesson 1 Case Scenarios 1–4 Answer Key.*

Enrollment Question Quiz Answer Key

Statement	True	False	Resource
All children have a right to attend public school in the United States, regardless of their residency status.	✓		Dear Colleague Letter, U.S. Department of Justice and U.S. Department of Education, 2015a, www2.ed.gov/about/offices/list/ocr/letters/colleague-el-201501.pdf Fact Sheet: Information on the Rights of All Children to Enroll in School, U.S. Department of Education, 2011, www.ed.gov/media/document/dcl-factsheet-201405pdf
Schools have the right to require a Social Security number for every student who enrolls in their school district.		✓	Fact Sheet: Information on the Rights of All Children to Enroll in School, U.S. Department of Education, 2011, www.ed.gov/media/document/dcl-factsheet-201405pdf
All families are required to provide proof of local residence in order to enroll in public school.	✓		Fact Sheet: Public Education for Immigrant Students: Understanding Plyler v. Doe, American Immigration Council, 2016, www.americanimmigrationcouncil.org/research/plyler-v-doe-public-education-immigrant-students

CONTINUED

	True	False	Resource
Free and reduced-price lunch is only available to families who are legally residing in the United States.			Applying for Free and Reduced-Price School Meals, U.S. Department of Agriculture, Food and Nutrition Services, n.d., www.fns.usda.gov/cn/applying-free-and-reduced-price-school-meals Non-Citizen Communities, U.S. Department of Agriculture, Food and Nutrition Services, n.d., www.fns.usda.gov/non-citizen-communities Translated Applications, U.S. Department of Agriculture, Food and Nutrition Services, n.d., www.fns.usda.gov/cn/translated-applications

Interpretation and Translation Rights Quiz Answer Key

Statement	True	False	Resource
Apps like Google Translate are appropriate methods of interpreting or translating for families.		✓	Information for Limited English Proficient (LEP) Parents and Guardians and for Schools and School Districts that Communicate with Them, U.S. Department of Justice and U.S. Department of Education, 2015c, www2.ed.gov/about/offices/list/ocr/docs/dcl-factsheet-lep-parents-201501.pdf
It is not appropriate to use multilingual students or siblings as interpreters in family meetings.	✓		

SLIFE and High School Attendance Quiz Answer Key

Statement	True	False	Resource
Students who arrive in the Unites States at the age of 18 are not allowed to enroll in school.		✓	Equal Educational Opportunities Act of 1974, www.justice.gov/crt/types-educational-opportunities-discrimination Fact Sheet: Information on the Rights of All Children to Enroll in School, U.S. Department of Education, 2011, www.ed.gov/media/document/dcl-factsheet-201405pdf Title VI of the Civil Rights Act of 1964, U.S. Department of Justice, n.d., https://www.justice.gov/crt/fcs/TitleVI
SLIFE who arrive after age 17 are better served in alternative schools to help them learn through modified instruction.		✓	

CONTINUED

Special Education and ELD Program Schedules Quiz Answer Key

Statement	True	False	Resource
School districts are not obligated to factor in the English language proficiency of multilingual learners of English when conducting evaluations to determine suitable assessments and other evaluation materials.		✓	Dear Colleague Letter, U.S. Department of Justice and U.S. Department of Education, 2015a, www2.ed.gov/about/offices/list/ocr/letters/colleague-el-201501.pdf
Schools only need to inform parents of multilingual learners of English about the details of the IEP and do not have to include information on how the language instruction education program aligns with the child's IEP objectives.		✓	
When a multilingual learner of English is identified with an IEP, the student should continue to receive both language instruction and specialized education support.	✓		

After working through one or all of those scenarios and quizzes, you may have gained insight into challenges that affect the lives of immigrant and refugee students in your school. At this point, you may wonder what you can do to help improve the learning environment for students and their families new to this country or developing their English language proficiency. In our next lesson, we pause to reflect on our learning up to this point and begin to think about actions we can take to advocate for our students.

Lesson 2: Federal Guidance Self-Assessment

As teachers, we know the power of reflecting on new learning. When we take the time to reflect after learning something new, it allows us to internalize new information and promotes a deeper understanding of the topic. Reflection also allows us to connect new knowledge with our current understanding, develop critical thinking skills, and transfer our new knowledge to real-world situations (Kember et al., 2008). Our next activity asks you to reflect on your previous learning and consider actions you might take to better support immigrant and refugee students in your school and classroom. If you are reading this chapter as a group, this activity naturally lends itself to a group discussion focused on identifying potential barriers for groups of students and families and solutions that teachers can take to address those barriers.

Activity   I Used to Think but Now I Know

Key Learning Target: I can evaluate my current knowledge of federal protections for multilingual learners of English and identify areas where I can improve my understanding.

Activity Goal: Reflect on previous learning and consider actions you might take to better support immigrant and refugee students in your school and classroom.

Step 1
- Take a moment to pause, breathe, and reflect on the main thoughts circulating in your mind after engaging with the first lesson in this chapter. You might have additional questions or be currently dealing with a topic in your school that is similar to the previous scenarios.
- Identify a method to store information about helpful resources. You may choose to store information in an electronic document that you can update and share with colleagues as appropriate.

Step 2
- Consider the resources presented in this chapter to support your next steps. Where can you store this information for future use?
- What are some additional resources in your school or community that you should share with your school and colleagues? Who would be the appropriate person in your school to connect with these school or community resources?

CONTINUED

Issue	I used to think...	Now I know...	Resource to support my position	Actions I can take moving forward
Example				
Translators at Parent-Teacher Conferences.	I used to think it was okay to ask a sibling or the student in my class to interpret for me and their parents.	Schools must provide translation or interpretation from appropriate and competent individuals and may not rely on or ask students, siblings, friends, or untrained school staff to translate or interpret for parents.	Federal document: Information for Limited English Proficient (LEP) Parents and Guardians and for Schools and School Districts That Communicate With Them.	Talk to my principal about locating local or online interpreters for parent-teacher conferences.

Your Turn

Issue	I used to think...	Now I know...	Resource to support my position	Actions I can take moving forward

Step 3

As you choose your first actions to take in advocacy, consider what you can do right now. Action and advocacy can take many forms. The more practical your initial action steps are, the more likely you are to complete them successfully.

Closing Questions and Suggestions for Each Teacher Role

Closing Questions and Suggestions for Each Teacher Role

Directions: Take a moment to write and reflect on your learning from Professional Learning Opportunity #16: Application of Federal Guidance. We have included a few role-specific questions and suggestions to prompt your thinking.

Professional Learning Providers

Closing Questions
- Which activities did you choose to facilitate?
- What went well?
- What might you want to improve?
- In what ways do you feel teachers are now able to locate federal guidance to support students and families?
- What follow-up opportunities may you want to plan to further support teachers in your school or district?

Suggestions for This Role
Before you begin planning professional development on the rights of immigrant and refugee families, you may want to survey your teachers to learn what questions they have about supporting multilingual learners of English in your school. A quick survey might help you target learning topics that are most needed in your school and raise awareness that all teachers need to be aware of legal protections for all students.

English Language Development Teachers

Closing Questions
- What were your key takeaways from these lessons?
- How did these lessons impact your work with your students and families?
- Are there barriers for your students and families that you could address by developing a deeper understanding of locating federal guidance to support students and families?
- Which aspects of these lessons would you like to address and collaborate on with general education teachers in your school or district?

Suggestions for This Role
If you are not familiar with the legal rights of multilingual learners of English and their families in U.S. schools, you may want first to explore the Dear Colleague Letter listed in activity four of Lesson 1. This document covers many key areas of support to inform your work with students and your general education colleagues.

General Education Teachers

Closing Questions
- How did this go?
- What went well?
- What were your key takeaways?
- How did this learning inform how you support immigrant and refugee students and their families in your school?
- How does locating federal guidance to support students and families support your practice as a teacher in your school?

CONTINUED

Professional Learning Opportunity #17: Advocate on Behalf of Multilingual Learners of English and Their Families

A broad meaning of advocacy is speaking or acting on behalf of another (Staehr Fenner, 2014). More specifically, advocacy for multilingual learners of English and their families requires taking appropriate actions on their behalf for equitable education and gradually removing advocacy support as they and their families become increasingly comfortable advocating for themselves (Staehr Fenner, 2014). Furthermore, because of a growing population of multilingual learners of English, advocacy for them and their families must be the responsibility of all teachers serving language learners, including the ELD teacher, general education teacher, and others serving multilingual learners of English (National Education Association, 2015; TESOL International Association, 2024).

Advocating on behalf of multilingual learners of English and their families supports a variety of TESOL's 6 Principles (TESOL International Association, 2024), including Principles 1, 2, 3, and 6 (see the Advocate on Behalf of Multilingual Learners of English and Their Families box for more details). Advocacy also allows teachers to apply knowledge of local and governmental policies and legislations that impact the educational rights of multilingual learners of English (Standard 5, Component 5b of the *Standards for Initial TESOL Pre-K–12 Teacher Preparation Programs*). The Advocate on Behalf of Multilingual Learners of English and Their Families box shows the components of Professional Learning Opportunity #17, Advocate on Behalf of Multilingual Learners of English and Their Families.

Advocate on Behalf of Multilingual Learners of English and Their Families

TESOL's 6 Principles (Grades K–12)	**Principle 1. Know Your Learners** **Principle 2. Create Conditions for Language Learning** **Principle 3. Design High-Quality Lessons for Language Development** **Principle 6. Engage and Collaborate Within a Community of Practice**
Standards for Initial TESOL Pre-K–12 Teacher Preparation Programs	**Standard 5: Professionalism and Leadership** **Component 5b.** Teachers apply knowledge of school, district, and governmental policies and legislations that impact multilingual learners of English and educational rights in order to advocate for multilingual learners of English.
Key Learning Target	I can build my capacity to advocate for multilingual learners of English and their families to ensure they are afforded an equitable education.

CONTINUED

Lessons and Activities	Lesson 1: Advocacy for Multilingual Learners of English and Their Families
	Activity 1. Sample Areas of Advocacy for Teachers of Multilingual Learners of English
	Lesson 2: How to Advocate for Multilingual Learners of English and Their Families
	Activities 1. Modeling With Five Steps to Advocacy 2. You Try It!
Notes for Each Teacher Role	**Professional Learning Providers:** In Lesson 1, you will help your participants build background for areas of advocacy relevant to multilingual learners of English and their families. You can facilitate a discussion around areas of advocacy and ask teachers to identify one area that applies most to their school or district context with multilingual learners of English and their families. Lesson 1 requires 20–30 minutes. In Lesson 2, you first help teachers build background for the National Education Association's (2015) five steps to advocacy for multilingual learners of English and then have them review a model scenario using the five steps. Reading about the five steps and completing the first activity of Lesson 2 requires about 20–30 minutes. After completing it, individuals or teams should feel prepared to complete the second activity outside of a professional learning session. They can apply the five steps to an advocacy issue they identified in Lesson 1. To support your professional learning efforts, you might also choose to print or download copies of online resources from the companion site for this book to enhance your professional learning sessions with teachers. **English Language Development Teachers:** This professional learning opportunity will provide you with a five-step process to support your advocacy efforts for multilingual learners of English and their families. It will also serve as a reminder of the many areas of advocacy for multilingual learners of English and their families and support you in choosing an area of focus for your continued advocacy efforts. **General Education Teachers:** In this professional learning opportunity, you will become familiar with several areas of advocacy for multilingual learners of English and their families. You will choose at least one area that resonates most with your work and use a five-step process to advocate for multilingual learners of English and their families.

Lesson 1: Advocacy for Multilingual Learners of English and Their Families

To support teachers of multilingual learners of English in their role of advocate, TESOL International Association (2024a) captured key areas of advocacy for teachers of multilingual learners of English that support TESOL's 6 Principles (Grades K–12). In Lesson 1, you will review these key areas of advocacy and identify an area that applies to your school or district context with multilingual learners of English and their families.

Sample Areas of Advocacy for Teachers of Multilingual Learners of English

Key Learning Target: I can build my capacity to advocate for multilingual learners of English and their families to ensure they are afforded an equitable education.

Activity Goal: Review a synthesis of sample areas of advocacy for teachers of multilingual learners of English that support TESOL's 6 Principles to identify potential areas of advocacy in your context with multilingual learners of English and their families.

Directions:
1. Review the first three columns of the following table.
   a. The first column lists six areas of advocacy supported by TESOL's 6 Principles.
   b. The second column identifies the TESOL Principle that supports the area of advocacy.
   c. The third column lists examples of advocacy issues for the six areas of advocacy with questions to help you identify potential areas of advocacy in your work with multilingual learners of English and their families.
2. In the final column, identify whether each area of advocacy (from the first column) is a potential area of advocacy (yes/no) in your school or district context with multilingual learners of English and their families. Also, list an example(s) of an advocacy issue (from the third column) that could apply to your school or district.
3. Finally, answer the reflection questions at the end of this activity.

Note: Focusing on areas of advocacy will also help you complete the You Try It! activity for this professional learning opportunity.

Area of Advocacy	TESOL Principle Supported	Examples of Advocacy Issues (with questions to help reflect upon areas of advocacy)	Is this a potential area of advocacy in your context? (Yes/No) (For which issue[s]?)
Advocate (Overall)	Principle 2. Create Conditions for Language Learning	• **Professional Learning Opportunities**: Are there professional learning opportunities in your school or district for teachers who feel underprepared to serve multilingual learners of English?	
Academics	Principle 3. Design High-Quality Lessons for Language Development	• **Instructional Materials:** Do you have access to content instructional materials and resources that are appropriate for multilingual learners of English (i.e., materials that are differentiated so language learners can access core content and that incorporate both language and content)?	
Academics	Principle 3. Design High-Quality Lessons for Language Development	• **Improved Programming:** Do achievement gaps exist between multilingual learners of English and non–multilingual learners of English? Have you seen beneficial results over time for multilingual learners of English?	

Academics	**Principle 3.** Design High-Quality Lessons for Language Development	• **Shared Responsibility:** Do English language development and general education teachers collaborate to implement content and academic language instruction? • **Assessment**: Do all teachers have access to and the ability to interpret multilingual learners of English–specific data? • **Pathways to Graduation:** Are there clear pathways to graduation for multilingual learners of English? • **Assets-Based Instruction:** Are cultural and language backgrounds of multilingual learners of English seen as assets? Are the cultures, languages, and prior knowledge of multilingual learners of English incorporated into instruction?	
Social and Emotional Needs	**Principle 1.** Know Your Learners	• **Know the Backgrounds of Your Multilingual Learners of English:** Is there a process to gather relevant background information on your multilingual learners of English? • **Address the Needs of the Whole Child:** Are appropriate counseling services available based on socioemotional needs? Do schools have counselors, school psychologists, social workers, and other specialists to support mental health needs? Do schools partner with community organizations to support the needs of the whole child (National Center on Safe Supportive Learning Environments, n.d.)?	
Access to Programs and Opportunities	**Principle 6.** Engage and Collaborate Within a Community of Practice	• **Curricular and Extracurricular Activities:** Are multilingual learners of English participating in programs such as prekindergarten, gifted and talented, career and technical education, arts, and athletics; Advanced Placement and International Baccalaureate courses; clubs; and honor societies in proportion to non–multilingual learners of English?	

CONTINUED

| Access to Programs and Opportunities | Principle 6. Engage and Collaborate Within a Community of Practice | • **Access to Language Programming:** Are multilingual learners of English identified in a timely manner for language programming based on clear entry criteria? Is there adequate staffing to support a language program that enables multilingual learners of English to become proficient in English and participate meaningfully in the standard content instructional program?
• **Special Education:** Are multilingual learners of English over- or under-identified for special education compared to non–multilingual learners of English? Are language learners appropriately identified using criteria specific to multilingual learners of English?
• **Gifted and Talented Programming:** Are multilingual learners of English over- or underidentified for gifted programming compared to non–multilingual learners of English? | |
| Support for Families | Principle 6. Engage and Collaborate Within a Community of Practice | • **Meaningful Communication:** Does the school or district communicate with the families of multilingual learners of English in a language most easily understood? Does the school or district provide information in a language most easily understood "about any program, service, or activity that is called to the attention of parents who are proficient in English" (U.S. Department of Justice & U.S. Department of Education, 2015c, p. 1)?
• **Welcoming Environment:** Is there a process to welcome new multilingual learners of English and their families into the school community (e.g., support with registration and completion of forms in a language most easily understood, information about health and other community services, school tour)? | |

CONTINUED

| Support for Families | Principle 6. Engage and Collaborate Within a Community of Practice | • **Family Engagement:**
  ◦ Has the school attempted to remove barriers to family engagement (e.g., language, time, childcare? For ideas, see SupportEd, 2022; supported.com/wp-content/uploads/2023/01/Barriers_and_Solutions-1.pdf).
  ◦ Do the parents of multilingual learners of English, their families, and caregivers have the opportunity to engage with teachers as partners? | |
| Societal and Legal Issues | Principle 1. Know Your Learners | • **Legal Rights:** Is the school aware that students are eligible for K–12 education regardless of immigration status?
• **Career and College:** Does the school support undocumented students with access to college opportunities? | |

Reflections Questions
- What **advocacy area** resonates most with you in your school or district context with multilingual learners of English and their families? For suggestions, refer to **Column 1** of the preceding table. Write that advocacy area in the space provided.
  - Area of Advocacy:

- What **advocacy issue** resonates with you within the area of advocacy that you chose? For suggestions, see **Columns 3 and 4** of the preceding table. Write that advocacy issue in the space provided.
  - Advocacy Issue:

- Why are the area of advocacy and advocacy issue you chose important to you? Write your why in the space provided.
  - Why:

Based on Staehr Fenner (2014), TESOL International Association (2024a), and U.S. Department of Justice & U.S. Department of Education (2015a, 2015c).

Lesson 2: How to Advocate for Multilingual Learners of English and Their Families

The National Education Association (NEA; 2015) identified five steps to advocate around issues related to multilingual learners of English. Snyder and Staehr Fenner (2021) and Staehr Fenner (2014) also emphasize the five steps in their advocacy work for multilingual learners of English and their families.

In this lesson you will first build some background for the NEA's five steps to advocacy. We will then model an advocacy process with the support of the NEA's five steps. Finally, you will apply the five steps to an advocacy issue that you identified as a potential area of advocacy in your context with multilingual learners of English and their families.

In the upcoming sections, you can read and reflect upon each step of the NEA's (2015) five steps to advocacy around issues related to multilingual learners of English and their families in more detail.

Step 1: Isolate the Issue

The first step is to isolate the issue. Step 1 means that teachers must recognize the heart of the issue. For example, what might the issue be if teachers notice that the families of multilingual learners of English have low attendance at parent-teacher conferences? The issue might be that the timing of conferences conflicts with families' work schedules, or there is a lack of interpreters to support families with languages they most easily understand, or there is a need for childcare. Possible solutions could be offering conferences at various times of the day, removing language barriers by providing interpreters, and providing childcare during conferences (Snyder & Staehr Fenner, 2021; SupportEd, 2022).

Step 2: Identify Your Allies

Once you have isolated the issues, you can identify your *allies,* or people with whom you can collaborate to address the issues. Some examples include ELD teachers, general education teachers, school and district administrators, community leaders, and state and national leaders (Linville & Whiting, 2022; Staehr Fenner, 2014). Staehr Fenner (2014) recommends working first within your "sphere of influence" (p. 56), or areas that are in your control. For example, you might start by advocating for one of the students in your classroom. You can then gradually expand your sphere of influence to other students, teachers, and administrators within your school and then to teachers at the district level. Additionally, advocacy can happen on a larger scale with community, state, and national leaders (Linville & Whiting, 2022; Snyder & Staehr Fenner, 2021; Staehr Fenner, 2014). If you expand your sphere of influence, much like the "ripple effect" (Staehr Fenner, 2014, p. 62), your influence and advocacy will slowly grow and potentially have an increasingly positive impact on multilingual learners of English.

Step 3: Be Clear on the Rights of Multilingual Learners of English and Their Families

Knowing these rights means understanding laws, legislation, and policies at the federal, state, and local levels and schools' obligations to ensure an equitable education for multilingual learners of English. In addition, you should share this information with your allies. You may revisit federal and state-level rights and obligations in Professional Learning Opportunities #15 and #16.

Step 4: Organize and Educate Others

The NEA (2015) reminds teachers: "Remember you are not alone" (p. 12). Step 4 involves sharing information and discussing advocacy issues for multilingual learners of English and their families with individuals in your "sphere of influence" (Staehr Fenner, 2014, p. 56; e.g., teachers, families, community organizations). This step also involves being open to divergent viewpoints and determining action steps so you can begin to address an issue or situation impacting the education of multilingual learners of English and their families.

Step 5: Identify Your Outlets for Change

Step 5 is to identify your outlets for change, or consider what you can do in your school or broader context based on what you can control. The NEA (2015, p. 13) recommends asking the following questions:

- What can I do in my classroom?
- What can I do in my school?
- What can I do in my district?
- What can I do in my community?
- How can I collaborate with other non-school-based communities?

Now that you are familiar with the NEA's (2015) five steps to advocacy for multilingual learners of English, you will review one model for how to apply these steps to an advocacy issue.

Activity   Modeling With Five Steps to Advocacy

Key Learning Target: I can build my capacity to advocate for multilingual learners of English and their families to ensure they are afforded an equitable education.

Activity Goal: Review a sample advocacy issue (or model) for how to advocate using the five steps to advocacy for multilingual learners of English and their families.

Directions
1. Review the five steps to advocacy for the sample advocacy issue related to meaningful communication with the families of multilingual learners of English.
2. Consider how you will apply the five steps to an advocacy issue in the second activity of Lesson 2, You Try It!

Sample Advocacy Issue for Multilingual Learners of English and Their Families

Area of Advocacy: Support for Families

Advocacy Issue: Meaningful Communication

Scenario: Teachers at your school struggle to communicate orally and in writing with the families of multilingual learners of English who do not speak English. As a result, many of these families do not attend school events, and their children miss school opportunities. Also, when the families of multilingual learners of English who need language assistance come to school, it is challenging for teachers to describe school processes, share student successes, and address their questions or concerns. They sometimes rely on other students to interpret information.

CONTINUED

Five Steps to Advocacy	Advocacy Discussion Questions
1. Isolate the issue. 	**What is the advocacy issue? What is the heart of the issue?** • There is a need to communicate meaningfully with the families of multilingual learners of English in a language most easily understood. Families need help understanding the oral or written messages they are receiving from the school. In addition, many are not attending school events. **What might be contributing to the issue?** • The school communicates with families only in English. • The school does not provide translations or oral interpretation in families' home languages.
2. Identify your allies. 	**Who might you seek out as allies to work on addressing this issue?** • At the school level, I could collaborate with other teachers on the same grade-level teams, the English language development teacher, and the principal to advocate for communication in families' home languages. • I could also contact state-level consultants or other leaders to inquire about a school's obligation to communicate in a language most easily understood.
3. Be clear on the rights of multilingual learners of English and their families. 	**What do you know about the rights of multilingual learners of English and their families related to this advocacy issue?** • The U.S. Department of Health, Education, and Welfare's May 25, 1970, Memorandum addresses meaningful communication as an area of school compliance. It explains that schools must notify the parents of multilingual learners of English of any school activities shared with other parents, preferably in a language best understood by parents. • The Dear Colleague Letter: English Learner Students and Limited English Proficient Parents (U.S. Department of Justice & U.S. Department of Education, 2015a) explains: ○ Limited English Proficient (LEP) parents are parents or guardians whose primary language is other than English and who have limited English proficiency in one of the four domains of language proficiency (speaking, listening, reading, or writing). School districts and SEAs [state education agencies] have an obligation to ensure meaningful communication with LEP parents in a language they can understand and to adequately notify LEP parents of information about any program, service, or activity of a school district or SEA that is called to the attention of non-LEP parents. At the school and district levels, this essential information includes but is not limited to information regarding: language assistance programs, special education and related services, IEP [Individualized Education Program] meetings, grievance procedures, notices of nondiscrimination, student discipline policies and procedures, registration and enrollment, report cards, requests for parent permission for student participation in district or school activities, parent-teacher conferences, parent handbooks, gifted and talented programs, magnet and charter schools, and any other school and program choice options. (pp. 37–38)

CONTINUED

- Additionally, the Information for Limited English Proficient Parents and for Schools and School Districts That Communicate With Them is available for families in multiple languages, describing their right to receive meaningful communication in a language most easily understood (U.S. Department of Justice & U.S. Department of Education, 2015c).
  - The Fact Sheet also states that "schools must provide translation or interpretation from appropriate and competent individuals and may not rely on or ask students, siblings, friends, or untrained school staff to translate or interpret for parents" (p.1).

How might you share this information with others?
- I could share this information in a face-to-face meeting and also provide resources electronically.

4. Organize and educate others.

What is an action step you can take to address this issue?
- Identify meaningful ways to communicate with the families of multilingual learners of English when language assistance is needed.

What pushback might you receive?
- Administrators might say translations are expensive.
- Teachers might share that finding interpreters for all the languages spoken in a school is difficult.

How can you respond to the pushback?
- The school team could be encouraged to reserve more expensive translations for official school documents.
- The school team could determine the best times to communicate messages using a face-to-face interpreter, a by-phone interpreter, bilingual staff in a school, or translation apps (Gardner, 2020). For example, it might be more appropriate to use a by-phone interpreter if interpreters are only available in the school or community for some languages spoken in the school.

CONTINUED

5. Identify your outlets for change

What can you (and your allies) do to address the advocacy issue in your classroom, school, district, and community? Remember it is recommended that you advocate within areas of your control.

- In My classroom?
  - I can work with my families to build awareness of their preferred language(s) to receive school communications.
  - I can use a two-way communication app like Talking Points to communicate with the families I serve via text messages. With Talking Points, teachers can send messages in English (or the language of the school), which are then translated into a family's preferred language. Similarly, families text in their preferred language and send the message to teachers in English. Talking Points is recommended for lower stakes communications.
- In my school?
  - Teachers can work toward creating a process in which families can indicate their preferred oral and written language to receive communications. For example, preferred languages are often indicated on the home language survey.
  - Professional learning providers can help staff in becoming familiar with Gardner's (2020) "spectrum of options" (www.immigrantsrefugeesandschools.org/post/how-to-fulfill-interpretation-translation-requirements-tools-for-guiding-decisions) to learn the pros and cons of various ways to meaningfully communicate with families when the English language is limited (e.g., with a trained face-to-face interpreter, a by-phone interpreter, a bilingual colleague, or a translation app).
  - Teams can investigate translation app options such as Talking Points for lower stakes communication between the school and home.
  - Schools can house translated high-stake documents related to information about programs, services, or activities that schools must provide to families needing language support on a shared server.
  - Professional learning providers can support school staff in best practices for working with interpreters. For example, school staff can build familiarity with a few common interpreting mistakes and how to correct them when working with an interpreter in an educational setting by viewing and discussing two videos available through Clarity Interpreting:
    - *Interpreter Training (Part 1)* discusses body positioning; speaking in first person; never add, omit, or substitute; and handling side conversations (Clarity Interpreting, 2011a; www.youtube.com/watch?v=3wg-qZjMhU4).
    - *Interpreter Training (Part 2)* focuses on clarifying and managing the session, as well as tone, register, and style (Clarity Interpreting, 2011b; www.youtube.com/watch?v=9e_nlDJV-Lk&t=0s).

CONTINUED

- In my district?
  - I can advocate for district leaders to establish a process to provide translated documents and other information about programs, services, or activities that schools are obligated to provide to families in need of language support (e.g., information regarding language assistance programs, special education and related services, IEP meetings, grievance procedures, notices of nondiscrimination, student discipline policies and procedures, registration and enrollment, report cards, requests for parent permission for student participation in district or school activities, parent-teacher conferences, parent handbooks, gifted and talented programs, magnet and charter schools, and any other school and program choice options (U.S. Department of Justice & U.S. Department of Education, 2015a).
- In my community?
  - Schools and districts can contract with trained community members for additional interpretation and translation services.
- With other non-school-based communities?
  - Schools and districts can contract non-school-based communities for additional interpretation and translation services.
  - In addition, the National Association of Educational Translators and Interpreters of Spoken Languages (2021) is an organization whose mission is "to establish a collective understanding of the standards, qualifications and accreditation requirements for educational translators and interpreters of spoken languages with the goal of enhancing EL [i.e., multilingual learner of English] family involvement, student achievement, and meaningful home-school connections." Many free resources are available at naetisl. org.

Based on National Education Association (2015), Snyder & Staehr Fenner (2021), Staehr Fenner (2014).

Activity You Try It!

Key Learning Target: I can build my capacity to advocate for multilingual learners of English and their families to ensure they are afforded an equitable education.

Activity Goal: Apply what you have learned about the five steps to advocacy for multilingual learners of English and their families to an advocacy issue in your educational context.

Directions
1. Identify an area of advocacy and an advocacy issue for your school or district context. The area and issue could be the ones you chose in the Sample Areas of Advocacy for Teachers of Multilingual Learners of English activity for Professional Learning Opportunity #17.
2. Then, write a brief scenario to describe the issue.
3. Finally, answer the advocacy discussion questions for the five steps to advocacy for multilingual learners of English and their families.

CONTINUED

Advocating for Multilingual Learners of English and Their Families

Area of Advocacy:

Advocacy Issue:

Scenario:

Five Steps to Advocacy	Advocacy Discussion Questions
1. Isolate the issue. 	**What is the advocacy issue? What is the heart of the issue? What might be contributing to the issue?**
2. Identify your allies. 	**Who might you seek out as allies to work on addressing this issue?**
3. Be clear on the rights of multilingual learners of English and their families. 	**What do you know about the rights of multilingual learners of English related to this advocacy issue? How might you share this information with others?**
4. Organize and educate others. 	**What is an action step you can take to address this issue? What pushback might you receive? How can you respond to the pushback?**
5. Identify your outlets for change. 	**What can you (and your allies) do to address the advocacy issue in your classroom, school, district, and community? Remember it is recommended that you advocate within areas of your control.**

Based on National Education Association (2015).

Closing Questions and Suggestions for Each Teacher Role

In Professional Learning Opportunity #17, Advocate on Behalf of Multilingual Learners of English and Their Families, you built your capacity to take appropriate action on behalf of multilingual learners of English and their families to address an issue that impacted equitable education. The following box offers some role-specific questions and suggestions to help you reflect upon and extend your learning after engaging in this professional learning opportunity.

Closing Questions and Suggestions for Each Teacher Role

Directions: Take a moment to write and reflect on your learning from Professional Learning Opportunity #17, Advocate on Behalf of Multilingual Learners of English and Their Families. We have included a few role-specific questions and suggestions to prompt your thinking.

Professional Learning Providers

Closing Questions
- What went well for this professional learning opportunity?
- What surprised you?
- What might you change for next time?
- What key advocacy areas and issues did your professional learning participants choose for the You Try It activity?

Suggestions for This Role
To get started, you might choose a schoolwide advocacy issue that impacts the majority of your multilingual learners and families. Your sphere of influence might be wider as a teacher of teachers, allowing you to reach out to allies at the district or community level to support your efforts.

English Language Development Teachers

Closing Questions
- How did the National Education Association's (2015) five steps to advocacy support your advocacy efforts?
- Are there any additional focus areas for your advocacy work beyond the area and issue you chose for the You Try It activity?

Suggestions for This Role
To expand your advocacy, you might bring your advocacy issue to a professional learning community or another school team to gradually create a ripple of advocacy around an issue for the multilingual learners of English and their families that you support.

General Education Teachers

Closing Questions
- What were your key takeaways about advocacy for multilingual learners of English and their families?
- What surprised you?
- How might your advocacy efforts continue?

CONTINUED

Wrapping Things Up

Postassessment

Complete the Postassessment for Professionalism and Leadership found in Table 6.5 by indicating with a date or other symbol your new perceived level of progress toward meeting learning targets for the Professionalism and Leadership pathway on a 1–5 continuum. As you may recall, the continuum starts with *1-Emerging* (little to no understanding), moves to *3-Developing* (somewhat familiar but still need information to take action), and ends in *5-Proficient* (I feel confident that I understand and can take action on this learning target). You can then compare your postassessment results to your preassessment to monitor and celebrate your growth. The postassessment can also guide future multilingual learners of English–specific continued learning choices.

Next Steps

Consider the following questions to guide your thinking around what you will do next to inform your future continued learning for the Professionalism and Leadership pathway.

1. What do I still need to know about this topic?
2. What are my next action steps for professional learning or professional practice related to professionalism and leadership?
3. To promote equity for multilingual learners of English and their families, how could I continue to expand my sphere of influence to colleagues within my school or district or even on a larger scale with community, state, and regional leaders?

Chapter Highlights

In Chapter 6, you had the opportunity to become familiar with the rights of multilingual learners of English and their families that impact their access to an equitable education. You also applied federal guidance to real-life K–12 educational contexts. In addition, there were opportunities to identify sample areas of advocacy for multilingual learners of English and their families and address an issue(s) that impacted equitable education.

In the final chapter, the conclusion, we reiterate our purpose of providing teachers with access to continued professional learning to increase their preparedness to serve multilingual learners of English. Additionally, we summarize key chapter concepts and emphasize the central theme of equity for both teachers and the students they support.

Table 6.5 *Postassessment for Professionalism and Leadership*

Professionalism and Leadership Professional Learning Opportunities #15–17		1 Emerging
#15 Know the Rights of Multilingual Learners of English and Their Families	1. I can identify key rights and policies that impact instruction and daily interaction with multilingual learners of English and their families.	
#16 Application of Federal Guidance	2. I can apply information from federal guidance to support immigrant and refugee families in our school.	
	3. I can evaluate my current knowledge of federal protections for multilingual learners of English and identify areas where I can improve my understanding.	
#17 Advocate on Behalf of Multilingual Learners of English and Their Families	4. I can build my capacity to advocate for multilingual learners of English and their families to ensure they are afforded an equitable education.	

2	3 Developing	4	5 Proficient

References

American Immigration Council. (2016). *Fact sheet: Public education for immigrant students: understanding Plyler v. Doe.* https://www.americanimmigrationcouncil.org/research/plyler-v-doe-public-education-immigrant-students

Castañeda v. Pickard, 648 F.2d 989 (U.S. App. 1981).

Civil Rights Act, 42 U.S.C. § 2000d (1964). *et seq.* (1964).

Clarity Interpreting. (2011a, September 28). *Interpreter training (Part 1)* [Video]. YouTube. https://www.youtube.com/watch?v=3wg-qZjMhU4

Clarity Interpreting. (2011b, September 28). *Interpreter training (Part 2)* [Video]. YouTube. https://www.youtube.com/watch?v=9e_nIDJV-Lk&t=0s

Elementary and Secondary Education Act of 1965, Pub. L. No. 118-42, 79 Stat. 27 (1965).

Equal Educational Opportunities Act of 1974, Pub. L. No. 93-380, 88 Stat. 514 (1974).

Every Student Succeeds Act, 20 U.S.C. § 6301 (2015). https://www.congress.gov/bill/114th-congress/senate-bill/1177

Gardner, L. (2020, December 17). *How to fulfill interpretation and translation requirements: Tools for guiding decisions.* Immigrant Connections. https://www.immigrantsrefugeesandschools.org/post/how-to-fulfill-interpretation-translation-requirements-tools-for-guiding-decisions

Kember, D., McKay, J., Sinclair, K., & Wong, F. K. (2008). A four-category scheme for coding and assessing the level of reflection in written work. *Assessment & Evaluation in Higher Education, 33*(4), 369–379. https://doi.org/10.1080/02602930701293355

Lau v. Nichols, 414 U.S. 563 (1974).

Linville, H., & Whiting, J. (2022). *Zip guide: Advocating for English learners.* TESOL Press.

Morando Rhim, L., Cortiella, C., Kubatzky, L., & VanderPloeg, L. (2023, January 3). Bracing for a tidal wave of unnecessary special education referrals. *The 74 Newsletter.* https://www.the74million.org/article/bracing-for-a-tidal-wave-of-unnecessary-special-education-referrals/

National Association of Educational Translators and Interpreters of Spoken Languages. (2021). *NAETISL.* https://naetisl.org/

National Center on Safe Supportive Learning Environments. (n.d.). *Back-to-school checklist for parents.* https://safesupportivelearning.ed.gov/resources/back-school-checklist-parents

National Education Association. (2015). *All in! How educators can advocate for English learners.* https://www.nea.org/sites/default/files/2020-07/ALL%20IN_%20NEA%20ELL_AdvocacyGuide2015_v7.pdf

No Child Left Behind Act of 2001, Pub. L. No. 107-110, § 115, Stat. 1425 (2002).

Plyler v. Doe, 457 U.S. 202 (1982).

Snyder, S., & Staehr Fenner, D. (2021). *Culturally responsive teaching for multilingual learners: Tools for equity.* Corwin.

Staehr Fenner, D. (2014). *Advocating for English learners: A guide for educators.* Corwin.

Stanford University. (2015). *Freedom to talk* [Video]. Vimeo. https://vimeo.com/133969433

SupportEd. (2022). *Possible barriers to ML family engagement and solutions.* Resource Library Advocacy. https://supported.com/wp-content/uploads/2023/01/Barriers_and_Solutions-1.pdf

TESOL International Association. (2019). *Standards for initial TESOL Pre-K–12 teacher preparation programs.* TESOL Press.

TESOL International Association. (2024a). *The 6 principles for exemplary teaching of English learners: Grades K–12* (2nd ed.). TESOL Press.

TESOL International Association. (2024b). *Common acronyms in the English language teaching field.* https://www.tesol.org/careers/career-tools/beginning-your-career/common-acronyms-in-the-english-language-teaching-profession

U.S. Department of Agriculture, Food and Nutrition Services. (n.d.a). *National school lunch program—Applying for free and reduced-price school meals.* https://www.fns.usda.gov/cn/applying-free-and-reduced-price-school-meals

U.S. Department of Agriculture, Food and Nutrition Services. (n.d.b). *National school lunch program translated applications.* https://www.fns.usda.gov/cn/translated-applications

U.S. Department of Agriculture, Food and Nutrition Services. (n.d.c). *Non-citizen communities.* https://www.fns.usda.gov/non-citizen-communities

U.S. Department of Education. (2011). *Fact sheet: Information on the rights of all children to enroll in school.* https://www2.ed.gov/about/offices/list/ocr/docs/dcl-factsheet-201101.html

U.S. Department of Health, Education, and Welfare (1970, May 25). *Memorandum: Identification of discrimination and denial of services on the basis of national origin.* http://www2.ed.gov/about/offices/list/ocr/docs/lau1970.html

U.S. Department of Justice & U.S. Department of Education. (2015a, January 7). *Dear colleague letter: English learner students and limited English proficient parents.* https://www2.ed.gov/about/offices/list/ocr/letters/colleague-el-201501.pdf

U.S. Department of Justice & U.S. Department of Education. (2015b). *Ensuring English learner students can participate meaningfully and equally in educational programs.* https://www2.ed.gov/about/offices/list/ocr/docs/dcl-factsheet-el-students-201501.pdf

U.S. Department of Justice & U.S. Department of Education. (2015c). *Information for limited English proficient parents and for schools and school districts that communicate with them.* https://www2.ed.gov/about/offices/list/ocr/docs/dcl-factsheet-lep-parents-201501.pdf

WIDA Consortium. (2015). *Tutorial: EL 101: Introduction to English learners* [Webinar]. https://www.isbe.net/Pages/ELLWebinarsandPresentations.aspx

Chapter 7

Conclusion

Teachers practice self-assessment and reflection, make adjustments for self-improvement, and plan for continuous professional development in the field of English language learning and teaching (TESOL International Association, 2019, p. 11).

In the concluding chapter of this book, we reiterate our purpose of providing teachers with access to ongoing professional learning to help them feel empowered and prepared to serve multilingual learners of English in their classrooms. We also revisit the self-assessments we introduced in Chapter 1 to help you celebrate the growth you have made on your learning journey and to encourage reflection on where you are now in your learning and where you want to go next. Finally, we invite you to ponder the next steps in your professional learning journey, whether at the individual, team, or school level.

Reiterating Our Purpose

This book prioritized professional learning for teachers of multilingual learners of English, specifically emphasizing the ongoing learning needs of professional learning providers, English language development (ELD) teachers, and K–12 general education teachers. By providing access to professional learning opportunities focused on multilingual learners of English, we aimed to reduce some of the inequities that teachers might experience when supporting multilingual learners of English. We believe preparedness to teach multilingual learners of English is an equity issue for teachers who deserve access to ongoing professional learning. Teacher preparedness is an equity issue for students whose academic achievement ultimately relies on having prepared teachers (Harper et al., 2008; National Education Association, 2015).

In this book, we also wanted professional learning opportunities to be relevant and practical for teachers of multilingual learners of English. To enhance the relevancy and practicality of the opportunities, we were guided by *The 6 Principles for Exemplary Teaching of English Learners: Grades K–12, Second Edition* (TESOL International Association, 2024) and, when applicable, the *Standards for Initial TESOL Pre-K–12 Teacher Preparation Programs* (TESOL International Association, 2019). Through these two lenses, we offered K–12 teachers of multilingual learners of English opportunities to build their knowledge in five crucial areas related to multilingual learners of English: sociocultural considerations, English language acquisition, high-quality lesson design, assessment and evaluation, and professionalism and leadership.

Revisiting the Self-Assessments

As stated in the opening of this chapter, Standard 5. Professionalism and Leadership from the *Standards for Initial TESOL Pre-K–12 Teacher Preparation Programs* (and more specifically Component 5c) recommends that "candidates practice self-assessment and reflection, make adjustments for self-improvement, and plan for continuous professional development in the field of English language learning and teaching" (TESOL International Association, 2019, p. 11). In this section, we encourage you to reflect upon your current level of learning, make adjustments for self-improvement, and plan for future continuous professional learning. We will revisit the larger overall self-assessments that we shared in Chapter 1 to help you reflect upon your current level of learning and the next steps in your learning journey.

Reflecting on Your Overall Level of Perceived Preparedness as a Teacher of Multilingual Learners of English Self-Assessment

In Chapter 1, we introduced Table 1.3, the Overall Level of Perceived Preparedness as a Teacher of Multilingual Learners of English Self-Assessment. We shared that this self-assessment was a dynamic tool that could be completed at the beginning of professional learning, midway or after engaging in a few professional learning opportunities, and at the end of this book or after concluding your professional learning. For this self-assessment, you rated your overall level of perceived preparedness as a teacher of multilingual learners of English on a *1-low* to *10-high* continuum. As a gentle reminder, please complete the self-assessment at this time as a postassessment and reflect upon your learning journey. To complete this self-assessment and reflection, follow the directions in Table 7.1.

Table 7.1 *Reflecting on Your Overall Level of Perceived Preparedness as a Teacher of Multilingual Learners of English Self-Assessment*

Directions

1. Locate the Overall Level of Perceived Preparedness as a Teacher of Multilingual Learners of English Self-Assessment in Chapter 1 (Table 1.3) or two versions on the companion site with the Chapter 1 online resources.
2. Complete the Overall Level of Perceived Preparedness as a Teacher of Multilingual Learners of English Self-Assessment as a postassessment by indicating your overall level of perceived preparedness as a teacher of multilingual learners of English on a *1-low* to *10-high* continuum.
3. Then, answer the following reflection questions.

Reflection Questions

- What is your current level of preparedness as a teacher of multilingual learners of English on a *1-low* to *10-high* continuum?
- Did your preparedness level change from the beginning to midway to the end of your learning journey? Why or why not?
- What do you want to celebrate?
- What might be the next step in your learning journey as a teacher of multilingual learners of English?

Reflecting on the Five Professional Learning Pathways Self-Assessment

Each of the professional learning opportunities chapters (Chapters 2 through 6) included pre- and post-self-assessments that enabled you to identify your current and changing levels of progress toward meeting learning targets in this book's five professional learning pathways: Sociocultural Considerations, English Language Acquisition, High-Quality Lesson Design, Assessment and Evaluation, and Professionalism and Leadership. These pre- and postassessments helped you monitor and celebrate your growth and determine the next steps for learning.

In addition, in Chapter 1, we referenced the Five Professional Learning Pathways Self-Assessment, a compiled version of the pre- and postassessments from each chapter. As a reminder, please complete the pathways self-assessment as you finish this book. Follow the directions in Table 7.2 to indicate your current level of progress toward meeting learning targets for each professional learning pathway, and then reflect on your current level of learning.

Table 7.2 *Reflecting on the Five Professional Learning Pathways Self-Assessment*

Directions

1. Locate the Five Professional Learning Pathways Self-Assessment on the companion site with the Chapter 1 online resources.
2. Complete the Five Professional Learning Pathways Self-Assessment as a postassessment by indicating with a date or other symbol your level of progress toward meeting learning targets for each professional learning pathway on a 1–5 continuum:
   - *1-Emerging* (I have little to no current understanding).
   - *3-Developing* (I am somewhat familiar but still need information to take action).
   - *5-Proficient* (I feel confident that I understand and can take action on this learning target).
3. Then, compare your pre- and postassessment results by answering the following reflection questions.

Reflection Questions

- In which of the five learning pathways did you grow (i.e., Sociocultural Considerations, English Language Acquisition, High-Quality Lesson Design, Assessment and Evaluation, Professionalism and Leadership)?
- Which of the 17 professional learning opportunities did you complete?
- In which of the five learning pathways would you still like to grow to support your students, team, or school?
- Which professional learning opportunities would you like to engage in next?

Continuing Your Learning Journey

At this reading juncture, we invite you to ponder the next steps in your professional learning journey, whether at the individual, team, or school level. Take a moment to complete Table 7.3.

Table 7.3 *Reflecting on the Next Steps in Your Professional Learning Journey as a Teacher of Multilingual Learners of English*

Directions: Indicate your role(s) and then answer any other questions that apply to your role(s) to help you reflect upon the next steps in your professional learning journey as a teacher of multilingual learners of English.	
What is your **role(s)**? Check all those that apply.	• ____ Professional learning provider • ____ English language development teacher • ____ General education teacher • ____ Other (please specify) _____ _____
What are your next steps **as an individual** in your professional learning journey as a teacher of multilingual learners of English?	
What are your next steps **as a team** in your professional learning journey as a teacher of multilingual learners of English?	
What are your next steps **at the school-based level** in your professional learning journey as a teacher of multilingual learners of English?	
Do you have **additional next steps or intentions** you would like to consider? If so, list them in the space provided.	

Closing Thoughts

Thank you for taking this professional learning journey with us. Throughout this journey, we hope you were able to access professional learning opportunities focused on multilingual learners of English to meet both your immediate and ongoing learning needs. We humbly extend our heartfelt gratitude to you, teachers of multilingual learners of English, recognizing and appreciating your dedication, creativity, and advocacy for students and families. Because of your support, multilingual learners of English can achieve greater academic and personal success. May your learning journey continue one professional learning opportunity at a time.

References

Harper, C. A., de Jong, E. J., & Platt, E. J. (2008). Marginalizing English as a second language teacher expertise: The exclusionary consequences of No Child Left Behind. *Language Policy, 7*(3), 267–284.

National Education Association. (2015). *All in! How educators can advocate for English language learners.* https://www.nea.org/sites/default/files/2020-07/ALL%20IN_%20NEA%20ELL_AdvocacyGuide2015_v7.pdf

TESOL International Association. (2019). *Standards for initial TESOL Pre-K–12 teacher preparation programs.* TESOL Press.

TESOL International Association. (2024). *The 6 principles for exemplary teaching of English learners: Grades K–12* (2nd ed.). TESOL Press.

About the Authors

Janet Eichenberger Hiatt, PhD, has worked in the field of K–12 English language teaching for over three decades as an English language development (ELD) teacher, ELD teacher leader, and professional learning provider. In these roles, she has taught in newcomer, bilingual literacy, and content-based programs, coached ELD and general education teachers, and designed and facilitated professional learning opportunities for teachers of multilingual learners of English. Most recently, Janet has served as an English language/diversity consultant in a regional education agency providing consultative services to K–12 teachers and leaders of multilingual learners of English. Additionally, she works at the higher education level as an adjunct professor specializing in ELD coursework tailored to general education teachers. Through her professional experiences, she has become a strong advocate for ensuring that multilingual learners of English receive an equitable education and that their teachers have access to the professional learning they need to support their students. Janet earned her PhD in education from Drake University with a research emphasis on expanding professional learning opportunities for teachers of multilingual learners of English. She is also a lifelong learner who enjoys travel, yoga, learning languages, and spending time with family and friends.

Cindra Porter, PhD, has worked in education for two decades as an English language development (ELD) teacher, ELD curriculum coordinator, adjunct professor, community ESL program director, and English language/diversity consultant. Cindra's commitment to social justice in English language education began during her MSW internship while working with Hmong and Lao women in her community. Through this experience, she initiated a community English language program, recognizing the challenges many immigrant women faced in securing local employment due to insufficient English proficiency for local job requirements. The lessons learned through those initial years of English language teaching guided her decision to explore social justice issues for all multilingual learners of English in the K–12 education setting. Upon completing her PhD in teaching and learning in foreign language and ESL education at the University of Iowa, Cindra focused on ELD education in K–12 settings. Her education interests include assessment practices for English learners and distinguishing language differences from learning disabilities. Cindra serves as an English language/diversity consultant at an education agency, providing guidance and support to administrators, ELD teachers, and general education teachers in K–12 classrooms.